This DRAFT Military Standard, MIL-STD-461G, titled "**Requirements for The Control of Electromagnetic Interference Characteristics of Subsystems and Equipment**" contains some of the most recent information on Electromagnetic Pulse (EMP) and protection of the Electromagnetic Environment (EME) for DoD equipment. Unfortunately, there is very little current information describing how best to protect an entire facility from intentional electromagnetic interference (IEMI). Although this standard is best suited for items such as electronic enclosures that are no larger than an equipment rack, electrical interconnections that are discrete wiring harnesses between enclosures, and electrical power input derived from prime power sources, the technical aspects are equally relevant to facilities design and construction. The principles in this standard may be useful as a basis for developing suitable requirements for facility design and construction.

This Mil Std provides guidance on frequency scanning, emission identification, susceptibility testing, susceptibility requirements, limits, and test procedures for equipment installed in mission-critical facilities. This book is even more important nowadays as nations like China combine information warfare, electronic warfare and space warfare to create "**intelligentized warfare**".

Each of the books we publish includes a list of cybersecurity publications produced by the National Institute of Standards and Technology (NIST), Unified Facilities Criteria (UFC), Mil Handbooks and other publications that are directly applicable to the topic for consideration during the planning process. These publications cover a wide range of topics that are carefully designed to work together to produce a holistic approach to cybersecurity primarily for government agencies and constitute the best practices used by industry. This holistic strategy to cybersecurity covers the gamut of security subjects from development of secure encryption standards for communication and storage of information while at rest to how best to recover from a cyber-attack.

Why buy a book you can download for free? We print this so you don't have to.

Some documents are only distributed in electronic media. Some online docs are missing some pages or the graphics are barely legible. When a new standard is released, an engineer prints it out, punches holes and puts it in a 3-ring binder. While this is not a big deal for a 5 or 10-page document, many cyber documents are over 100 pages and printing a large document is a time-consuming effort. So, an engineer that's paid $75 an hour is spending hours simply printing out the tools needed to do the job. That's time that could be better spent doing engineering. We publish these documents so engineers can focus on what they were hired to do – engineering.

Here is a partial list of some other books we print that are available on Amazon.com

Information Operations Army, Navy, Air Force, Marines
TOP 01-2-620   **High-Altitude Electromagnetic Pulse (HEMP) Testing**
Electromagnetic Compatibility and Smart Grid Interoperability Issues
MIL-HDBK-419A   **Grounding, Bonding, and Shielding for Electronic Equipment and Facilities**
DOD Dictionary of Military and Associated Terms
Advanced Cyber Industrial Control System Tactics, Techniques, and Procedures (ACITTP)
CJCSM 6510.01B   **Cyber Incident Handling Program**
Federal Acquisition Regulation – Also complete for Kindle
DFARS – Also complete for Kindle
Financial Management Regulation – Also complete for Kindle
Defense Acquisition Guidebook
GAO Government Auditing Standards (Yellow Book)
GAO Standards for Internal Control in the Federal Government (Green Book)
2017 DoD **Operational Law Handbook**
2016 DoD **Law of War Manual**
GAO Financial Audit Manual
Federal Information System Controls Audit Manual (FISCAM)
China's **The Science of Military Strategy** (2013 English translation)
China's **The Science of Campaigns** (2006 English Translation)
Information Operations Army, Navy, Air Force, Marines
Comprehensive Security for Data Centers and Mission Critical Facilities
Cyber Warfare in the 21st Century: Threats, Challenges, and Opportunities
DoDM 7600.07   **DoD Audit Manual**
DoD 5220.22-M   **National Industrial Security Program Operating Manual** (NISP)
DoDI 5200.02   DoD **Personnel Security Program**
DODI 8500.01   **Cybersecurity**
DoDI 3020.40   **DoD Mission Assurance** - Includes DoDI 3020.45 - DoDI 3020.45

METRIC

MIL-STD-461G
DRAFT

SUPERSEDING
MIL-STD-461F
10 December 2007

DEPARTMENT OF DEFENSE INTERFACE STANDARD

REQUIREMENTS FOR THE CONTROL OF ELECTROMAGNETIC INTERFERENCE CHARACTERISTICS OF SUBSYSTEMS AND EQUIPMENT

AMSC ####

AREA EMCS

FOREWORD

1. This standard is approved for use by all Departments and Agencies of the Department of Defense.

2. The stated interface requirements are considered necessary to provide reasonable confidence that a particular subsystem or equipment complying with these requirements will function within their designated design tolerances when operating in their intended electromagnetic environment (EME). The procuring activity should consider tailoring the individual requirements to be more or less severe based on the design features of the intended platform and its mission in concert with personnel knowledgeable about electromagnetic compatibility (EMC) issues affecting platform integration.

3. An appendix is included which provides the rationale and background for each requirement and verification section.

4. A committee consisting of representatives of the Army, Air Force, Navy, other DoD agencies, and industry prepared this document.

5. Comments, suggestions, or questions on this document should be addressed to AFLCMC/ENRS, Bldg 28, 2145 Monahan Way, Wright-Patterson AFB OH 45433-7017 or emailed to AFLCMC/EN_EZ_Engineering.Standards@us.af.mil. Since contact information can change, you may want to verify the currency of this address information using the ASSIST Online database at http://assist.dla.mil.

CONTENTS

CONTENTS

CONTENTS

CONTENTS

CONTENTS

CONTENTS

CONTENTS

CONTENTS

CONTENTS

FIGURE

MIL-STD-461G
DRAFT DATED 2 MARCH 2015

CONTENTS

CONTENTS

CONTENTS

1. SCOPE

1.1 Purpose.

This standard establishes interface and associated verification requirements for the control of the electromagnetic interference (EMI) emission and susceptibility characteristics of electronic, electrical, and electromechanical equipment and subsystems designed or procured for use by activities and agencies of the Department of Defense (DoD). Such equipment and subsystems may be used independently or as an integral part of other subsystems or systems. This standard is best suited for items that have the following features: electronic enclosures that are no larger than an equipment rack, electrical interconnections that are discrete wiring harnesses between enclosures, and electrical power input derived from prime power sources. This standard should not be directly applied to items such as modules located inside electronic enclosures or entire platforms. The principles in this standard may be useful as a basis for developing suitable requirements for those applications. Data item requirements are also included.

1.2 Application.

1.2.1 General applicability.

The applicability of the emission and susceptibility requirements is dependent upon the types of equipment or subsystems and their intended installations as specified herein.

1.2.2 Tailoring of requirements.

Application-specific environmental criteria may be derived from operational and engineering analyses on equipment or subsystems being procured for use in specific systems or platforms. When analyses reveal that the requirements in this standard are not appropriate for that procurement, the requirements may be tailored and incorporated into the request-for-proposal, specification, contract, order, and so forth, prior to the start of the test program. The test procedures contained in this document are generic test methods and should be adapted as necessary for each application, while maintaining the intent of the test, and subject to approval by the procuring activity. The adapted test procedures should be documented in the Electromagnetic Interference Test Procedures (EMITP) (see 6.3).

1.3 Structure.

The standard has two primary sections, the main body and the appendix. The main body contains the interface and verification requirements of this standard. The appendix is non-contractual and provides rationale for the requirements and guidance on their interpretation and use. The paragraph numbering scheme for the appendix parallels the numbering for the main body requirements except that an "A" is included (for example, A.4.2 rather than 4.2). Occasionally, there are references in the main body to appendix material where an obvious need exists for the appendix information to be examined.

1.4 Emission and susceptibility designations.

The emissions and susceptibility and associated test procedure requirements in this standard are designated in accordance with an alphanumeric coding system. Each requirement is identified by a two letter combination followed by a three digit number. The number is for reference purposes only. The meaning of the individual letters is as follows:

C = Conducted

R = Radiated

E = Emission

S = Susceptibility

a. <u>Conducted emissions</u> requirements are designated by "CE---."

b. <u>Radiated emissions</u> requirements are designated by "RE---."

c. <u>Conducted susceptibility</u> requirements are designated by "CS---."

d. <u>Radiated susceptibility</u> requirements are designated by "RS---."

e. "---" = numerical order of requirement from 101 to 199.

2. APPLICABLE DOCUMENTS

2.1 General.
The documents listed in this section are specified in sections 3, 4, or 5 of this standard. This section does not include documents cited in other sections of this standard or recommended for additional information or as examples. While every effort has been made to ensure the completeness of this list, document users are cautioned that they must meet all specified requirements of documents cited in sections 3, 4, or 5 of this standard, whether or not they are listed.

2.2 Government documents.

2.2.1 Other Government documents, drawings, and publications.
The following other Government documents, drawings, and publications form a part of this document to the extent specified herein. Unless otherwise specified, the issues of these documents are those cited in the solicitation or contract.

DEPARTMENT OF DEFENSE (DoD)

DoDI 6055.11   Protecting Personnel from Electromagnetic Fields

(Copies of this document are available online at http://www.dtic.mil/whs/directives/.)

DEFENSE STANDARDIZATION PROGRAM OFFICE (DSPO)

SD-2   DoD Acquisitions Buying Commercial Items and Nondevelopmental Items

(Copies of this document are available online at http://quicksearch.dla.mil.)

2.3 Non-Government publications.
The following documents form a part of this document to the extent specified herein. Unless otherwise specified, the issues of these documents are those cited in the solicitation or contract.

IEEE/ASTM INTERNATIONAL

IEEE/ASTM SI 10   American National Standard for Metric Practice

(IEEE and ASTM International publish this standard jointly. Copies are available from www.ieee.org or www.astm.org..)

AMERICAN NATIONAL STANDARDS INSTITUTE (ANSI)/IEEE

ANSI C63.2   American National Standard for Electromagnetic Noise and Field Strength Instrumentation, 10 Hz to 40 GHz Specifications

ANSI C63.14   American National Standard Dictionary for Technologies of Electromagnetic Compatibility (EMC) including Electromagnetic Environmental Effects (E3)

(ANSI and IEEE publish these documents jointly. Copies are available from www.ieee.org or www.ansi.org.)

AMERICAN SOCIETY FOR QUALITY (ASQ)

ANSI/ISO/IEC 17025   General Requirements for the competence of testing and calibration laboratories

(Copies of this document are available from http://standardsgroup.asq.org.)

INTERNATIONAL ORGANIZATION FOR STANDARDIZATION (ISO)

ISO 10012   Measurement management systems – Requirements for measurement processes and measuring equipment

(Copies of this document are available from www.iso.org.)

SAE INTERNATIONAL

AEROSPACE RECOMMENDED PRACTICE

ARP958   Electromagnetic Interference Measurement Antennas; Standard Calibration Method

(Copies of this document are available from http://www.sae.org.)

2.4 Order of precedence.
Unless otherwise noted herein or in the contract, in the event of a conflict between the text of this document and the references cited herein, the text of this document takes precedence. Nothing in this document, however, supersedes applicable laws and regulations unless a specific exemption has been obtained.

3. DEFINITIONS

3.1 General.
The terms used in this standard are defined in ANSI C63.14. In addition, the following definitions are applicable for the purpose of this standard.

3.2 Above deck.
All shipboard areas outside the skin of the ship which are continuously exposed to the external electromagnetic environment.

3.3 Below deck.
Areas in ships that are surrounded by a metallic structure such as the hull or superstructure of metallic surface ships, the screened areas or rooms of non-metallic ships, the screened areas of ships utilizing a combination of metallic/non-metallic material for hull and superstructure or a deck mounted metallic shelter.

3.4 Exposed below deck.
Areas within the skin of the ship that have electrically large openings which when open expose the equipment and cables in those spaces to the external electromagnetic environment. This can also include spaces that are surrounded by material that does not have at least as much shielding effectiveness as the structure. Examples of these areas may include the bridge, hangar, boat bay, mooring stations, and intakes, and uptake trunks.

3.5 External installation.
An equipment location on a platform which is exposed to the external electromagnetic environment (EME), such as an aircraft cockpit which does not use electrically conductive treatments on the canopy or windscreen, electronic systems mounted outside of a tactical ground platform.

3.6 Flight-line equipment.
Any support equipment that is attached to or used next to an aircraft during pre-flight or post-flight operations, such as uploading or downloading data, maintenance diagnostics, or equipment functional testing.

3.7 Internal installation.
An equipment location on a platform which is totally inside an electrically conductive structure, such as a typical avionics bay in aluminum skin aircraft, metallic hull of a tactical ground platform.

3.8 Metric units.
Metric units are a system of basic measures which are defined by the International System of Units based on "Le System International d'Unites (SI)," of the International Bureau of Weights and Measures. These units are described in IEEE/ASTM SI 10.

3.9 Non-developmental item (NDI).
Non-developmental item is a broad, generic term that covers material available from a wide variety of sources both industry and Government with little or no development effort required by the procuring activity.

3.10 Safety critical.

Unless otherwise defined in the procurement specification, a term applied to a condition, event, operation, process, or item whose proper recognition, control, performance or tolerance is essential to safe system operation or use; for example, safety critical function, safety critical path, or safety critical component. A term also used when a failure or malfunction of a system or subsystem can cause death or serious injury to personnel.

3.11 Test setup boundary.

The test setup boundary includes all enclosures of the Equipment Under Test (EUT), exposed interconnecting leads and power leads required by 4.3.8.6.

3.2 Acronyms used in this standard.

ASW	Anti-Submarine Warfare
BIT	Built-in Test
CI	Commercial Item
DoD	Department of Defense
EMC	Electromagnetic Compatibility
EME	Electromagnetic Environment
EMI	Electromagnetic Interference
EMICP	Electromagnetic Interference Control Procedures
EMITP	Electromagnetic Interference Test Procedures
EMITR	Electromagnetic Interference Test Report
ERP	Effective Radiated Power
ESD	Electrostatic Discharge
EUT	Equipment Under Test
FCC	Federal Communication Commission
FFT	Fast Fourier Transform
GFE	Government Furnished Equipment
LISN	Line Impedance Stabilization Network
MAD	Magnetic Anomaly Detectors
NDI	Non-Developmental Item
RF	Radio Frequency
RMS	Root Mean Square
TEM	Transverse Electromagnetic
TPD	Terminal Protection Device

4. GENERAL REQUIREMENTS

4.1 General.
Electronic, electrical, and electromechanical equipment and subsystems shall comply with the applicable general interface requirements in 4.2. General requirements for verification shall be in accordance with 4.3. These general requirements are in addition to the applicable detailed emission and susceptibility requirements and associated test procedures defined in 5.

4.2 Interface requirements.

4.2.1 Joint procurement.
Equipment or subsystems procured by one DoD activity for multi-agency use shall comply with the requirements of the user agencies.

4.2.2 Filtering (Navy only).
The use of line-to-ground filters for EMI control shall be minimized. Such filters establish low impedance paths for structure (common-mode) currents through the ground plane and can be a major cause of interference in systems, platforms, or installations because the currents can couple into other equipment using the same ground plane. If such a filter must be employed, the line-to-ground capacitance for each line shall not exceed 0.1 microfarads (µF) for 60 Hertz (Hz) equipment or 0.02 µF for 400 Hz equipment. For DC-powered equipment, the filter capacitance from each line-to-ground at the user interface shall not exceed 0.075 µF/kW of connected load. For DC loads less than 0.5 kW, the filter capacitance shall not exceed 0.03 µF. The filtering employed shall be fully described in the equipment or subsystem technical manual and the Electromagnetic Interference Control Procedures (EMICP) (see 6.3).

4.2.3 Self-compatibility.
The operational performance of an equipment or subsystem shall not be degraded, nor shall it malfunction, when all of the units or devices in the equipment or subsystem are operating together at their designed levels of efficiency or their design capability.

4.2.4 Non-developmental items (NDI).
In accordance with the guidance provided by the SD-2, the requirements of this standard shall be met when applicable and warranted by the intended installation and platform requirements.

4.2.4.1 Commercial items (CI).

4.2.4.1.1 Selected by contractor.
When it is demonstrated that a CI selected by the contractor is responsible for equipment or subsystems failing to meet the contractual EMI requirements, either the CI shall be modified or replaced or interference suppression measures shall be employed, so that the equipment or subsystems meet the contractual EMI requirements.

4.2.4.1.2 Specified by procuring activity.
When it is demonstrated by the contractor that a CI specified by the procuring activity for use in an equipment or subsystem is responsible for failure of the equipment or subsystem to meet its contractual EMI requirements, the data indicating such failure shall be included in the Electromagnetic Interference Test Report (EMITR) (see 6.3). No modification or replacement shall be made unless authorized by the procuring activity.

4.2.4.2 Procurement of equipment or subsystems having met other EMI requirements.
Procurement of equipment and subsystems electrically and mechanically identical to those previously procured by activities of DoD or other Federal agencies, or their contractors, shall

meet the EMI requirements and associated limits, as applicable in the earlier procurement, unless otherwise specified by the Command or agency concerned.

4.2.5 Government furnished equipment (GFE).
When it is demonstrated by the contractor that a GFE is responsible for failure of an equipment or subsystem to meet its contractual EMI requirements, the data indicating such failure shall be included in the EMITR. No modification shall be made unless authorized by the procuring activity.

4.2.6 Switching transients.
Switching transient emissions that result at the moment of operation of manually actuated switching functions are exempt from the requirements of this standard. Other transient type conditions, such as automatic sequencing following initiation by a manual switching function, shall meet the emissions requirements of this standard.

4.2.7 Interchangeable modular equipment
The requirements of this standard are verified at the Shop Replaceable Unit, Line Replaceable Unit, or Integrated Equipment Rack assembly level. When modular equipment such as line replaceable modules are replaced or interchanged within the assembly, additional testing or a similarity assessment is required. The type of assessment shall be approved by the procuring agency.

4.3 Verification requirements.
The general requirements related to test procedures, test facilities, and equipment stated below, together with the detailed test procedures included in section 5, shall be used to determine compliance with the applicable emission and susceptibility requirements of this standard. Any procuring activity approved exceptions or deviations from these general requirements shall be documented in the Electromagnetic Interference Test Procedures (EMITP) (see 6.3). Equipment intended to be operated as a subsystem shall be tested as such to the applicable emission and susceptibility requirements whenever practical. Formal testing is not to commence without approval of the EMITP by the Command or agency concerned. Data that is gathered as a result of performing tests in one electromagnetic discipline may be sufficient to satisfy requirements in another. Therefore, to avoid unnecessary duplication, a single test program should be established with tests for similar requirements conducted concurrently whenever possible.

4.3.1 Measurement tolerances.
Unless otherwise stated for a particular measurement, the tolerance shall be as follows:

    a.   Distance: ±5%

    b.   Frequency: ±2%

    c.   Amplitude, measurement receiver: ±2 dB

    d.   Amplitude, measurement system (includes measurement receivers, transducers, cables, and so forth): ±3 dB

    e.   Time (waveforms): ±5%

    f.   Resistors: ±5%

    g.   Capacitors: ±20%

4.3.2 Shielded enclosures.

To prevent interaction between the EUT and the outside environment, shielded enclosures will usually be required for testing. These enclosures prevent external environment signals from contaminating emission measurements and susceptibility test signals from interfering with electrical and electronic items in the vicinity of the test facility. Shielded enclosures shall have adequate attenuation such that the ambient requirements of 4.3.4 are satisfied. The enclosures shall be sufficiently large such that the EUT arrangement requirements of 4.3.8 and antenna positioning requirements described in the individual test procedures are satisfied.

4.3.2.1 Radio frequency (RF) absorber material.

RF absorber material (carbon impregnated foam pyramids, ferrite tiles, and so forth) shall be used when performing electric field radiated emissions or radiated susceptibility testing inside a shielded enclosure to reduce reflections of electromagnetic energy and to improve accuracy and repeatability. The RF absorber shall be placed above, behind, and on both sides of the EUT, and behind the radiating or receiving antenna as shown on Figure 1. Minimum performance of the material shall be as specified in Table I. The manufacturer's certification of their RF absorber material (basic material only, not installed) is acceptable.

TABLE I. Absorption at normal incidence.

Frequency	Minimum absorption
80 MHz - 250 MHz	6 dB
above 250 MHz	10 dB

4.3.3 Other test sites.

If other test sites are used, the ambient requirements of 4.3.4 shall be met.

4.3.4 Ambient electromagnetic level.

During testing, the ambient electromagnetic level measured with the EUT de-energized and all auxiliary equipment turned on shall be at least 6 dB below the allowable specified limits when the tests are performed in a shielded enclosure. Ambient conducted levels on power leads shall be measured with the leads disconnected from the EUT and connected to a resistive load which draws the same rated current as the EUT. When tests are performed in a shielded enclosure and the EUT is in compliance with required limits, the ambient profile need not be recorded in the EMITR. When measurements are made outside a shielded enclosure, the tests shall be performed during times and conditions when the ambient is at its lowest level. The ambient shall be recorded in the EMITR and shall not compromise the test results.

4.3.5 Ground plane.

The EUT shall be installed on a ground plane that simulates the actual installation. If the actual installation is unknown or multiple installations are expected, then a metallic ground plane shall be used. Unless otherwise specified below, ground planes shall be 2.25 square meters or larger in area with the smaller side no less than 76 centimeters (cm). When a ground plane is not present in the EUT installation, the EUT shall be placed on a non-conductive table, such as wood or foam.

4.3.5.1 Metallic ground plane.

When the EUT is installed on a metallic ground plane, the ground plane shall have a surface resistance no greater than 0.1 milliohms per square. The DC resistance between metallic ground planes and the shielded enclosure shall be 2.5 milliohms or less. The metallic ground planes shown on Figures 2 through 5 shall be electrically bonded to the floor or wall of the basic shielded room structure at least once every 1 meter. The metallic bond straps shall be solid and maintain a five-to-one ratio or less in length to width. Metallic ground planes used outside a shielded enclosure shall extend at least 2.5 meters beyond the test setup boundary in each direction.

4.3.5.2 Composite ground plane.
When the EUT is installed on a conductive composite ground plane, the surface resistivity of the typical installation shall be used. Composite ground planes shall be electrically bonded to the enclosure with means suitable to the material.

4.3.6 Power source impedance.
The impedance of power sources providing input power to the EUT shall be controlled by Line Impedance Stabilization Networks (LISNs) for all measurement procedures of this document unless otherwise stated in a particular test procedure. LISNs shall not be used on output power leads. The LISNs shall be located at the power source end of the exposed length of power leads specified in 4.3.8.6.2. LISNs shall be electrically bonded to the test ground plane or facility ground as required and the bond resistance shall not exceed 2.5 milliohms. The LISN circuit shall be in accordance with the schematic shown on Figure 6. The LISN impedance characteristics shall be in accordance with Figure 7. The LISN impedance shall be measured at least annually under the following conditions:

a. The impedance shall be measured between the power output lead on the load side of the LISN and the metal enclosure of the LISN.

b. The signal output port of the LISN shall be terminated in fifty ohms.

c. The power input terminal on the power source side of the LISN shall be unterminated.

The impedance measurement results shall be provided in the EMITR.

4.3.7 General test precautions.

4.3.7.1 Accessory equipment.
Accessory equipment used in conjunction with measurement receivers shall not degrade measurement integrity.

4.3.7.2 Excess personnel and equipment.
The test area shall be kept free of unnecessary personnel, equipment, cable racks, and desks. Only the equipment essential to the test being performed shall be in the test area or enclosure. Only personnel actively involved in the test shall be permitted in the enclosure. Remove all equipment and ancillary gear not required, including antennas, from shielded enclosures not being actively used for a particular subset of radiated tests.

4.3.7.3 Overload precautions.
Measurement receivers and transducers are subject to overload, especially receivers without pre-selectors and active transducers. Periodic checks shall be performed to assure that an overload condition does not exist. Instrumentation changes shall be implemented to correct any overload condition.

4.3.7.4 RF hazards.
Some tests in this standard will result in electromagnetic fields which are potentially dangerous to personnel. The permissible exposure levels in DoDI 6055.11 shall not be exceeded in areas

where personnel are present. Safety procedures and devices shall be used to prevent accidental exposure of personnel to RF hazards.

4.3.7.5 Shock hazard.
Some of the tests require potentially hazardous voltages to be present. Extreme caution must be taken by all personnel to assure that all safety precautions are observed.

4.3.7.6 Federal Communications Commission (FCC) restrictions.
Some of the tests require high level signals to be generated that could interfere with normal FCC approved frequency assignments. All such testing should be conducted in a shielded enclosure. Some open site testing may be feasible if prior FCC coordination is accomplished.

4.3.8 EUT test configurations.
The EUT shall be configured as shown in the general test setups of Figures 1 through 5 as applicable. These setups shall be maintained during all testing unless other direction is given for a particular test procedure.

4.3.8.1 EUT design status.
EUT hardware, software and firmware shall be representative of production. Software may be supplemented with additional code that provides diagnostic capability to assess performance.

4.3.8.2 Bonding of EUT.
Only the provisions included in the design of the EUT shall be used to bond units such as equipment case and mounting bases together, or to the ground plane. When bonding straps are required, they shall be identical to those specified in the installation drawings. Before testing and completing the cable connections, bonding of the EUT to the ground plane shall be verified to be in accordance with the installation drawings or equipment specification. The verification process and results shall be recorded in the EMITR.

4.3.8.3 Shock and vibration isolators.
EUTs shall be secured to mounting bases having shock or vibration isolators if such mounting bases are used in the installation. The bonding straps furnished with the mounting base shall be connected to the ground plane. When mounting bases do not have bonding straps, bonding straps shall not be used in the test setup.

4.3.8.4 Safety grounds.
When external terminals, connector pins, or equipment grounding conductors are available for safety ground connections and are used in the actual installation, they shall be connected to the ground plane. Arrangement and length shall be in accordance with 4.3.8.6.1.

4.3.8.5 Orientation of EUTs.
EUTs shall be oriented such that surfaces which produce maximum radiated emissions and respond most readily to radiated signals face the measurement antennas. Bench mounted EUTs shall be located 10 ±2 cm from the front edge of the ground plane subject to allowances for providing adequate room for cable arrangement as specified below.

4.3.8.6 Construction and arrangement of EUT cables.
Electrical cable assemblies shall simulate actual installation and usage. Shielded cables or shielded leads within cables shall be used only if they have been specified in installation requirements. Input (primary) power leads, returns, and wire grounds shall not be shielded. Cables shall be checked against installation requirements to verify proper construction

techniques such as use of twisted pairs, shielding, and shield terminations. Details on the cable construction used for testing shall be included in the EMITP.

4.3.8.6.1 Interconnecting leads and cables.

Individual leads shall be grouped into cables in the same manner as in the actual installation. Total interconnecting cable lengths in the setup shall be the same as in the actual platform installation. If a cable is longer than 10 meters, at least 10 meters shall be included. When cable lengths are not specified for the installation, cables shall be sufficiently long to satisfy the conditions specified below. At least the first 2 meters (except for cables which are shorter in the actual installation) of each interconnecting cable associated with each enclosure of the EUT shall be run parallel to the front boundary of the setup. Remaining cable lengths shall be routed to the back of the setup, positioned 5 cm above the ground plane, and shall be placed in a zig-zagged arrangement, minimizing cable overlap or crossing. When the setup includes more than one cable, individual cables shall be separated by 2 cm measured from their outer circumference. For bench top setups using ground planes, the cable closest to the front boundary shall be placed 10 cm from the front edge of the ground plane. All cables shall be supported 5 cm above the ground plane with non-conductive material such as wood or foam. If the EUT is a tall cabinet and the cables are routed from top or near the top, then the cables shall be routed down to the ground plane bench and then 2 meters shall be run parallel to the front edge of the boundary. If the EUT is a floor standing unit and the cables are routed from the top, then the cables shall be routed down to the ground plane bench and then 2 meters shall be run parallel to the front edge of the boundary. If the cables are routed from the bottom, then the cables shall be routed up to the ground plane bench and then 2 meters shall be run parallel to the front edge of the boundary.

4.3.8.6.2 Input (primary) power leads.

Two meters of input power leads (including neutrals and returns) shall be routed parallel to the front edge of the setup in the same manner as the interconnecting leads. Each input power lead, including neutrals and returns, shall be connected to a LISN (see 4.3.6). Power leads that are bundled as part of an interconnecting cable in the actual installation shall be separated from the bundle and routed to the LISNs (outside the shield of shielded cables). After the 2 meter exposed length, the power leads shall be terminated at the LISNs in as short a distance as possible. The total length of power lead from the EUT electrical connector to the LISNs shall not exceed 2.5 meters, except for large EUTs, where the cables are routed from the top of a tall EUT or bottom of a floor standing cabinet, then the total length may exceed 2.5 meters, but shall be kept at a minimum. All power leads shall be supported 5 cm above the ground plane. If the power leads are twisted in the actual installation, they shall be twisted up to the LISNs.

4.3.8.7 Electrical and mechanical interfaces.

All electrical input and output interfaces shall be terminated with either the actual equipment from the platform installation or loads which simulate the electrical properties (impedance, grounding, balance, and so forth) present in the actual installation. Signal inputs shall be applied to all applicable electrical interfaces to exercise EUT circuitry. EUTs with mechanical outputs shall be suitably loaded. When variable electrical or mechanical loading is present in the actual installation, testing shall be performed under expected worst case conditions. When active electrical loading (such as a test set) is used, precautions shall be taken to insure the active load meets the ambient requirements of 4.3.4 when connected to the setup, and that the active load does not respond to susceptibility signals. Antenna ports on the EUT shall be terminated with shielded, matched loads.

4.3.9 Operation of EUT.
During emission measurements, the EUT shall be placed in an operating mode which produces maximum emissions. During susceptibility testing, the EUT shall be placed in its most susceptible operating mode. For EUTs with several available modes (including software/firmware controlled operational modes), a sufficient number of modes shall be tested for emissions and susceptibility such that all circuitry is evaluated. The rationale for modes selected shall be included in the EMITP.

4.3.9.1 Operating frequencies for tunable RF equipment.
Measurements shall be performed with the EUT tuned to not less than three frequencies within each tuning band, tuning unit, or range of fixed channels, consisting of one mid-band frequency and a frequency within ±5 percent from each end of each band or range of channels.

4.3.9.2 Operating frequencies for spread spectrum equipment.
Operating frequency requirements for two major types of spread spectrum equipment shall be as follows:

a. Frequency hopping. Measurements shall be performed with the EUT utilizing a hop set which contains a minimum of 30% of the total possible frequencies. This hop set shall be divided equally into three segments at the low, mid, and high end of the EUTs operational frequency range.

b. Direct sequence. Measurements shall be performed with the EUT processing data at the highest possible data transfer rate.

4.3.9.3 Susceptibility monitoring.
The EUT shall be monitored during susceptibility testing for indications of degradation or malfunction. This monitoring is normally accomplished through the use of built-in-test (BIT), visual displays, aural outputs, and other measurements of signal outputs and interfaces. Monitoring of EUT performance through installation of special circuitry in the EUT is permissible; however, these modifications shall not influence test results.

4.3.10 Use of measurement equipment.
Measurement equipment shall be as specified in the individual test procedures of this standard. Any frequency selective measurement receiver may be used for performing the testing described in this standard provided that the receiver characteristics (that is, sensitivity, selection of bandwidths, detector functions, dynamic range, and frequency of operation) meet the constraints specified in this standard and are sufficient to demonstrate compliance with the applicable limits. Typical instrumentation characteristics may be found in ANSI C63.2. Measurement receivers using Fast Fourier Transform (FFT) time domain measurement techniques are acceptable for use, as long as Table II parameters are directly user accessible and can be verified.

4.3.10.1 Detector.
A peak detector shall be used for all frequency domain emission and susceptibility measurements. This device detects the peak value of the modulation envelope in the receiver bandpass. Measurement receivers are calibrated in terms of an equivalent Root Mean Square (RMS) value of a sine wave that produces the same peak value. When other measurement devices such as oscilloscopes, non-selective voltmeters, or broadband field strength sensors are used for susceptibility testing, correction factors shall be applied for test signals to adjust the reading to equivalent RMS values under the peak of the modulation envelope.

4.3.10.2 Computer-controlled instrumentation.

A description of the operations being directed by software for computer-controlled instrumentation shall be included in the EMITP. Verification techniques used to demonstrate proper performance of the software shall also be included. If commercial software is being used then, as a minimum, the manufacturer, model and revision of the software needs to be provided. If the software is developed in-house, then documentation needs to be included that describes the methodology being used for the control of the test instrumentation and how the software revisions are handled.

4.3.10.3 Emission testing.

4.3.10.3.1 Bandwidths.

The measurement receiver bandwidths listed in Table II shall be used for emission testing. These bandwidths are specified at the 6 dB down points for the overall selectivity curve of the receivers. Video filtering shall not be used to bandwidth limit the receiver response. If a controlled video bandwidth is available on the measurement receiver, it shall be set to its greatest value. Larger receiver bandwidths may be used; however, they may result in higher measured emission levels. NO BANDWIDTH CORRECTION FACTORS SHALL BE APPLIED TO TEST DATA DUE TO THE USE OF LARGER BANDWIDTHS.

TABLE II. Bandwidth and measurement time.

| Frequency Range | 6 dB Resolution Bandwidth | Dwell Time | | Minimum Measurement Time Analog-Tuned Measurement Receiver [1] |
		Stepped-Tuned Receiver [1] (Seconds)	FFT Receiver [2] (Seconds/ Measurement Bandwidth)	
30 Hz - 1 kHz	10 Hz	0.15	1	0.015 sec/Hz
1 kHz - 10 kHz	100 Hz	0.015	1	0.15 sec/kHz
10 kHz - 150 kHz	1 kHz	0.015	1	0.015 sec/kHz
150 kHz - 10 MHz	10 kHz	0.015	1	1.5 sec/MHz
10 MHz - 30 MHz	10 kHz	0.015	0.15	1.5 sec/MHz
30 MHz - 1 GHz	100 kHz	0.015	0.15	0.15 sec/MHz
Above 1 GHz	1 MHz	0.015	0.015	15 sec/GHz

[1] **Alternative scanning technique.** Multiple faster sweeps with the use of a maximum hold function may be used if the total scanning time is equal to or greater than the Minimum Measurement Time defined above.

[2] **FFT Receivers.** FFT measurement techniques may be used provided that FFT operation is in accordance with ANSI C63.2. The user interface of the measurement receiver must allow for the direct input of the parameters in Table II for both FFT Time Domain and Frequency Stepped modes of measurement in the same manner, without the necessity or opportunity to control FFT functions directly.

4.3.10.3.2 Emission identification.

All emissions regardless of characteristics shall be measured with the measurement receiver bandwidths specified in Table II and compared against the applicable limits. Identification of emissions with regard to narrowband or broadband categorization is not applicable.

4.3.10.3.3 Frequency scanning.

For emission measurements, the entire frequency range for each applicable test shall be scanned. Minimum measurement time for analog measurement receivers during emission testing shall be as specified in Table II. Synthesized measurement receivers shall step in one-half bandwidth increments or less, and the measurement dwell time shall be as specified in Table II. For equipment that operates such that potential emissions are produced at only infrequent intervals, times for frequency scanning shall be increased as necessary to capture any emissions.

4.3.10.3.4 Emission data presentation.

Amplitude versus frequency profiles of emission data shall be automatically generated and displayed at the time of test and shall be continuous. The displayed information shall account for all applicable correction factors (transducers, attenuators, cable loss, and the like) and shall include the applicable limit. Manually gathered data is not acceptable except for verification of the validity of the output. Plots of the displayed data shall provide a minimum frequency resolution of 1% or twice the measurement receiver bandwidth, whichever is less stringent, and minimum amplitude resolution of 1 dB. The above resolution requirements shall be maintained in the reported results of the EMITR.

4.3.10.4 Susceptibility testing.

4.3.10.4.1 Frequency scanning.

For susceptibility measurements, the entire frequency range for each applicable test shall be scanned. For swept frequency susceptibility testing, frequency scan rates and frequency step sizes of signal sources shall not exceed the values listed in Table III. The rates and step sizes are specified in terms of a multiplier of the tuned frequency (f_o) of the signal source. Analog scans refer to signal sources which are continuously tuned. Stepped scans refer to signal sources which are sequentially tuned to discrete frequencies. Stepped scans shall dwell at each tuned frequency for the greater of 3 seconds or the EUT response time. Scan rates and step sizes shall be decreased when necessary to permit observation of a response.

4.3.10.4.2 Modulation of susceptibility signals.

Susceptibility test signals for CS114 and RS103 shall be pulse modulated (on/off ratio of 40 dB minimum) at a 1 kHz rate with a 50% duty cycle.

TABLE III. Susceptibility scanning.

Frequency Range	Analog Scans Maximum Scan Rates	Stepped Scans Maximum Step Size
30 Hz - 1 MHz	0.0333 f/sec	0.05 f
1 MHz – 30 MHz	0.00667 f/sec	0.01 f
30 MHz - 1 GHz	0.00333 f/sec	0.005 f
1 GHz - 40 GHz	0.00167 f/sec	0.0025 f

4.3.10.4.3 Thresholds of susceptibility.
Susceptibilities and anomalies that are not in conformance with contractual requirements are not acceptable. However, all susceptibilities and anomalies observed during conduct of the test shall be documented. When susceptibility indications are noted in EUT operation, a threshold level shall be determined where the susceptible condition is no longer present. Thresholds of susceptibility shall be determined as follows and described in the EMITR:

a. When a susceptibility condition is detected, reduce the interference signal until the EUT recovers.

b. Determine the worst-case failure frequency within the failure bandwidth by manually tuning the frequency, iteratively reducing the step size by a factor of two until the lowest threshold is determined.

c. Reduce the interference signal by an additional 6 dB.

d. Gradually increase the interference signal until the susceptibility condition reoccurs. The resulting level is the threshold of susceptibility.

e. Record this level, frequency range of occurrence, frequency and level of greatest susceptibility, and other test parameters, as applicable.

4.3.11 Calibration of measuring equipment.
Primary measurement devices and accessories required for measurement in accordance with this standard shall be calibrated in accordance with ANSI/ISO/IEC 17025 or ISO 10012 or under an approved calibration program traceable to the National Institute for Standards and Technology. After the initial calibration, for passive devices such as measurement antennas, current probes, and LISNs, require no further formal calibration. The measurement system integrity check in the procedures is sufficient to determine acceptability of passive devices.

4.3.11.1 Measurement system test.
At the start of each emission test, the complete test system (including measurement receivers, cables, attenuators, couplers, and so forth) shall be verified by injecting a known signal, as stated in the individual test procedure, while monitoring system output for the proper indication. When the emission test involves an uninterrupted set of repeated measurements (such as evaluating different operating modes of the EUT) using the same measurement equipment, the measurement system test needs to be accomplished only one time.

4.3.11.2 Antenna factors.
Factors for test antennas shall be determined in accordance with SAE ARP958.

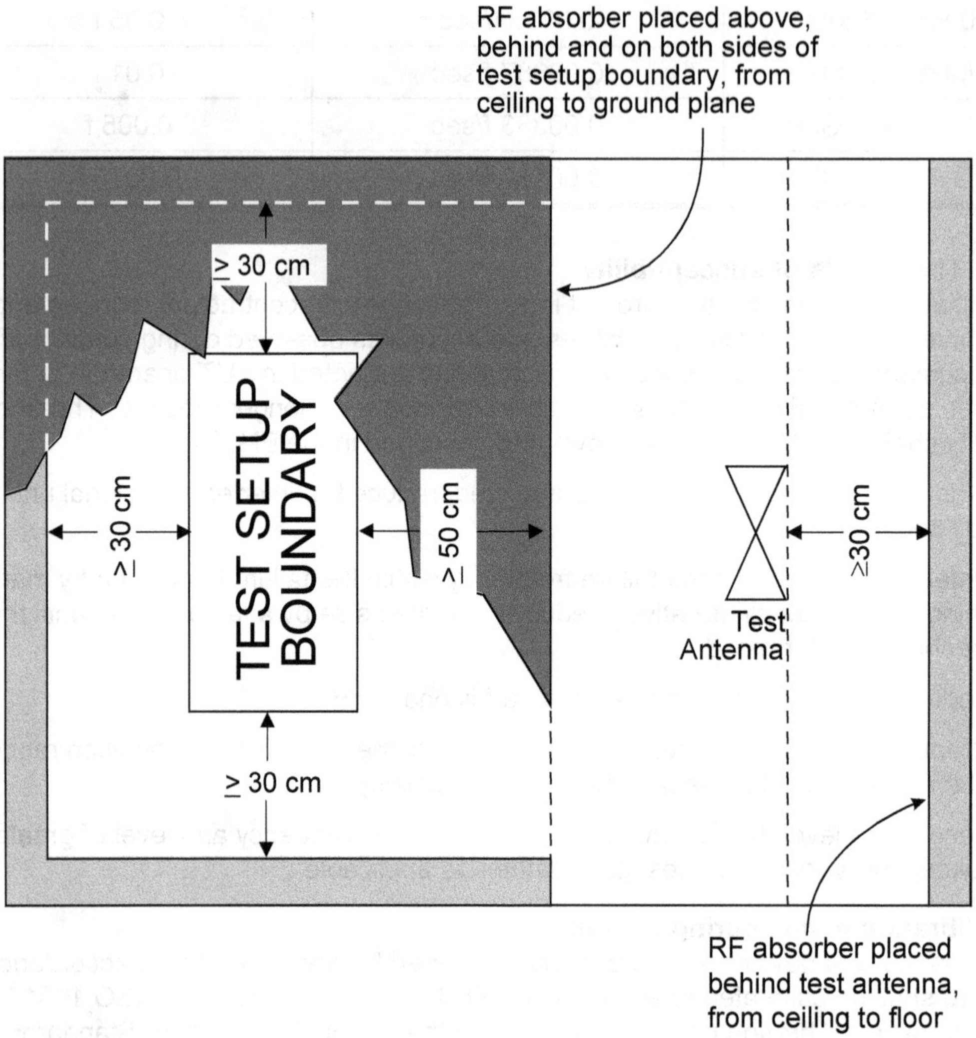

RF absorber placed above, behind and on both sides of test setup boundary, from ceiling to ground plane

≥ 30 cm

≥ 30 cm

≥ 50 cm

TEST SETUP BOUNDARY

≥ 30 cm

Test Antenna

≥30 cm

RF absorber placed behind test antenna, from ceiling to floor

FIGURE 1. RF absorber loading diagram.

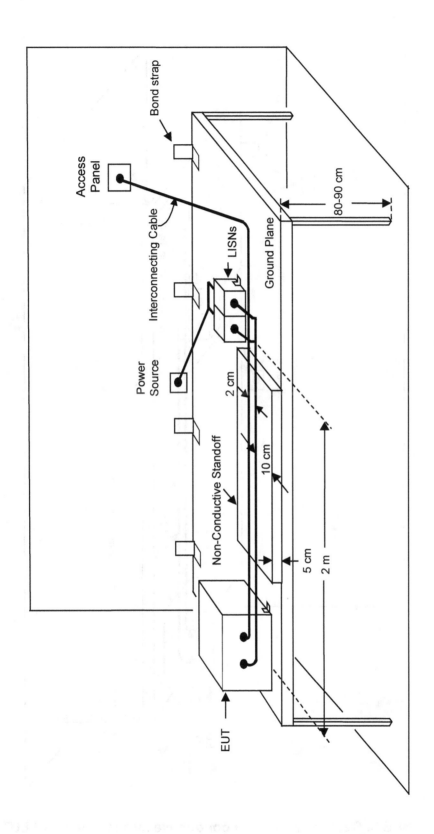

FIGURE 2. General test setup.

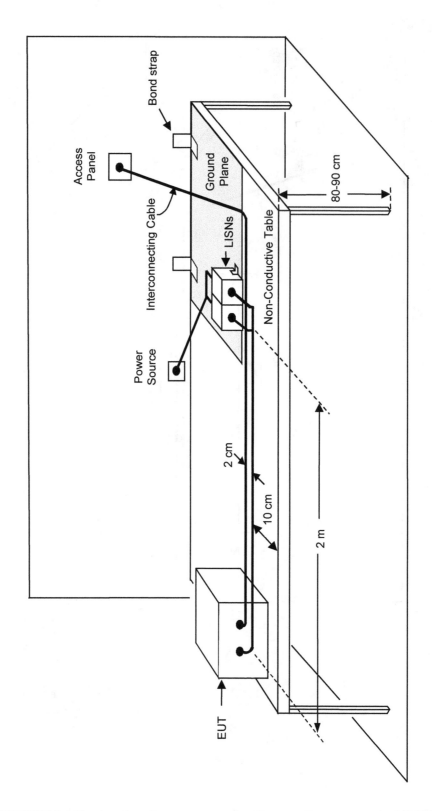

FIGURE 3. Test setup for non-conductive surface mounted EUT.

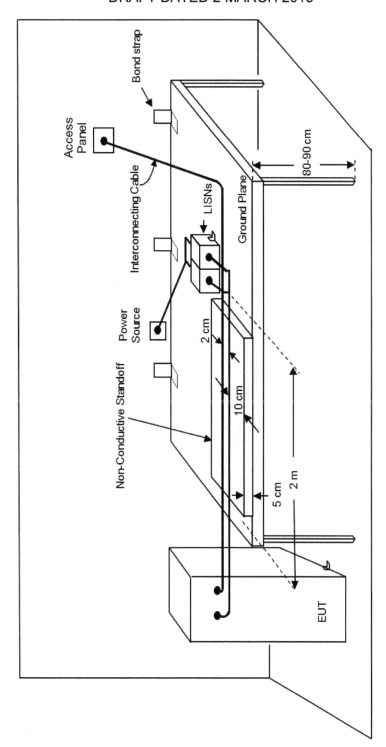

FIGURE 4. Test setup for free standing EUT in shielded enclosure.

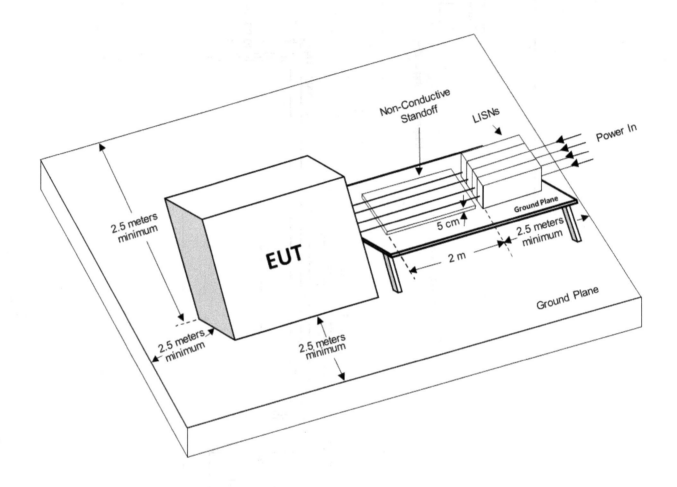

FIGURE 5. Test setup for free standing EUT.

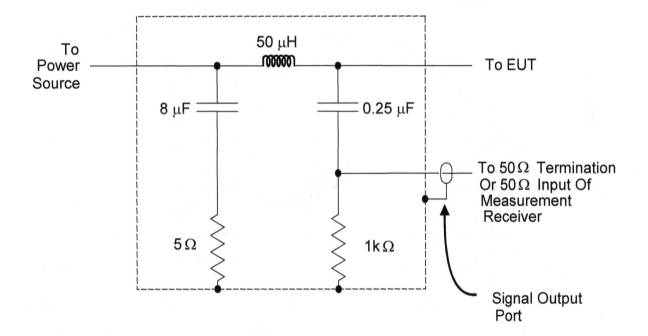

FIGURE 6. LISN schematic.

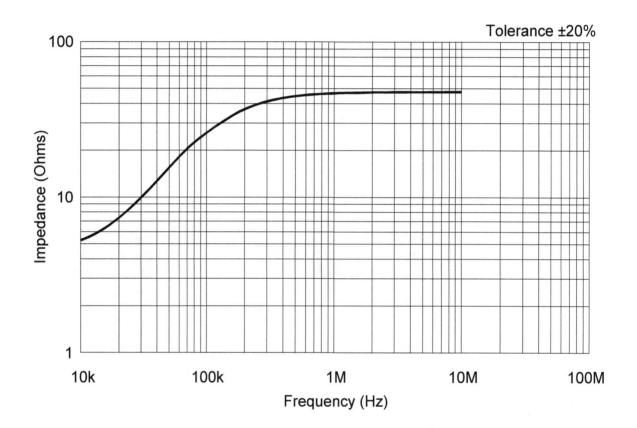

FIGURE 7. LISN impedance.

5. DETAILED REQUIREMENTS

5.1 General.

This section specifies detailed emissions and susceptibility requirements and the associated test procedures. Table IV is a list of the specific requirements established by this standard identified by requirement number and title. General test procedures are included in this section. Specific test procedures are implemented by the Government approved EMITP (in accordance with DI-EMCS-80201). All results of tests performed to demonstrate compliance with the requirements are to be documented in the EMITR (in accordance with DI-EMCS-80200C) and forwarded to the Command or agency concerned for evaluation prior to acceptance of the equipment or subsystem. Design procedures and techniques for the control of EMI shall be described in the EMICP. Approval of design procedures and techniques described in the EMICP does not relieve the supplier of the responsibility of meeting the contractual emission, susceptibility, and design requirements.

5.1.1 Units of frequency domain measurements.

All frequency domain limits are expressed in terms of equivalent Root Mean Square (RMS) value of a sine wave as would be indicated by the output of a measurement receiver using peak envelope detection (see 4.3.10.1).

5.2 EMI control requirements versus intended installations.

Table V summarizes the requirements for equipment and subsystems intended to be installed in, on, or launched from various military platforms or installations. When an equipment or subsystem is to be installed in more than one type of platform or installation, it shall comply with the most stringent of the applicable requirements and limits. An "A" entry in the table means the requirement is applicable. An "L" entry means the applicability of the requirement is limited as specified in the appropriate requirement paragraphs of this standard; the limits are contained herein. An "S" entry means the procuring activity must specify the applicability, limit, and verification procedures in the procurement specification. Absence of an entry means the requirement is not applicable.

5.3 Emission and .

Individual emission or susceptibility requirements and their associated limits and test procedures are grouped together in the following sections. The applicable frequency range and limit of many emission and susceptibility requirements varies depending on the particular platform or installation. The test procedures included in this section are valid for the entire frequency range specified in the procedure; however, testing only needs to be performed over the frequency range specified for the particular platform or installation.

TABLE IV. Emission and susceptibility requirements.

Requirement	Description
CE101	Conducted Emissions, Power Leads
CE102	Conducted Emissions, Power Leads
CE106	Conducted Emissions, Antenna Terminal
CS101	Conducted Susceptibility, Power Leads
CS103	Conducted Susceptibility, Antenna Port, Intermodulation
CS104	Conducted Susceptibility, Antenna Port, Rejection of Undesired Signals
CS105	Conducted Susceptibility, Antenna Port, Cross-Modulation
CS109	Conducted Susceptibility, Structure Current
CS114	Conducted Susceptibility, Bulk Cable Injection
CS115	Conducted Susceptibility, Bulk Cable Injection, Impulse Excitation
CS116	Conducted Susceptibility, Damped Sinusoidal Transients, Cables and Power Leads
CS117	Conducted Susceptibility, Lightning Induced Transients, Cables and Power Leads
CS118	Conducted Susceptibility, Personnel Borne Electrostatic Discharge
RE101	Radiated Emissions, Magnetic Field
RE102	Radiated Emissions, Electric Field
RE103	Radiated Emissions, Antenna Spurious and Harmonic Outputs
RS101	Radiated Susceptibility, Magnetic Field
RS103	Radiated Susceptibility, Electric Field
RS105	Radiated Susceptibility, Transient Electromagnetic Field

TABLE V. Requirement matrix.

Equipment and Subsystems Installed In, On, or Launched From the Following Platforms or Installations	Requirement Applicability																		
	CE101	CE102	CE106	CS101	CS103	CS104	CS105	CS109	CS114	CS115	CS116	CS117	CS118	RE101	RE102	RE103	RS101	RS103	RS105
Surface Ships	A	A	L	A	S	L	S	L	A	S	A	L	A	A	A	L	L	A	L
Submarines	A	A	L	A	S	L	S	L	A	S	L		A	A	A	L	L	A	L
Aircraft, Army, Including Flight Line	A	A	L	A	S	S	S		A	A	A	L	A	A	A	L	A	A	L
Aircraft, Navy	L	A	L	A	S	S	S		A	A	A	L	A	L	A	L	S	A	L
Aircraft, Air Force		A	L	A	S	S	S		A	A	A	L		A	L		A		
Space Systems, Including Launch Vehicles		A	L	A	S	S	S		A	A	A	L		A	L		A		
Ground, Army		A	L	A	S	S	S		A	A	A	S	A		A	L	L	A	
Ground, Navy		A	L	A	S	S	S		A	A	A		A		A	L	L	A	L
Ground, Air Force		A	L	A	S	S	S		A	A	A		A		A	L		A		

Legend:

A: Applicable

L: Limited as specified in the individual sections of this standard.

S: Procuring activity must specify in procurement documentation.

5.4 CE101, conducted emissions, power leads.

5.4.1 CE101 applicability.

This requirement is applicable from 30 Hz to 10 kHz for power leads, including returns, that obtain power from other sources not part of the EUT for surface ships, submarines, Army aircraft[&] (including flight line) and Navy aircraft[*&]

*For equipment intended to be installed on Navy aircraft, this requirement is applicable only if the platform contains Anti-Submarine Warfare (ASW) equipment, which operate between 30 Hz and 10 kHz, such as Acoustic (Sonobouy) Receivers or Magnetic Anomaly Detectors (MAD).

[&]For AC applications, this requirement is applicable starting at the second harmonic of the EUT power frequency.

5.4.2 CE101 limits.

Conducted emissions on power leads shall not exceed the applicable values shown on Figures CE101-1 through CE101-3, as appropriate, for submarines and Figure CE101-4 for Army aircraft (including flight line) and Navy ASW aircraft.

5.4.3 CE101 test procedure.

5.4.3.1 Purpose.

This test procedure is used to verify that electromagnetic emissions from the EUT do not exceed the specified requirements for power input leads including returns.

5.4.3.2 Test equipment.

The test equipment shall be as follows:

- a. Measurement receivers
- b. Current probes
- c. Signal generator
- d. Data recording device
- e. Oscilloscope
- f. Resistor (R)
- g. LISNs

5.4.3.3 Setup.

The test setup shall be as follows:

- a. Maintain a basic test setup for the EUT as shown and described on Figures 2 through 5 and 4.3.8. The LISN may be removed or replaced with an alternative stabilization device when approved by the procuring activity.

- b. Measurement system integrity check. Configure the test setup for the measurement system check as shown on Figure CE101-5.

- c. EUT testing.

  (1) Configure the test setup for compliance testing of the EUT as shown on Figure CE101-6.

  (2) Position the current probe 5 cm from the LISN.

5.4.3.4 Procedures.

The test procedures shall be as follows:

- a. Turn on the measurement equipment and allow a sufficient time for stabilization.

- b. Measurement system integrity check. Evaluate the overall measurement system from the current probe to the data output device.

  (1) Apply a calibrated signal level, which is at least 6 dB below the applicable limit at 1.1 kHz, 3 kHz, and 9.9 kHz, to the current probe.

  (2) Verify the current level, using the oscilloscope and load resistor; also, verify that the current waveform is sinusoidal.

  (3) Scan the measurement receiver for each frequency in the same manner as a normal data scan. Verify that the data recording device indicates a level within ±3 dB of the injected level.

  (4) If readings are obtained which deviate by more than ±3 dB, locate the source of the error and correct the deficiency prior to proceeding with the testing.

26

c.   EUT testing. Determine the conducted emissions from the EUT input power leads, including returns.

(1)   Turn on the EUT and allow sufficient time for stabilization.

(2)   Select an appropriate lead for testing and clamp the current probe into position.

(3)   Scan the measurement receiver over the applicable frequency range, using the bandwidths and minimum measurement times specified in Table II.

(4)   Repeat 5.4.3.4c(3) for each power lead.

5.4.3.5 Data presentation.

Data presentation shall be as follows:

a.   Continuously and automatically plot amplitude versus frequency profiles on X-Y axis outputs. Manually gathered data is not acceptable except for plot verification.

b.   Display the applicable limit on each plot.

c.   Provide a minimum frequency resolution of 1% or twice the measurement receiver bandwidth, whichever is less stringent, and a minimum amplitude resolution of 1 dB for each plot.

d.   Provide plots for both the measurement and system check portions of the procedure.

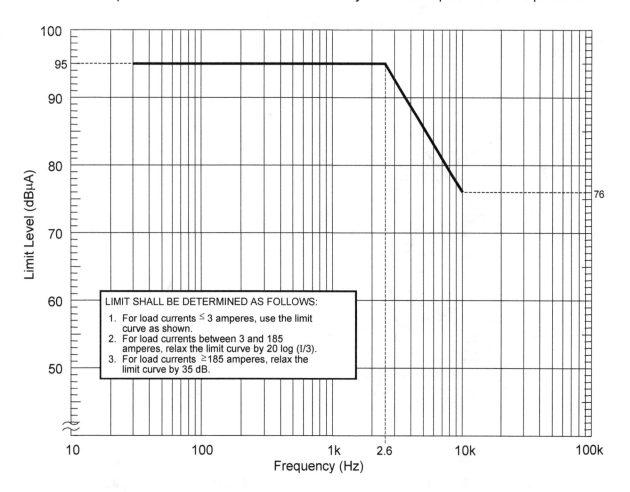

FIGURE CE101-1. CE101 limit for surface ships and submarine applications, DC.

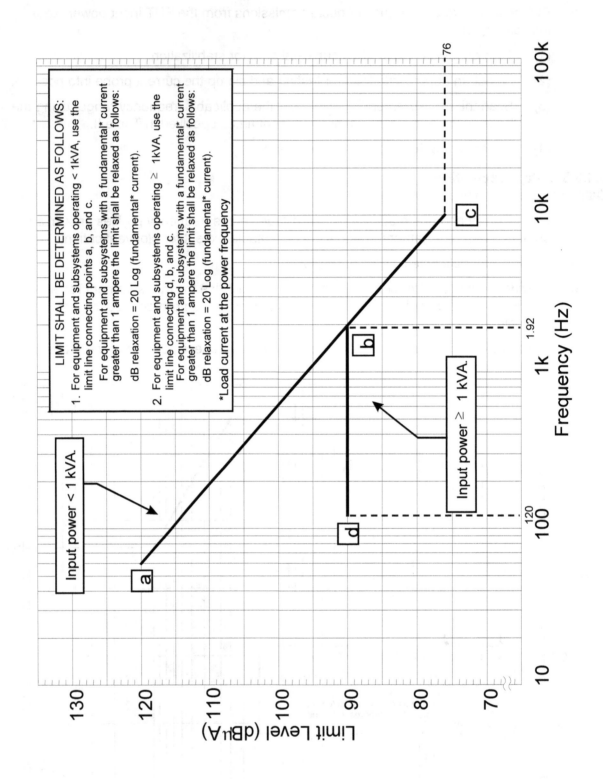

FIGURE CE101-2. CE101 limit for surface ships and submarine applications, 60 Hz.

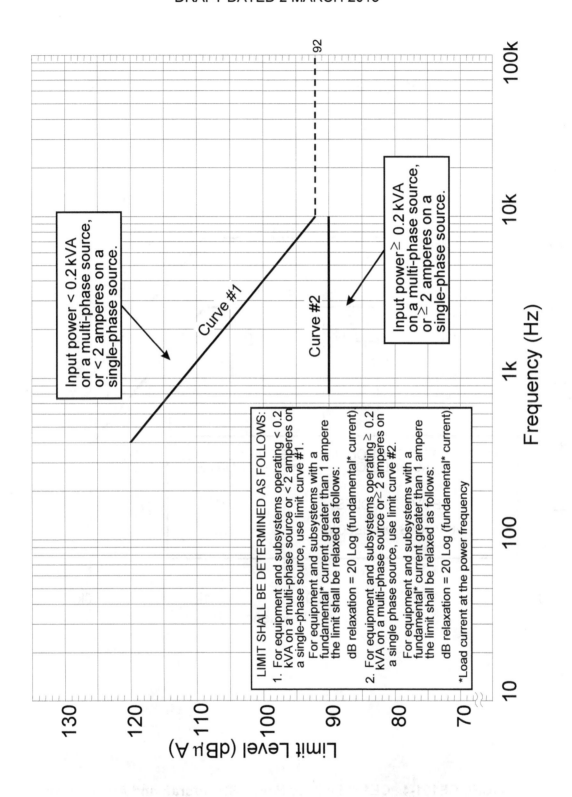

FIGURE CE101-3. CE101 limit for surface ships and submarine applications, 400 Hz.

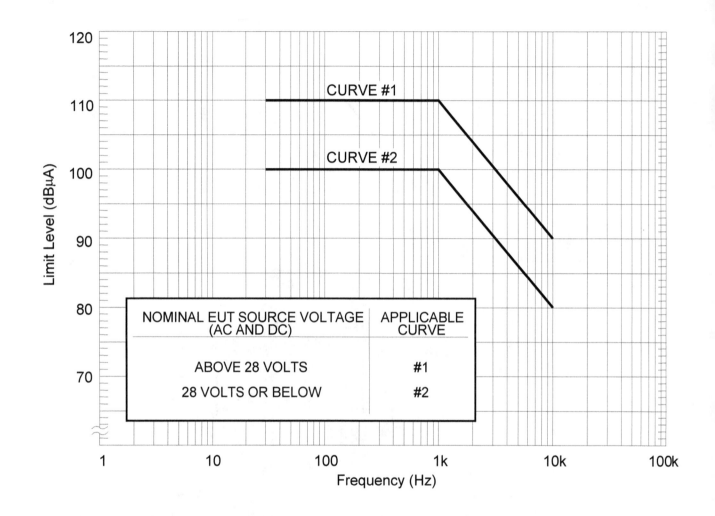

FIGURE CE101-4. CE101 limit for Navy ASW aircraft and Army aircraft (including flight line) applications.

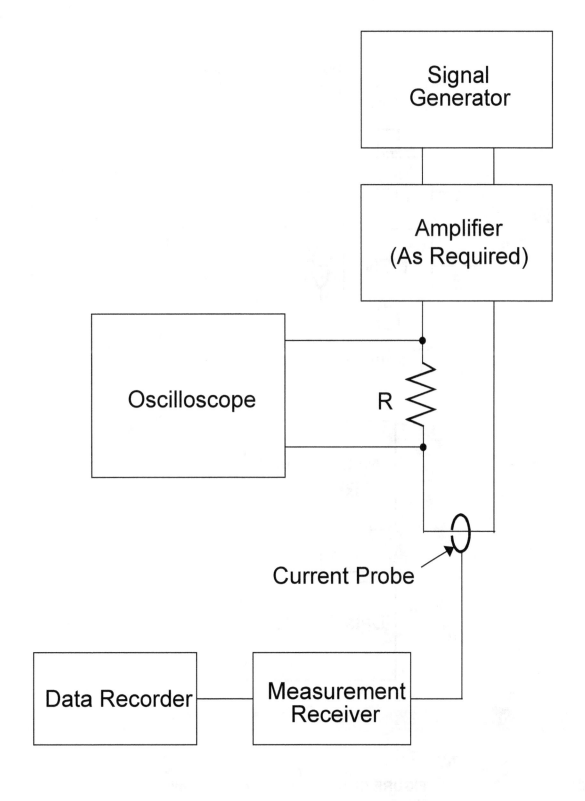

FIGURE CE101-5. Measurement system check.

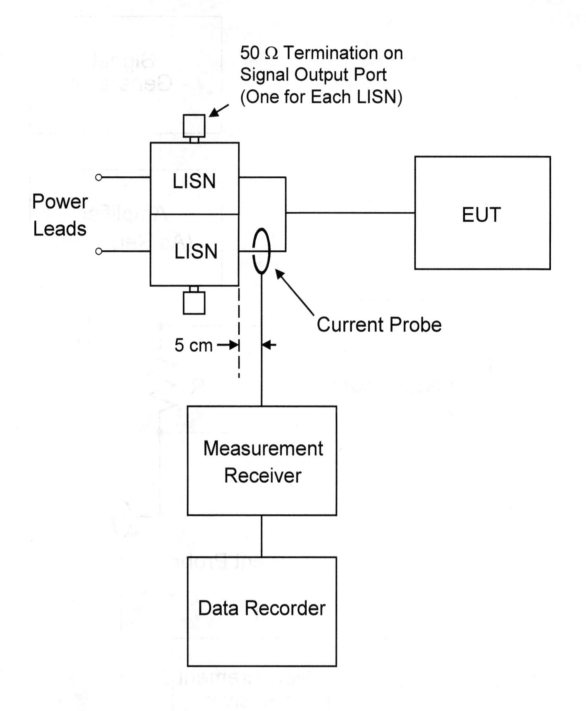

FIGURE CE101-6. Measurement setup.

5.5 CE102, conducted emissions, power leads.

5.5.1 CE102 applicability.

This requirement is applicable from 10 kHz to 10 MHz for all power leads, including returns, which obtain power from other sources not part of the EUT.

5.5.2 CE102 limits.

Conducted emissions on power leads shall not exceed the applicable values shown on Figure CE102-1.

5.5.3 CE102 test procedure.

5.5.3.1 Purpose.

This test procedure is used to verify that electromagnetic emissions from the EUT do not exceed the specified requirements for power input leads, including returns.

5.5.3.2 Test equipment.

The test equipment shall be as follows:

   a.   Measurement receiver

   b.   Data recording device

   c.   Signal generator

   d.   Attenuator, 20 dB, 50 ohm

   e.   Oscilloscope

   f.   LISNs

5.5.3.3 Setup.

The test setup shall be as follows:

   a.   Maintain a basic test setup for the EUT as shown and described on Figures 2 through 5 and 4.3.8.

   b.   Measurement system integrity check.

      (1)   Configure the test setup for the measurement system check as shown on Figure CE102-2. Ensure that the EUT power source is turned off.

      (2)   Connect the measurement receiver to the 20 dB attenuator on the signal output port of the LISN.

   c.   EUT testing.

      (1)   Configure the test setup for compliance testing of the EUT as shown on Figure CE102-3.

      (2)   Connect the measurement receiver to the 20 dB attenuator on the signal output port of the LISN.

5.5.3.4 Procedures.

The test procedures shall be as follows:

   a.   Measurement system integrity check. Perform the measurement system check using the measurement system check setup of Figure CE102-2.

      (1)   Turn on the measurement equipment and allow a sufficient time for stabilization.

(2) Apply a signal level of 90 dBµV at 10 kHz and 100 kHz to the power output terminal of the LISN. At 10 kHz and 100 kHz, use an oscilloscope to verify that there is a proper signal level at the LISN and verify that it is sinusoidal. After establishing the proper signal at the LISN, disconnect LISN and measure resulting voltage using a 50 Ohm termination. The ratio of the LISN voltage to the 50 ohm voltage measurement must be within the following tolerances: at 10 kHz = -14 dB (+1 dB/-2 dB) and at 100 kHz = -3 dB (+1 dB/-2 dB).

(3) Apply a signal level that is at least 6 dB below the limit at 10.5 kHz, 100 kHz, 1.95 MHz and 9.8 MHz to the power output terminal of the LISN. At 10 kHz and 100 kHz, use an oscilloscope to calibrate the signal level. At 1.95 MHz and 9.8 MHz, use a calibrated output level directly from a 50 Ω signal generator.

(4) Scan the measurement receiver for each frequency in the same manner as a normal data scan. Verify that the measurement receiver indicates a level within ±3 dB of the injected level. Correction factors shall be applied for the 20 dB attenuator and the voltage drop due to the LISN 0.25 µF coupling capacitor (see Figure 6).

(5) If readings are obtained which deviate by more than ±3 dB, locate the source of the error and correct the deficiency prior to proceeding with the testing.

(6) Repeat 5.5.3.4a(2) through 5.5.3.4a(5) for each LISN.

b. EUT testing. Perform emission data scans using the measurement setup of Figure CE102-3.

(1) Turn on the EUT and allow a sufficient time for stabilization.

(2) Select an appropriate lead for testing.

(3) Scan the measurement receiver over the applicable frequency range, using the bandwidths and minimum measurement times in the Table II.

(4) Repeat 5.5.3.4b(2) and 5.5.3.4b(3) for each power lead.

5.5.3.5 Data presentation.
Data presentation shall be as follows:

a. Continuously and automatically plot amplitude versus frequency profiles on X-Y axis outputs. Manually gathered data is not acceptable except for plot verification.

b. Display the applicable limit on each plot.

c. Provide a minimum frequency resolution of 1% or twice the measurement receiver bandwidth, whichever is less stringent, and a minimum amplitude resolution of 1 dB for each plot.

d. Provide plots for both the measurement system check and measurement portions of the procedure.

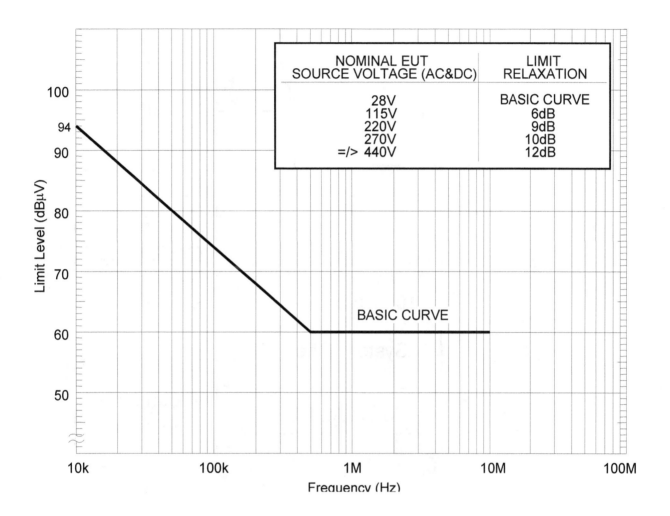

FIGURE CE102-1. CE102 limit (EUT power leads, AC and DC) for all applications.

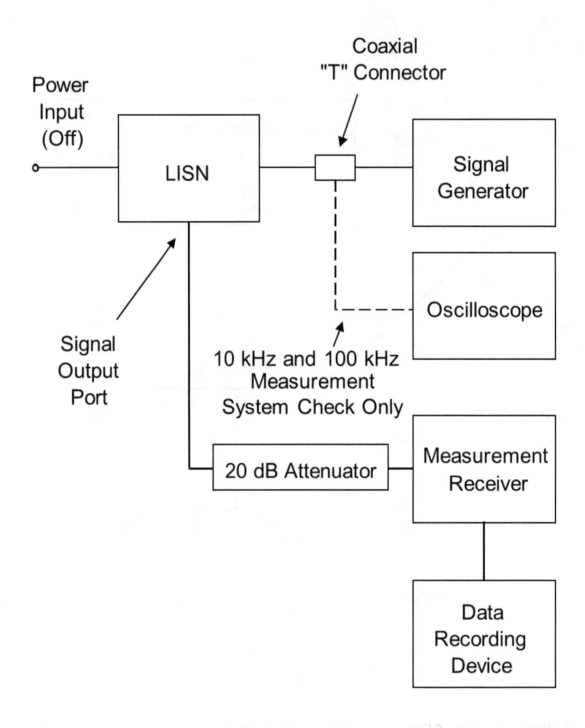

FIGURE CE102-2. Measurement system check setup.

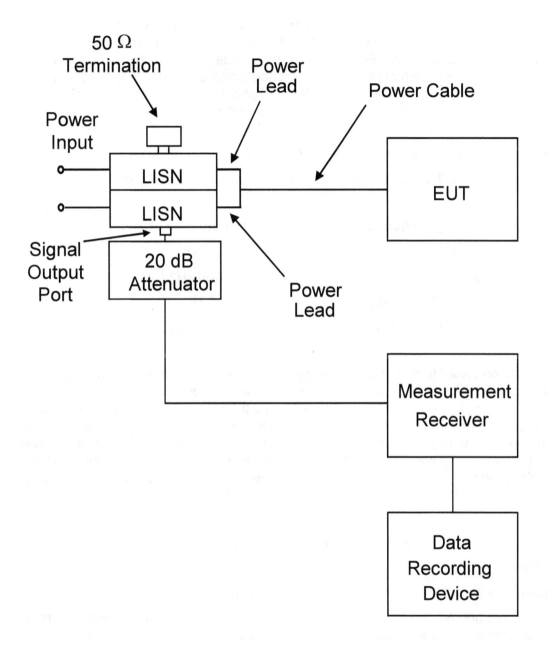

FIGURE CE102-3. Measurement setup.

5.6 CE106, conducted emissions, antenna terminal.

5.6.1 CE106 applicability.

This requirement is applicable from 10 kHz to 40 GHz for the antenna ports of transmitters, receivers, and amplifiers. The requirement is not applicable to equipment designed with antennas permanently mounted to the EUT. The transmit mode portion of this requirement is not applicable within the bandwidth of the EUT transmitted signal or within ±5 percent of the fundamental frequency, whichever is larger. For Navy shipboard applications with peak transmitter power greater than 1 kW, the 5% frequency exclusion will be increased by an additional 0.1% of the fundamental frequency for each dB above 1 kW of peak power.

Frequency Exclusion = $\pm$ f * (0.05 + (0.001/dB) * (P_{tPk} [dBm] – 60 [dBm]))

Depending on the operating frequency range of the EUT, the start frequency of the test is as follows:

EUT Operating Frequency Range	Start Frequency of Test
10 kHz to 3 MHz	10 kHz
3 MHz to 300 MHz	100 kHz
300 MHz to 3 GHz	1 MHz
3 GHz to 40 GHz	10 MHz

The equipment will be tested to an upper frequency limit based on the highest frequency generated or received by the EUT. For systems with the frequencies generated or received less than 1 GHz, the upper frequency limit will be 20 times the highest frequency or 18 GHz whichever is greater. For systems with frequencies generated or received greater than or equal to 1 GHz, the upper frequency limit will be 10 times the highest frequency or 40 GHz whichever is less. For equipment using waveguide, the requirement does not apply below eight-tenths of the waveguide's cutoff frequency. RE103 may be used as an alternative for CE106 for testing transmitters with their operational antennas.

5.6.2 CE106 limits.

Conducted emissions at the EUT antenna terminal shall not exceed the values given below.

    a.   Receivers: 34 dBμV

    b.   Transmitters and amplifiers (standby mode): 34 dBμV

    c.   Transmitters and amplifiers (transmit mode): Harmonics, except the second and third, and all other spurious emissions shall be at least 80 dB down from the level at the fundamental. The second and third harmonics shall be suppressed to a level of -20 dBm or 80 dB below the fundamental, whichever requires less suppression. For Navy shipboard applications, the second and third harmonics will be suppressed to a level of -20 dBm and all other harmonics and spurious emissions shall be suppressed to -40 dBm, except if the duty cycle of the emissions are less than 0.2%, then the limit may be relaxed to 0 dBm.

5.6.3 CE106 test procedure.

5.6.3.1 Purpose.

This test procedure is used to verify that conducted emissions appearing at the antenna terminal of the EUT do not exceed specified requirements.

5.6.3.2 Test equipment.
The test equipment shall be as follows:

a.   Measurement receiver

b.   Attenuators, 50 ohm

c.   Rejection networks

d.   Directional couplers

e.   Dummy loads, 50 ohm

f.   Signal generators. For amplifier testing, a signal generator is required to drive the amplifier that provides the modulation used in the intended application and that has spurious and harmonic outputs that are down at least 6 dB greater than the applicable limit.

g.   Data recording device

5.6.3.3 Setup.
It is not necessary to maintain the basic test setup for the EUT as shown and described on Figures 2 through 5 and 4.3.8. The test setup shall be as follows:

a.   Measurement system integrity check. Configure the test setup for the signal generator path shown on Figures CE106-1 through CE106-3 as applicable. The choice of Figure CE106-1 or CE106-2 is dependent upon the capability of the measuring equipment to handle the transmitter power.

b.   EUT testing. Configure the test setup for the EUT path shown on Figures CE106-1 through CE106-3 as applicable. The choice of Figure CE106-1 or CE106-2 is dependent upon the capability of the measuring equipment to handle the transmitter power.

5.6.3.4 Procedures.

5.6.3.4.1 Transmit mode for transmitters and amplifiers.
The test procedure shall be as follows:

a.   Turn on the measurement equipment and allow a sufficient time for stabilization.

b.   Measurement system integrity check.

(1)   Apply a known calibrated signal level from the signal generator through the system check path at a mid-band fundamental frequency (f_o).

(2)   Scan the measurement receiver in the same manner as a normal data scan. Verify the measurement receiver detects a level within ±3 dB of the expected signal.

(3)   If readings are obtained which deviate by more than ±3 dB, locate the source of the error and correct the deficiency prior to proceeding with the test.

(4)   Repeat 5.6.3.4.1b(1) through 5.6.3.4.1b(3) at the end points of the frequency range of test.

c.   EUT testing.

(1)   Turn on the EUT and allow sufficient time for stabilization.

(2)   For transmitters, tune the EUT to the desired test frequency and apply the appropriate modulation for the EUT as indicated in the equipment specification. For amplifiers, apply an input signal to the EUT that has the appropriate frequency, power level, and modulation as indicated in the equipment specification. For transmitters and amplifiers for which these parameters vary, test parameters shall be chosen such that the worst case emissions spectrum will result.

(3)   Use the measurement path to complete the rest of this procedure.

(4)   Tune the test equipment to the operating frequency (f_o) of the EUT and adjust for maximum indication.

(5)   Record the power level of the fundamental frequency (f_o) and the measurement receiver bandwidth.

(6)   Insert the fundamental frequency rejection network, when applicable.

(7)   Scan the frequency range of interest and record the level of all harmonics and spurious emissions. Add all correction factors for cable loss, attenuators and rejection networks. Maintain the same measurement receiver bandwidth used to measure the power level of the fundamental frequency (f_o) in 5.6.3.4.1c(5).

(8)   Verify spurious outputs are from the EUT and not spurious responses of the measurement system.

(9)   Repeat 5.6.3.4.1c(2) through 5.6.3.4.1c(8) for other frequencies as required by 4.3.9.1 and 4.3.9.2.

(10)   Determine measurement path losses at each spurious frequency as follows:

      (a)   Replace the EUT with a signal generator.

      (b)   Retain all couplers and rejection networks in the measurement path.

      (c)   Determine the losses through the measurement path. The value of attenuators may be reduced to facilitate the end-to-end check with a low level signal generator.

5.6.3.4.2 Receivers and stand-by mode for transmitters and amplifiers.
The test procedure shall be as follows:

a.   Turn on the measurement equipment and allow a sufficient time for stabilization.

b.   Measurement system integrity check.

      (1)   Apply a calibrated signal level, which is 6 dB below the applicable limit, from the signal generator through the system check path at a midpoint test frequency.

      (2)   Scan the measurement receiver in the same manner as a normal data scan. Verify the measurement receiver detects a level within ±3 dB of the injected signal.

      (3)   If readings are obtained which deviate by more than ±3 dB, locate the source of the error and correct the deficiency prior to proceeding with the test.

      (4)   Repeat 5.6.3.4.2b(1) through 5.6.3.4.2b(3) at the end points of the frequency range of test.

c. EUT testing.

(1) Turn on the EUT and allow sufficient time for stabilization.

(2) Tune the EUT to the desired test frequency and use the measurement path to complete the rest of this procedure.

(3) Scan the measurement receiver over the applicable frequency range, using the bandwidths and minimum measurement times of Table II.

(4) Repeat 5.6.3.4.2c(2) and 5.6.3.4.2c(3) for other frequencies as required by 4.3.9.1 and 4.3.9.2.

5.6.3.5 Data presentation.

5.6.3.5.1 Transmit mode for transmitters and amplifiers.
The data presentation shall be as follows:

a. Continuously and automatically plot amplitude versus frequency profiles for each tuned frequency. Manually gathered data is not acceptable except for plot verification.

b. Provide a minimum frequency resolution of 1% or twice the measurement receiver bandwidth, whichever is less stringent, and a minimum amplitude resolution of 1 dB for each plot.

c. Provide tabular data showing f_o and frequencies of all harmonics and spurious emissions measured, power level of the fundamental and all harmonics and spurious emissions, dB down level, and all correction factors including cable loss, attenuator pads, and insertion loss of rejection networks.

d. The relative dB down level is determined by subtracting the level in 5.6.3.4.1c(7) from that obtained in 5.6.3.4.1c(5).

5.6.3.5.2 Receivers and stand-by mode for transmitters and amplifiers.
The data presentation shall be as follows:

a. Continuously and automatically plot amplitude versus frequency profiles for each tuned frequency. Manually gathered data is not acceptable except for plot verification.

b. Display the applicable limit on each plot.

c. Provide a minimum frequency resolution of 1% or twice the measurement receiver bandwidth, whichever is less stringent, and a minimum amplitude resolution of 1 dB for each plot.

d. Provide plots for both the measurement and system check portions of the procedure.

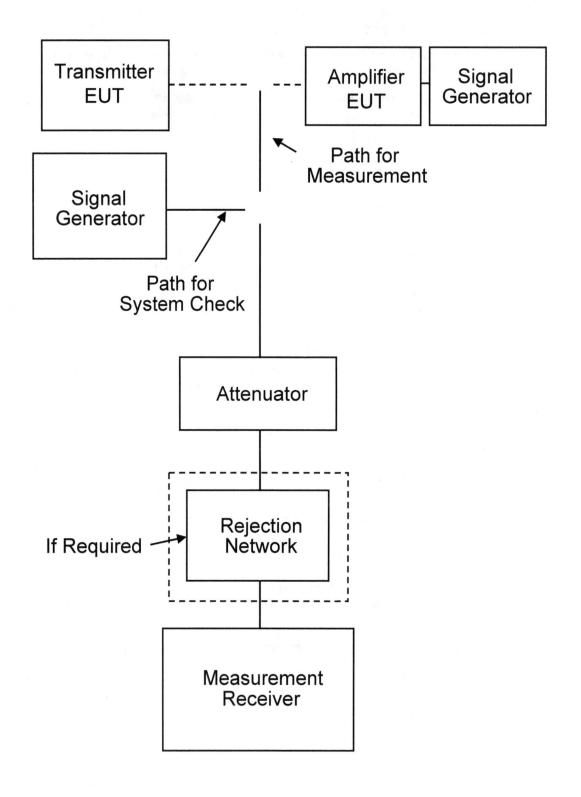

FIGURE CE106-1. Setup for low power transmitters and amplifiers.

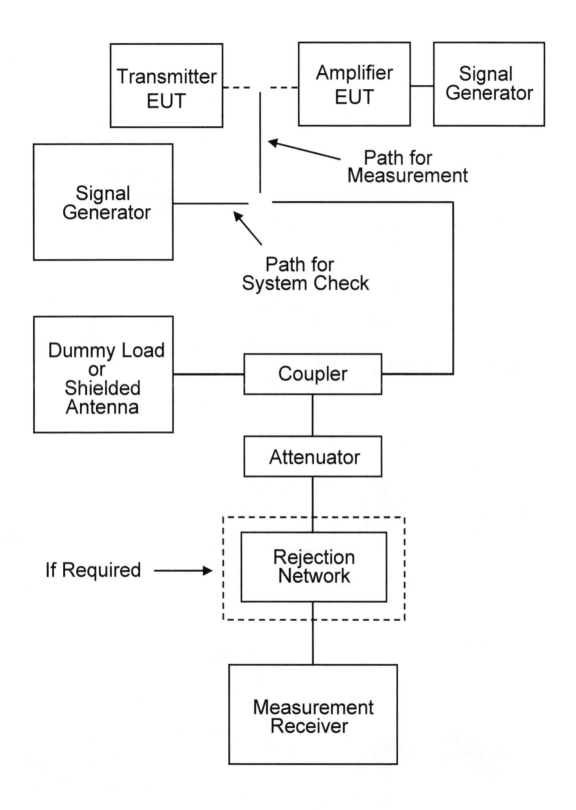

FIGURE CE106-2. Setup for high power transmitters and amplifiers.

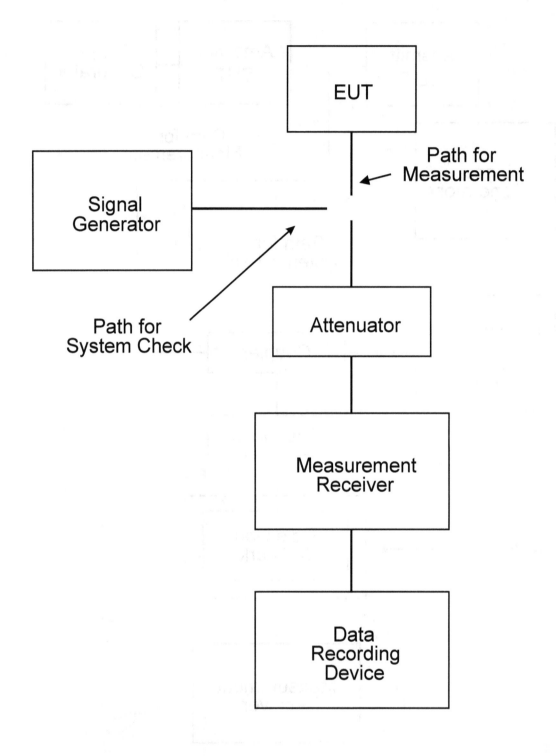

FIGURE CE106-3. Setup for receivers and stand-by mode for transmitters and amplifiers.

5.7 CS101, conducted susceptibility, power leads.

5.7.1 CS101 applicability.

This requirement is applicable from 30 Hz to 150 kHz for equipment and subsystem AC, limited to current draws ≤ 30 amperes per phase, and DC input power leads, not including returns. If the EUT is DC operated, this requirement is applicable over the frequency range of 30 Hz to 150 kHz. If the EUT is AC operated, this requirement is applicable starting from the second harmonic of the EUT power frequency and extending to 150 kHz.

5.7.2 CS101 limit.

The EUT shall not exhibit any malfunction, degradation of performance, or deviation from specified indications, beyond the tolerances indicated in the individual equipment or subsystem specification, when subjected to a test signal with voltage levels as specified on Figure CS101-1. The requirement is also met when the power source is adjusted to dissipate the power level shown on Figure CS101-2 in a 0.5 ohm load and the EUT is not susceptible.

5.7.3 CS101 test procedure.

5.7.3.1 Purpose.

This test procedure is used to verify the ability of the EUT to withstand signals coupled onto input power leads. There are two methods provided for making measurements of the applied signal. The first uses an oscilloscope with a power input isolation transformer. The second uses a measurement receiver together with a transducer. The transducer is intended to electrically isolate the receiver from the EUT power and reduce the signal levels to protect the receiver.

5.7.3.2 Test equipment.

The test equipment shall be as follows:

    a.   Signal generator

    b.   Power amplifier

    c.   Oscilloscope or measurement receiver

    d.   Coupling transformer

    e.   Capacitor, 10 µF

    f.   Isolation transformer

    g.   Resistor, 0.5 ohm

    h.   LISNs

    i.   Transducer for measurement receiver use

5.7.3.3 Setup.

The test setup shall be as follows:

    a.   Maintain a basic test setup for the EUT as shown and described on Figures 2 through 5 and 4.3.8.

    b.   Calibration. Configure the test equipment in accordance with Figure CS101-3. Set up the oscilloscope or measurement receiver/transducer to monitor the voltage across the 0.5 ohm resistor.

    c.   EUT testing.

    (1)   For DC or single phase AC power, configure the test equipment as shown on Figure CS101-4.

    (2)   For three phase ungrounded power, configure the test setup as shown on Figure CS101-5.

    (3)   For three phase wye power (four power leads), configure the test setup as shown on Figure CS101-6.

5.7.3.4 Procedures.

The test procedures shall be as follows:

  a. Turn on the measurement equipment and allow sufficient time for stabilization.

  b. Calibration.

    (1)   Set the signal generator to the lowest test frequency.

    (2)   Increase the applied signal until the oscilloscope or measurement receiver indicates the voltage level corresponding to the maximum required power level specified for the limit on Figure CS101-2. Verify the output waveform is sinusoidal for oscilloscope measurements.

    (3)   Record the setting of the signal source.

    (4)   Scan the required frequency range for testing and record the signal source setting needed to maintain the required power level.

  c. EUT testing.

    (1)   Turn on the EUT and allow sufficient time for stabilization. CAUTION: Exercise care when performing this test since the "safety ground" of the oscilloscope is disconnected due to the isolation transformer and a shock hazard may be present.

    (2)   Set the signal generator to the lowest test frequency. Increase the signal level until the required voltage or power level is reached on the power lead. (NOTE: Power is limited to the level calibrated in 5.7.3.4b(2).)

    (3)   While maintaining at least the required signal level, scan through the required frequency range at a rate no greater than specified in Table III.

    (4)   Susceptibility evaluation.

        (a) Monitor the EUT for degradation of performance.

        (b) If susceptibility is noted, determine the threshold level in accordance with 4.3.10.4.3.

    (5)   Repeat 5.7.3.4c(2) through 5.7.3.4c(4) for each power lead, as required. For three phase ungrounded power, the measurements shall be made as specified below:

Coupling Transformer in Line	Voltage Measurement From
A	A to B
B	B to C
C	C to A

For three phase wye power (four leads) the measurements shall be made as specified below:

Coupling Transformer in Line	Voltage Measurement From
A	A to neutral
B	B to neutral
C	C to neutral

5.7.3.5 Data presentation.

Data presentation shall be as follows:

a. Provide graphical or tabular data showing the frequencies and amplitudes at which the test was conducted for each lead.

b. Provide data on any susceptibility thresholds and the associated frequencies that were determined for each power lead.

c. Provide indications of compliance with the applicable requirements for the susceptibility evaluation specified in 5.7.3.4c for each lead.

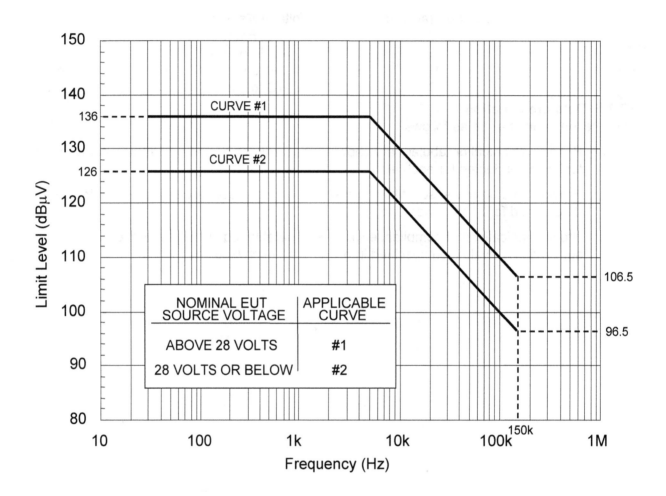

FIGURE CS101-1. CS101 voltage limit for all applications.

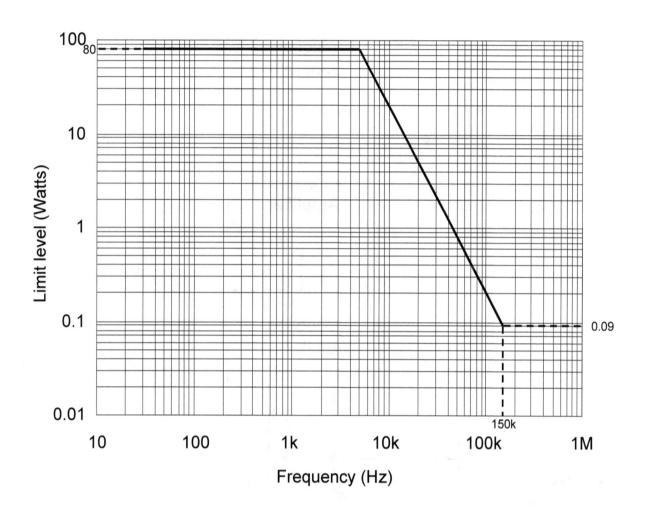

FIGURE CS101-2. CS101 power limit for all applications.

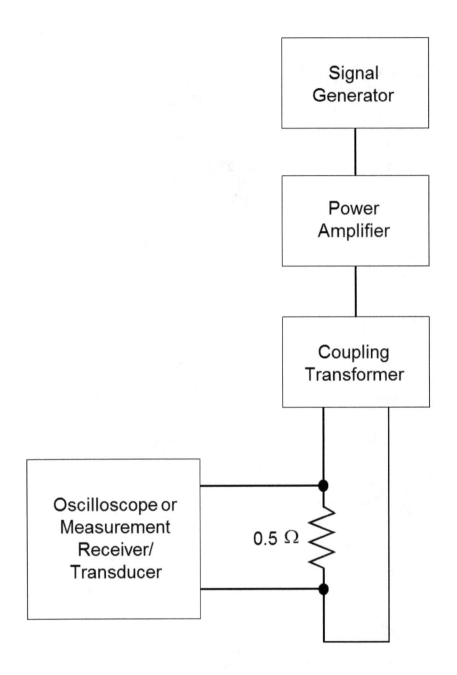

FIGURE CS101-3. Calibration.

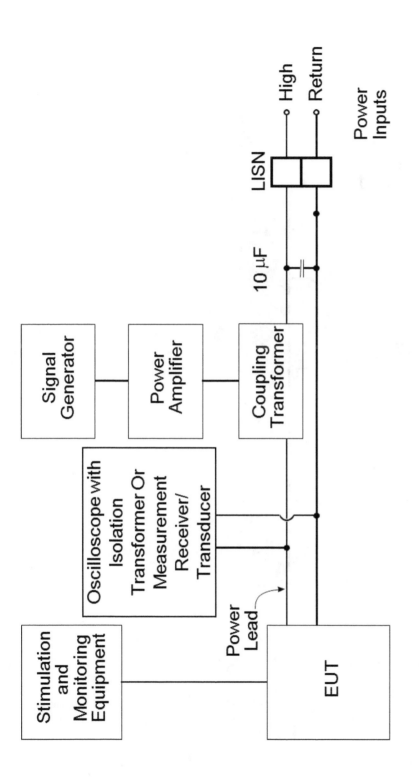

FIGURE CS101-4. Signal injection, DC or single phase AC.

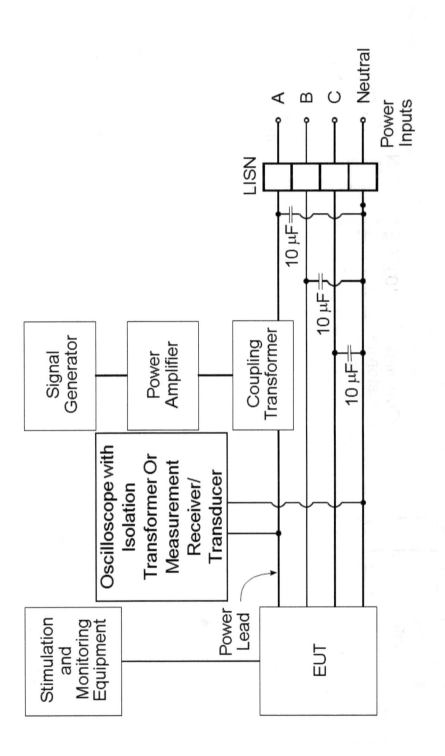

FIGURE CS101-5. Signal injection, 3-phase wye.

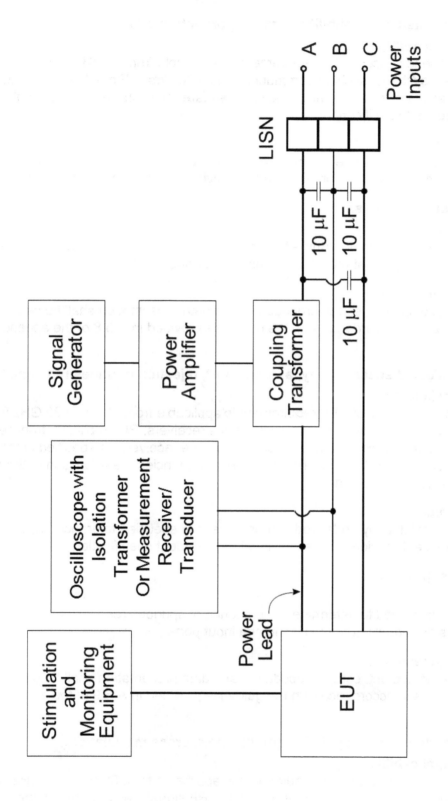

FIGURE CS101-6. Signal injection, 3-phase delta.

5.8 CS103, conducted susceptibility, antenna port, intermodulation.

5.8.1 CS103 applicability.

This receiver front-end susceptibility requirement is applicable from 15 kHz to 10 GHz for equipment and subsystems, such as communications receivers, RF amplifiers, transceivers, radar receivers, acoustic receivers, and electronic warfare receivers as specified in the individual procurement specification.

5.8.2 CS103 limit.

The EUT shall not exhibit any intermodulation products beyond specified tolerances when subjected to the limit requirement provided in the individual procurement specification.

5.8.3 CS103 test procedures.

5.8.3.1 Purpose.

This test procedure is used to determine the presence of intermodulation products that may be caused by undesired signals at the EUT antenna input ports.

5.8.3.2 Test requirements.

The required test equipment, setup, procedures, and data presentation shall be determined on a case-by-case basis in accordance with the guidance provided in A.5.8 of the appendix of this standard.

5.9 CS104, conducted susceptibility, antenna port, rejection of undesired signals.

5.9.1 CS104 applicability.

This receiver front-end susceptibility requirement is applicable from 30 Hz to 20 GHz for equipment and subsystems, such as communications receivers, RF amplifiers, transceivers, radar receivers, acoustic receivers, and electronic warfare receivers as specified in the individual procurement specification. The applicable frequencies are a function of the frontend design of the unit being evaluated.

5.9.2 CS104 limit.

The EUT shall not exhibit any undesired response beyond specified tolerances when subjected to the limit requirement provided in the individual procurement specification.

5.9.3 CS104 test procedures.

5.9.3.1 Purpose.

This test procedure is used to determine the presence of spurious responses that may be caused by undesired signals at the EUT antenna input ports.

5.9.3.2 Test requirements.

The required test equipment, setup, procedures, and data presentation shall be determined on a case-by-case basis in accordance with the guidance provided in A.5.9 of the appendix of this standard.

5.10 CS105, conducted susceptibility, antenna port, cross modulation.

5.10.1 CS105 applicability.

This receiver front-end susceptibility requirement is applicable from 30 Hz to 20 GHz only for receivers that normally process amplitude-modulated RF signals, as specified in the individual procurement specification.

5.10.2 CS105 limit.

The EUT shall not exhibit any undesired response, due to cross modulation, beyond specified tolerances when subjected to the limit requirement provided in the individual procurement specification.

5.10.3 CS105 test procedures.

5.10.3.1 Purpose.

This test procedure is used to determine the presence of cross-modulation products that may be caused by undesired signals at the EUT antenna ports.

5.10.3.2 Test requirements.

The required test equipment, setup, procedures, and data presentation shall be determined in accordance with the guidance provided in A.5.10 of the appendix of this standard.

5.11 CS109, conducted susceptibility, structure current.

5.11.1 CS109 applicability.

This requirement is applicable from 60 Hz to 100 kHz for equipment and subsystems that have an operating frequency of 100 kHz or less and an operating sensitivity of 1 μV or better (such as 0.5 μV). Handheld equipment is exempt from this requirement.

5.11.2 CS109 limit.

The EUT shall not exhibit any malfunction, degradation of performance, or deviation from specified indications, beyond the tolerances indicated in the individual equipment or subsystem specification, when subjected to the values shown on Figure CS109-1.

5.11.3 CS109 test procedures.

5.11.3.1 Purpose.

This test procedure is used to verify the ability of the EUT to withstand structure currents.

5.11.3.2 Test equipment.

The test equipment shall be as follows:

    a.   Signal generator

    b.   Amplifier (if required)

    c.   Isolation transformers

    d.   Current probe

    e.   Measurement receiver

    f.   Resistor, 0.5 ohm

    g.   Coupling transformer

5.11.3.3 Setup.

The test setup shall be as follows:

    a.   It is not necessary to maintain the basic test setup for the EUT as shown and described on Figures 2 through 5 and in 4.3.8.

    b.   Calibration. No special calibration is required.

    c.   EUT testing.

(1)   As shown on Figure CS109-2, configure the EUT and the test equipment (including the test signal source, the test current measurement equipment, and the equipment required for operating the EUT or measuring performance degradation) to establish a single-point ground for the test setup using the EUT ground terminal.

      (a)   Using isolation transformers, isolate all AC power sources. For DC power, isolation transformers are not applicable.

      (b)   Disconnect the safety ground leads of all input power cables.

      (c)   Place the EUT and the test equipment on non-conductive surfaces to enable a single point ground to be established.

(2)   The test points for the injected currents shall be as follows:

      (a)   Equipment that will not be rack mounted: At diagonal extremes across only the mounting surface.

      (b)   Rack mounted equipment: At diagonal extremes across all surfaces of the equipment.

      (c)   Deck resting equipment: At diagonal extremes across all surfaces of the equipment.

      (d)   Bulkhead mounted equipment: At diagonal extremes across rear surface of the equipment.

      (e)   Cables (all mounting methods): Between cable armor, which is terminated at the EUT, and the single point ground established for the test setup. This requirement shall also apply to cable shields and conduit, unless they have a single point ground.

(3)   Connect the signal generator and resistor to a selected set of test points. Attachment to the test points shall be by conductors that are perpendicular to the test surface for a length of at least 50 cm.

5.11.3.4 Procedures.

The test procedures shall be as follows:

a.   Turn on the EUT and measurement equipment and allow sufficient time for stabilization.

b.   Set the signal generator to the lowest required frequency. Adjust the signal generator to the required level as a minimum. Monitor the current with the current probe and measurement receiver.

c.   Scan the signal generator over the required frequency range in accordance with Table III while maintaining the current level at least to the level specified in the applicable limit. Monitor the EUT for susceptibility.

d.   If susceptibility is noted, determine the threshold level in accordance with 4.3.10.4.3.

e.   Repeat 5.11.3.4b through 5.11.3.4d for each diagonal set of test points on each surface of the EUT to be tested.

5.11.3.5 Data presentation.

Data presentation shall be as follows:

a. Provide a table showing the mode of operation, susceptible frequency, current threshold level, current limit level, and susceptible test points.

b. Provide a diagram of the EUT showing the location of each set of test points.

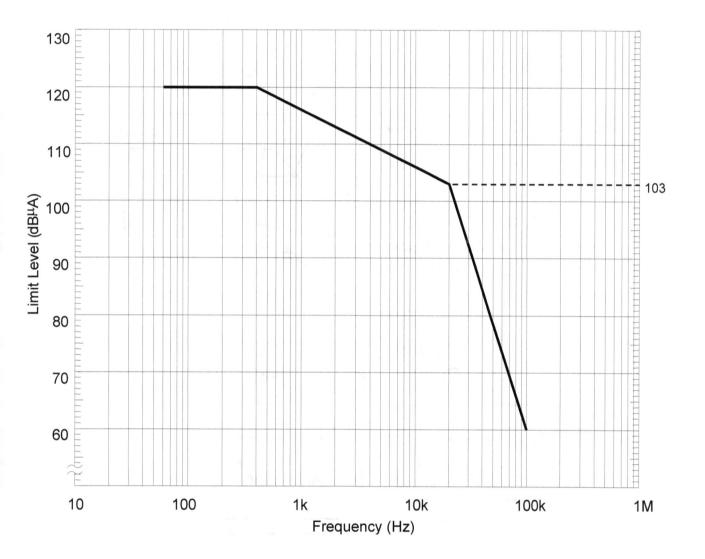

FIGURE CS109-1. CS109 limit.

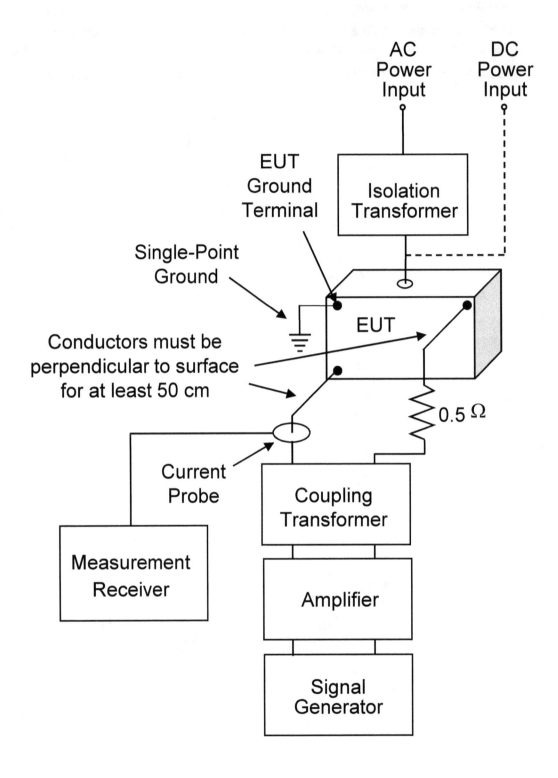

FIGURE CS109-2. Test configuration.

5.12 CS114, conducted susceptibility, bulk cable injection.

5.12.1 CS114 applicability.

This requirement is applicable from 10 kHz to 200 MHz for all interconnecting cables, including power cables. For EUTs intended to be installed on ships or submarines, an additional common mode limit of 77 dBµA is applicable from 4 kHz to 1 MHz on complete power cables (highs and returns - common mode test).

5.12.2 CS114 limit.

The EUT shall not exhibit any malfunction, degradation of performance, or deviation from specified indications beyond the tolerances indicated in the individual equipment or subsystem specification, when subjected to an injection probe drive level which has been pre-calibrated to the appropriate current limit shown on Figure CS114-1 and is modulated as specified below. The appropriate limit curve on Figure CS114-1 shall be selected from Table VI. Requirements are also met if the EUT is not susceptible at forward power levels sensed by the directional coupler that are below those determined during calibration provided that the actual current induced in the cable under test is Curve 5 = 115 dBµA, Curve 4 = 103 dBµA, Curve 3 = 95 dBµA, Curve 2 = 88 dBµA and Curve 1 = 83 dBµA across the frequency range.

The requirement is not applicable for coaxial cables to antenna ports of antenna-connected receivers except for surface ships and submarines.

5.12.3 CS114 test procedures.

5.12.3.1 Purpose.

This test procedure is used to verify the ability of the EUT to withstand RF signals coupled onto EUT associated cabling.

5.12.3.2 Test equipment.

The test equipment shall be as follows:

    a.   Measurement receivers

    b.   Current injection probes (maximum and minimum insertion loss shown on Figure CS114-2)

    c.   Current probes

    d.   Calibration fixture: coaxial transmission line with 50 ohm characteristic impedance, coaxial connections on both ends, and space for an injection probe around the center conductor.

    e.   Directional couplers

    f.   Signal generators

    g.   Plotter

    h.   Attenuators, 50 ohm

    i.   Coaxial loads, 50 ohm

    j.   Power amplifiers

    k.   LISNs

5.12.3.3 Setup.

The test setup shall be as follows:

a. Maintain a basic test setup for the EUT as shown and described on Figures 2 through 5 and in 4.3.8.

b. Calibration. Configure the test equipment in accordance with Figure CS114-3 for calibrating injection probes.

    (1) Place the injection probe around the center conductor of the calibration fixture and the monitor probe around a second fixture. Terminate the monitor probe with a 50 ohm load. This compensates for the monitor probe loading effects to be encountered in the EUT test.

    (2) Terminate one end of the calibration fixture with a 50 ohm load and terminate the other end with an attenuator connected to measurement receiver A.

c. EUT testing. Configure the test equipment as shown on Figure CS114-5 for testing of the EUT.

    (1) Place the injection and monitor probes around a cable bundle interfacing with EUT connector.

    (2) To minimize errors, maintain the same signal circuit that was used for calibration between the attenuator at the calibration fixture (oscilloscope, coaxial cables, bulkhead connectors, additional attenuators, etc.) and connect the circuit to the monitor probe. Additional attenuation may be used, if necessary.

    (3) Locate the monitor probe 5 cm from the connector. If the overall length of the connector and backshell exceeds 5 cm, position the monitor probe as close to the connector's backshell as possible.

    (4) Position the injection probe 5 cm from the monitor probe.

5.12.3.4 Procedures.

The test procedures shall be as follows:

a. Turn on the measurement equipment and allow sufficient time for stabilization.

b. Calibration. Perform the following procedures using the calibration setup.

    (1) Set the signal generator to 10 kHz, unmodulated.

    (2) Increase the applied signal until measurement receiver A indicates the current level specified in the applicable limit is flowing in the center conductor of the calibration fixture.

    (3) Record the "forward power" to the injection probe indicated on measurement receiver B.

    (4) Scan the frequency band from 10 kHz to 200 MHz and record the forward power needed to maintain the required current amplitude.

c. Verification. With the probes still in the calibration setup, configure the verification of the test system using Figure CS114-4. Conduct a scan as though this is a test of an EUT cable.

    (1) Set the signal generator to 10 kHz (modulation is optional and should not have an effect.

(2)   Apply the forward power level determined under 5.12.3.4b(4) to the injection probe while monitoring the induced current on the monitor probe.

(3)   Scan the required frequency range with minimal dwell times and step sizes twice those in Table II with while maintaining the forward power level at the calibrated level determined under 5.12.3.4b(4). Verify that the forward power follows the calibration and that the developed current is within a 3 dB tolerance of the current test limit.

d.   EUT testing. Configure the test as indicated on Figure CS114-5. Perform the following procedures on each cable bundle interfacing with each electrical connector on the EUT including complete power cables (high sides and returns). Also perform the procedures on power cables with the power returns and chassis grounds (green wires) excluded from the cable bundle. For connectors which include both interconnecting leads and power, perform the procedures on the entire bundle, on the power leads (including returns and grounds) grouped separately, and on the power leads grouped with the returns and grounds removed.

(1)   Turn on the EUT and allow sufficient time for stabilization.

(2)   Susceptibility evaluation.

(a)   Set the signal generator to 10 kHz with 1 kHz pulse modulation, 50% duty cycle. Verify that the modulation is present on the drive signal for each signal generator/modulation source combination. Ensure that the modulation frequency, waveform and depth (40 dB minimum from peak to baseline) are correct.

(b)   Apply the forward power level determined under 5.12.3.4b(4) to the injection probe while monitoring the induced current. For shielded cables or low impedance circuits, it may be preferable to increase the signal gradually to limit the current.

(c)   Scan the required frequency range in accordance with 4.3.10.4.1 and Table III while maintaining the forward power level at the calibration level determined under 5.12.3.4b(4), or the maximum current level for the applicable limit, whichever is less stringent.

(d)   Monitor the EUT for degradation of performance during testing.

(e)   Whenever susceptibility is noted, determine the threshold level in accordance with 4.3.10.4.3.

(f)   For EUTs with redundant cabling for safety critical reasons such as multiple data buses, use simultaneous multi-cable injection techniques.

5.12.3.5 Data presentation.
Data presentation shall be as follows:

a.   Provide amplitude versus frequency plots for the forward power levels required to obtain the calibration level as determined in 5.12.3.4b.

b.   Provide tables showing scanned frequency ranges and statements of compliance with the requirements for the susceptibility evaluation of 5.12.3.4c(2) for each interface connector. Provide any susceptibility thresholds that were determined, along with their associated frequencies.

TABLE VI. CS114 limit curves.

PLATFORM / FREQUENCY RANGE		AIRCRFAFT (EXTERNAL OR SAFETY CRITICAL)	AIRCRAFT INTERNAL	ALL SHIPS (ABOVE DECKS) AND SUBMARINES (EXTERNAL)*	SHIPS (METALLIC) (BELOW DECKS)	SHIPS (NON-METALLIC) (BELOW DECK)**	SUBMARINE (INTERNAL)	GROUND	SPACE
4 kHz to 1MHz	N	-	-	77 dBµA	77 dBµA	77 dBµA	77 dBµA	-	-
10 kHz to 2 MHz	A	5	5	2	2	2	1	3	3
	N	5	3	2	2	2	1	2	3
	AF	5	3	-	-	-	-	2	3
2 MHz to 30 MHz	A	5	5	5	2	4	1	4	3
	N	5	5	5	2	4	1	2	3
	AF	5	3	-	-	-	-	2	3
30 MHz to 200 MHZ	A	5	5	5	2	2	2	4	3
	N	5	5	5	2	2	2	2	3
	AF	5	3	-	-	-	-	2	3

Table heading: LIMIT CURVE NUMBERS SHOWN IN FIGURE CS-114-1 AND LIMITS

* For equipment located external to the pressure hull of a submarine but within the superstructure, use SHIPS (METALLIC) (BELOW DECKS)

** For equipment located in the hanger deck of Aircraft Carriers

KEY: A = Army
N = Navy
AF = Air Force

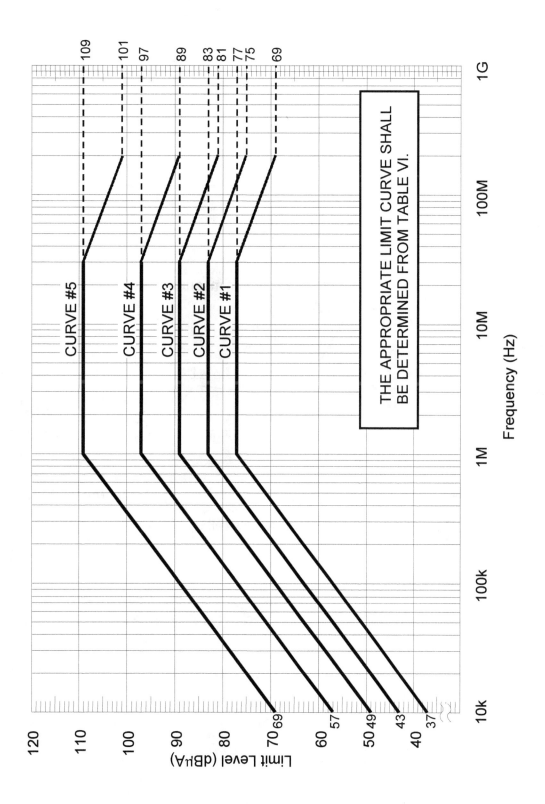

FIGURE CS114-1. CS114 calibration limits.

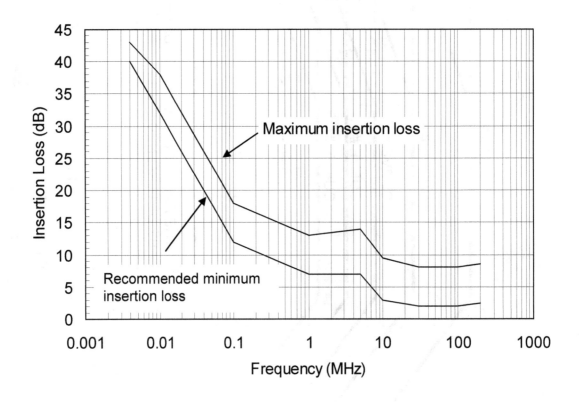

FIGURE CS114-2. Maximum insertion loss for injection probes.

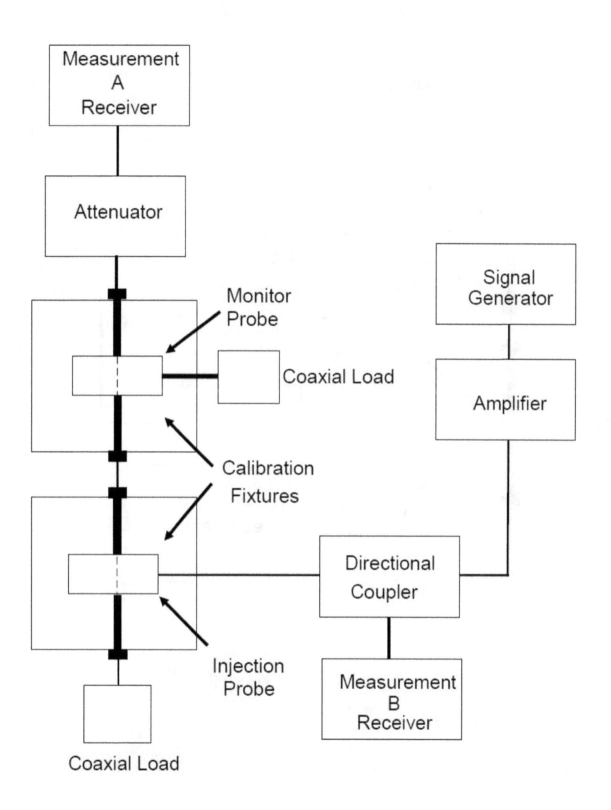

FIGURE CS114-3. Calibration setup.

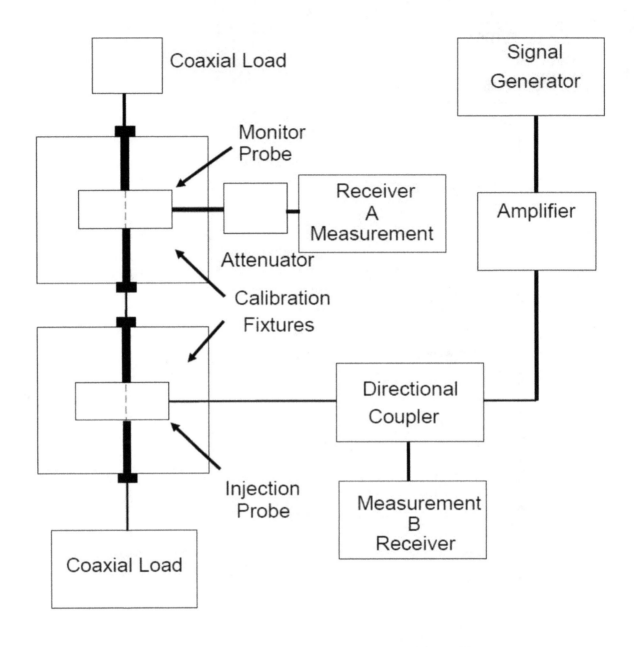

FIGURE CS114-4. Verification setup.

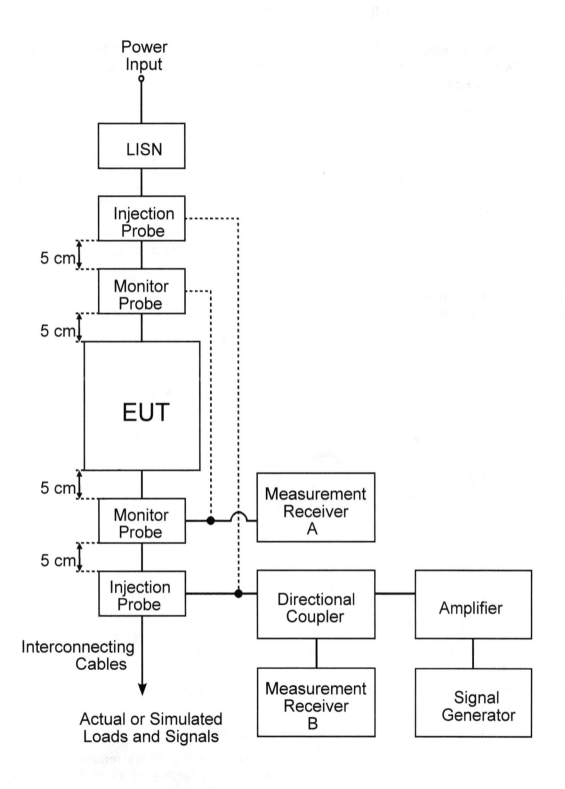

FIGURE CS114-5. Bulk cable injection evaluation.

5.13 CS115, conducted susceptibility, bulk cable injection, impulse excitation.

5.13.1 CS115 applicability.

This requirement is applicable to all aircraft, space, and ground system interconnecting cables, including power cables. The requirement is also applicable for surface ship and submarine subsystems and equipment when specified by the procuring activity.

5.13.2 CS115 limit.

The EUT shall not exhibit any malfunction, degradation of performance, or deviation from specified indications, beyond the tolerances indicated in the individual equipment or subsystems specification, when subjected to a pre-calibrated signal having rise and fall times, pulse width, and amplitude as specified on Figure CS115-1 at a 30 Hz rate for one minute.

5.13.3 CS115 test procedures.

5.13.3.1 Purpose.

This test procedure is used to verify the ability of the EUT to withstand impulse signals coupled onto EUT associated cabling.

5.13.3.2 Test equipment.

The test equipment shall be as follows:

    a.   Pulse generator, 50 ohm, charged line (coaxial)

    b.   Current injection probe

    c.   Drive cable, 50 ohm, 2 meters, 0.5 dB or less insertion loss at 500 MHz

    d.   Current probe

    e.   Calibration fixture: coaxial transmission line with 50 ohm characteristic impedance, coaxial connections on both ends, and space for an injection probe around the center conductor.

    f.   Oscilloscope, 50 ohm input impedance

    g.   Attenuators, 50 ohm

    h.   Coaxial loads, 50 ohm

    i.   LISNs

5.13.3.3 Setup.

The test setup shall be as follows:

    a.   Maintain a basic test setup for the EUT as shown and described on Figures 2 through 5 and 4.3.8.

    b.   Calibration. Configure the test equipment in accordance with Figure CS115-2 for calibrating the injection probe.

        (1)   Place the injection probe around the center conductor of the calibration fixture.

        (2)   Terminate one end of the calibration fixture with a coaxial load and terminate the other end with an attenuator connected to an oscilloscope with 50 ohm input impedance.

    c.   EUT testing. Configure the test equipment as shown on Figure CS115-3 for testing of the EUT.

(1) Place the injection and monitor probes around a cable bundle interfacing with an EUT connector.

(2) To minimize errors, maintain the same signal circuit that was used for calibration between the attenuator at the calibration fixture (oscilloscope, coaxial cables, bulkhead connectors, additional attenuators, etc.) and connect the circuit to the monitor probe. Additional attenuation may be used, if necessary.

(3) Locate the monitor probe 5 cm from the connector. If the overall length of the connector and backshell exceeds 5 cm, position the monitor probe as close to the connector's backshell as possible.

(4) Position the injection probe 5 cm from the monitor probe.

5.13.3.4 Procedures.
The test procedures shall be as follows:

a. Turn on the measurement equipment and allow sufficient time for stabilization.

b. Calibration. Perform the following procedures using the calibration setup.

  (1) Adjust the pulse generator source for the risetime, pulse width, and pulse repetition rate requirements specified in the requirement.

  (2) Increase the signal applied to the calibration fixture until the oscilloscope indicates that the current level specified in the requirement is flowing in the center conductor of the calibration fixture.

  (3) Verify that the rise time, fall time, and pulse width portions of the waveform have the correct durations and that the correct repetition rate is present. The precise pulse shape will not be reproduced due to the inductive coupling mechanism.

  (4) Record the pulse generator amplitude setting.

c. EUT testing.

  (1) Turn on the EUT and allow sufficient time for stabilization.

  (2) Susceptibility evaluation.

    (a) Adjust the pulse generator, as a minimum, for the amplitude setting determined in 5.13.3.4b(4).

    (b) Apply the test signal at the pulse repetition rate and for the duration specified in the requirement.

    (c) Monitor the EUT for degradation of performance during testing.

    (d) Whenever susceptibility is noted, determine the threshold level in accordance with 4.3.10.4.3.

    (e) Record the peak current induced in the cable as indicated on the oscilloscope.

    (f) Repeat 5.13.3.4c(2)(a) through 5.13.3.4c(2)(e) on each cable bundle interfacing with each electrical connector on the EUT. For power cables, perform 5.13.3.4c(2)(a) through 5.13.3.4c(2)(e) on complete power cables (high sides and returns) and on the power cables with the power returns and chassis grounds (green wires) excluded from the cable bundle. For connectors which include both interconnecting leads and power, perform 5.13.3.4c(2)(a) through 5.13.3.4c(2)(e) on the entire bundle, on the power leads (including returns and grounds) grouped separately, and on the power leads grouped with the returns and grounds removed.

5.13.3.5 Data presentation.
Data presentation shall be as follows:

a. Provide tables showing statements of compliance with the requirement for the susceptibility evaluation of 5.13.3.4c(2) and the induced current level for each interface connector.

b. Provide any susceptibility thresholds that were determined.

c. Provide oscilloscope photographs of injected waveforms with test data.

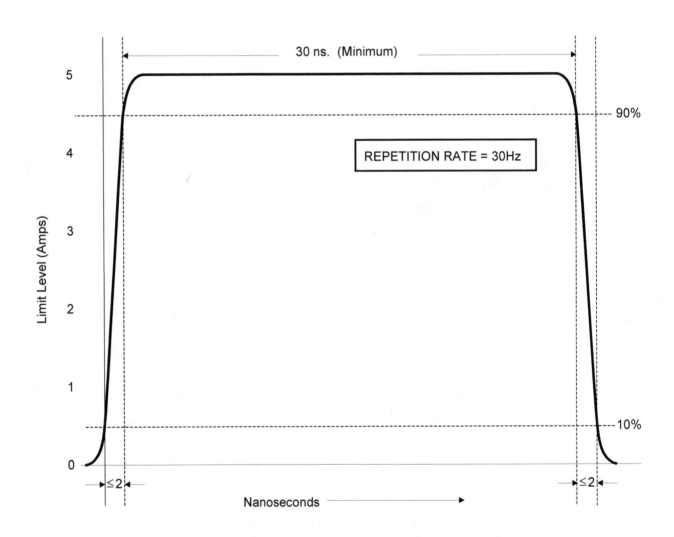

FIGURE CS115-1. CS115 signal characteristics for all applications.

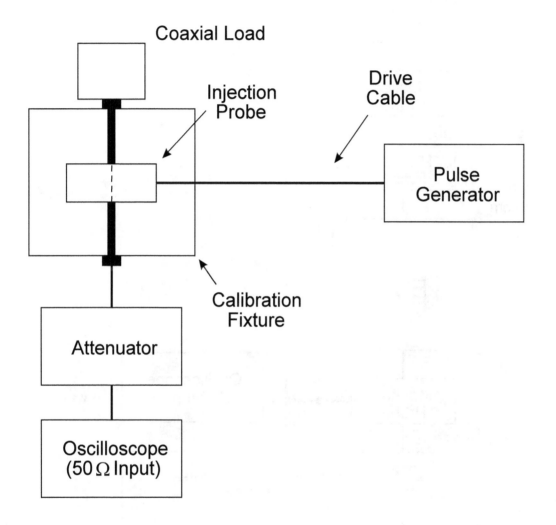

FIGURE CS115-2. Calibration setup.

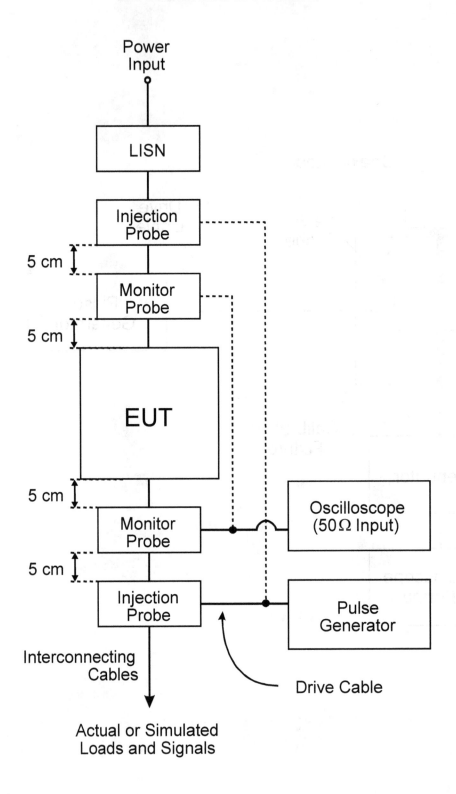

FIGURE CS115-3. Bulk cable injection.

5.14 CS116, conducted susceptibility, damped sinusoidal transients, cables and power leads.

5.14.1 CS116 applicability.

This requirement is applicable from 10 kHz to 100 MHz for all interconnecting cables, including power cables, and individual high side power leads. Power returns and neutrals need not be tested individually. For submarine applications, this requirement is applicable only to cables and leads external to or that exit the pressure hull.

5.14.2 CS116 limit.

The EUT shall not exhibit any malfunction, degradation of performance, or deviation from specified indications, beyond the tolerances indicated in the individual equipment or subsystem specification, when subjected to a signal having the waveform shown on Figure CS116-1 and having a maximum current as specified on Figure CS116-2. The limit is applicable across the entire specified frequency range. As a minimum, compliance shall be demonstrated at the following frequencies: 0.01, 0.1, 1, 10, 30, and 100 MHz. If there are other frequencies known to be critical to the equipment installation, such as platform resonances, compliance shall also be demonstrated at those frequencies. The test signal repetition rate shall be no greater than one pulse per second and no less than one pulse every two seconds. The pulses shall be applied for a period of five minutes.

5.14.3 CS116 test procedures.

5.14.3.1 Purpose.

This test procedure is used to verify the ability of the EUT to withstand damped sinusoidal transients coupled onto EUT associated cables and power leads.

5.14.3.2 Test equipment.

The test equipment shall be as follows:

    a. Damped sinusoid transient generator, $\leq$ 100 ohm output impedance

    b. Current injection probe

    c. Oscilloscope, 50 ohm input impedance

    d. Calibration fixture: Coaxial transmission line with 50 ohm characteristic impedance, coaxial connections on both ends, and space for an injection probe around the center conductor

    e. Current probes

    f. Waveform recording device

    g. Attenuators, 50 ohm

    h. Measurement receivers

    i. Coaxial loads, 50 ohm

    j. LISNs

5.14.3.3 Setup.

The test setup shall be as follows:

    a. Maintain a basic test setup for the EUT as shown and described on Figures 2 through 5 and 4.3.8.

b. Calibration. Configure the test equipment in accordance with Figure CS116-3 for verification of the waveform.

c. EUT testing:

(1) Configure the test equipment as shown on Figure CS116-4.

(2) To minimize errors, maintain the same signal circuit that was used for calibration between the attenuator at the calibration fixture (oscilloscope, coaxial cables, bulkhead connectors, additional attenuators, etc.) and connect the circuit to the monitor probe. Additional attenuation may be used, if necessary.

(3) Place the injection and monitor probes around a cable bundle interfacing an EUT connector.

(4) Locate the monitor probe 5 cm from the connector. If the overall length of the connector and backshell exceeds 5 cm, position the monitor probe as close to the connector's backshell as possible.

(5) Position the injection probe 5 cm from the monitor probe.

5.14.3.4 Procedures.

The test procedures shall be as follows:

a. Turn on the measurement equipment and allow sufficient time for stabilization.

b. Calibration. Perform the following procedures using the calibration setup for waveform verification.

(1) Set the frequency of the damped sine generator at 10 kHz.

(2) Adjust the amplitude of the signal from the damped sine generator to the level specified in the requirement.

(3) Record the damped sine generator settings.

(4) Verify and record that the waveform complies with the requirements. Calculate and record the damping factor (Q).

(5) Repeat 5.14.3.4b(2) through 5.14.3.4b(4) for each frequency specified in the requirement and those identified in 5.14.3.4c(2).

c. EUT testing. Perform the following procedures, using the EUT test setup on each cable bundle interfacing with each connector on the EUT including complete power cables. Also perform tests on each individual high side power lead (individual power returns and neutrals are not required to be tested). For delta configured power leads, test each power lead separately in addition to bulk cable.

(1) Turn on the EUT and measurement equipment to allow sufficient time for stabilization.

(2) Set the damped sine generator to a test frequency.

(3) Apply the calibrated test signals to each cable or power lead of the EUT sequentially. Reduce the signal, if necessary, to produce the required current. For shielded cables or low impedance circuits, it may be preferable to increase the signal gradually to limit the current. Record the peak current obtained.

(4) Monitor the EUT for degradation of performance.

(5)   If susceptibility is noted, determine the threshold level in accordance with 4.3.10.4.3.

(6)   Repeat 5.14.3.4c(2) through 5.14.3.4c(5) for each test frequency as specified in the requirement.

5.14.3.5 Data presentation.
Data presentation shall be as follows:

a.   Provide a list of the frequencies and amplitudes at which the test was conducted for each cable and lead.

b.   Provide data on any susceptibility thresholds and the associated frequencies that were determined for each connector and power lead.

c.   Provide indications of compliance with the requirements for the susceptibility evaluation specified in 5.14.3.4c for each interface connector.

d.   Provide oscilloscope photographs of calibrated (with Q values) and injected waveforms with test data.

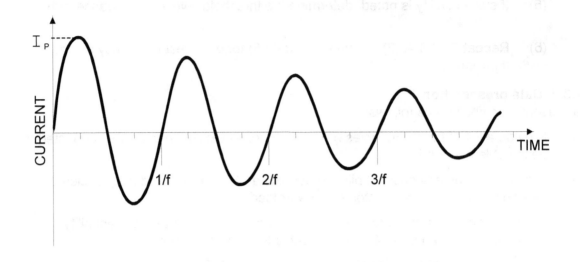

NOTES: 1. Normalized waveform: $e^{-(\pi f\,t)/Q}\sin(2\pi ft)$

Where:
f = Frequency (Hz)
t = Time (sec)
Q = Damping factor, 15 ± 5

2. Damping factor (Q) shall be determined as follows:

$$Q = \frac{\pi(N-1)}{\ln(I_P/I_N)}$$

Where:
Q = Damping factor
N = Cycle number (i.e. N = 2, 3, 4, 5,...)
I_P = Peak current at 1st cycle
I_N = Peak current at cycle closest to 50% decay
ln = Natural log
3. I_P as specified in Figure CS116-2

FIGURE CS116-1. Typical CS116 damped sinusoidal waveform.

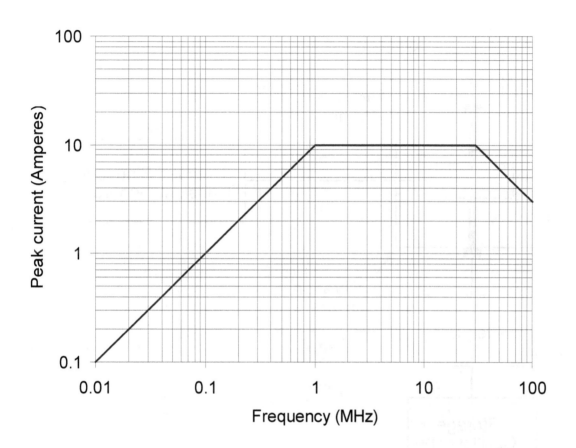

FIGURE CS116-2. CS116 limit for all applications.

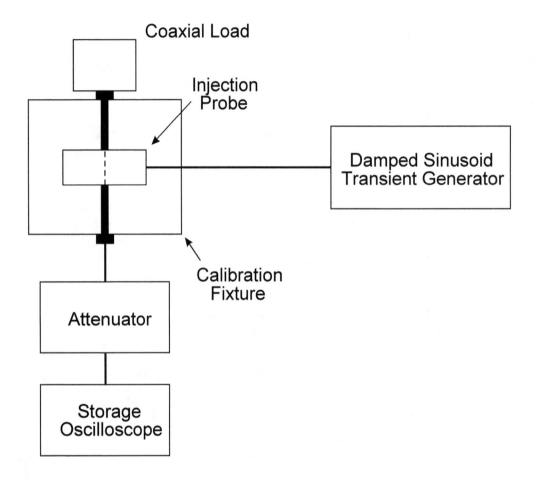

FIGURE CS116-3. Typical test setup for calibration of test waveform.

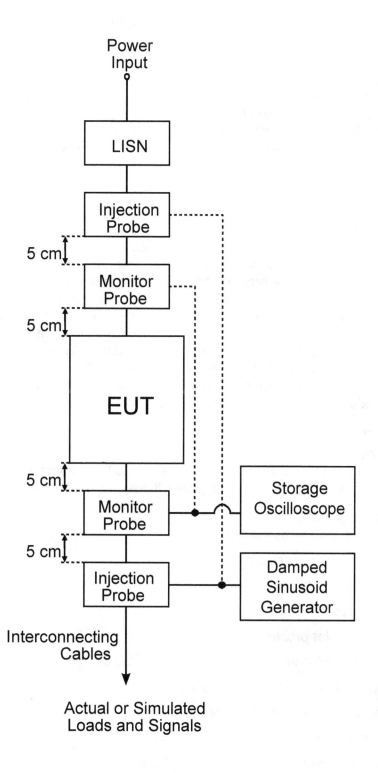

FIGURE CS116-4. Typical set up for bulk cable injection of damped sinusoidal transients.

5.15 CS117, conducted susceptibility, lightning induced transients, cables and power leads.

5.15.1 CS117 applicability.

This requirement is applicable to all aircraft safety-critical equipment interconnecting cables, including complete power cables, and individual high side power leads. It is also applicable to non-safety critical equipment with interconnecting cables/electrical interfaces that are part of or connected to equipment performing safety critical functions. It may be applicable to aircraft equipment performing non-safety critical functions when specified by the procuring activity. This requirement applies to surface ship equipment which is located above deck or has interconnecting cables which are routed above deck.

5.15.2 CS117 limit.

The EUT shall not exhibit any malfunction, degradation of performance, or deviation from specified indications, beyond the tolerances indicated in the individual equipment or subsystem specification, when subjected to the levels and lightning transients specified in Table CS117-1 and supplemented by the waveform and timing definitions shown on Figures CS117-1 through CS117-8. The applicable transients of Table CS117-1 are considered default values and waveforms based upon previous experience and shall be used for the defined equipment functionality when the host platform lightning transient data does not exist. In the event that there is platform lightning transient data available, this data may be used to tailor the requirements with different selected levels or waveforms, pending approval by the procuring activity. Note that the power lines are tested separately as well as within the bundle as defined in the test procedures section and are tested at the levels defined in Table CS117-1.

5.15.3 CS117 test procedures.

5.15.3.1 Purpose.

This test procedure is used to verify the ability of the EUT to withstand lightning transients coupled onto EUT associated cables and power leads.

5.15.3.2 Test equipment.

The test equipment shall be as follows:

a. Lightning transient generator

b. Injection Transformers

c. Oscilloscope

d. Current monitor probes

e. Attenuators, 50 ohm, as needed on current monitor probes

f. Voltage monitor probes, high impedance

g. Monitor loop, low impedance wire loop

h. Calibration loop, low impedance wire loop

i. Capacitor, >28,000 µF for DC power inputs

j. LISNs

5.15.3.3 Setup.

The test setup shall be as follows:

a. Maintain a basic test setup for the EUT as shown and described on Figure CS117-9, Figure CS117-10, Figure CS117-11, Figure CS117-12 and section 4.3.8. The power input side of the LISN shall have a >28,000bμF capacitor between the high and return for DC power.

b. Calibration. Configure the test equipment in accordance with Figure CS117-9 for verification of the waveform, both short circuit current and open circuit voltage.

c. EUT testing:

    (1) Configure the test equipment as shown on Figure CS117-10, Figure CS117-11 or Figure CS117-12.

    (2) Place the injection transformer and current monitor probe(s) around a cable bundle interfacing an EUT connector.

    (3) Locate the current monitor probe 5-15 cm from the connector. If the overall length of the connector and backshell exceeds 15 cm, position the current monitor probe as close to the connector's backshell as possible.

    (4) Position the injection transformer 5-50 cm from the current monitor probe.

    (5) Place a monitor loop in the injection transformer and connect a voltage monitor probe.

5.15.3.4 Procedures.
The test procedures shall be as follows:

a. Turn on the measurement equipment and allow sufficient time for stabilization.

b. Calibration. Perform the following procedures using the calibration setup for waveform verification.

    (1) Connect the transient generator to the primary input of the injection transformer.

    (2) For each waveform, at the designated test level (V_T or I_T), record the voltage waveform with the calibration loop open and the current waveform with the calibration loop shorted. Verify that each waveform complies with the relevant waveshape parameters shown on Figure CS117-1 through Figure CS117-6. It is not necessary for the transient generator to produce the associated voltage or current limit level (V_L or I_L) and waveshape. However, if the transient generator is capable of reaching the designated limit level (V_L or I_L), record and verify the limit waveform at that generator setting.

    (3) For the Multiple Stroke and Multiple Burst tests, also verify the applicable pulse patterns and timing identified on Figure CS117-7 and Figure CS117-8.

    (4) Reverse the transient generator polarity and repeat 5.15.3.4b(2) through 5.15.3.4b(3).

c. EUT testing.

    (1) Turn on the EUT and measurement equipment to allow sufficient time for stabilization.

    (2) While applying transients, increase the generator setting until the designated test level (V_T or I_T) or the limit level (V_L or I_L) is reached. Adjustments shall be made in the generator settings and/or injection transformer configuration as necessary to

enable the required test level (V_T or I_T) to be achieved in the tested cable unless the corresponding limit level (V_L or I_L) is reached first. Calibration shall then be repeated if changes are made to the injection transformer configuration. Record the waveforms and amplitude levels obtained. If the limit level (V_L or I_L) is reached before the test level (V_T or I_T), the test shall be reevaluated to determine if the test is acceptable as follows:

(a) If the transient generator produced a compliant limit waveform (amplitude and waveshape) during calibration, the test is acceptable.

(b) If the specified limit waveform is achieved during the test and is within the waveshape tolerances shown on Figure CS117-1 through Figure CS117-6, the test is acceptable.

(c) If one of the above criteria is not met, then the test shall be repeated for that cable bundle using another transient generator that can meet the limit waveform requirements. In this case, the associated limit level (V_L or I_L) now becomes the test level (V_T or I_T) and the test level now becomes the limit level. Calibration shall be repeated using the substitute transient generator.

When measuring voltage or current waveform levels, short duration spikes or high frequency noise due to instrument noise, switching transients, or loading effects shall be ignored.

(3) For the Multiple Stroke test, at the generator setting established in 5.15.3.4c(2), apply a minimum of ten multiple stroke applications while monitoring the operation of the EUT. The maximum time between application of each Multiple Stroke transient shall be no greater than 5 minutes.

(4) For the Multiple Burst test, at the generator setting established in 5.15.3.4c(2), apply a multiple burst application every 3 seconds (3 seconds between the start of each set of three bursts) continuously for at least 5 minutes.

(5) Reverse the transient generator polarity and repeat 5.15.3.4c(2) through 5.15.3.4c(4).

(6) Repeat 5.15.3.4c(2) through 5.15.3.4c(5) on each cable bundle interfacing with each electrical connector on the EUT. For power cables, perform 5.15.3.4c(2) through 5.15.3.4c(5) on complete power cables (high sides and returns) and on the power cables with the power returns and chassis grounds (green wires) excluded from the cable bundle. For connectors which include both interconnecting leads and power, perform 5.15.3.4c(2) through 5.15.3.4c(5) on the entire bundle, on the power leads (including returns and grounds) grouped separately, and on the power leads grouped with the returns and grounds removed.

5.15.3.5. Data presentation.
Data presentation shall be as follows:

a. Provide a list of the waveforms and amplitudes at which the test was conducted for each cable and lead.

b. Provide oscilloscope photographs of calibration waveforms.

c. Provide oscilloscope photographs of test waveforms for each cable and lead tested; one sample for each polarity.

d. Provide data on any susceptibility thresholds and the associated waveforms that were determined for each connector and power lead.

e. Provide probe correction factors and attenuator data (if used) on the data plots if not automatically applied to the displayed waveforms.

f. Provide indications of compliance with the requirements for the susceptibility evaluation specified in 5.15.3.4c for each interface connector.

TABLE CS117-1. CS117 Test and limit levels for multiple stroke and multiple burst lightning tests.

Test Number	Test Description/Applicability	Internal Equipment Limits [1]	External Equipment limits [1]
1	Multiple Stroke –Waveforms 1 and 2. Applicable to all aircraft.	Initial Stroke V_L = 300 volts (WF #2) I_T = 600 amps (WF #1) I_L = 60 amps [2] Subsequent Strokes V_L = 150 volts (WF #2) I_T = 150 amps (WF #1) I_L = 30 amps [2]	Initial Stroke V_L = 750 volts (WF #2) I_T = 1500 amps (WF #1) I_L = 150 amps [2] Subsequent Strokes V_L = 375 volts (WF #2) I_T = 375 amps (WF #1) I_L = 75 amps [2]
2	Multiple Stroke – Waveform 3, (apply at both 1 and 10 MHz) Applicable to all aircraft.	Initial Stroke V_T = 600 volts (WF #3) I_L = 120 amps (WF #3) I_T = 12 amps [2] Subsequent Strokes V_T = 300 volts (WF #3) I_L = 60 amps (WF #3) I_T = 12 amps [2]	Initial Stroke V_T = 1500 volts (WF #3) I_L = 300 amps (WF #3) I_T = 60 amps [2] Subsequent Strokes V_T = 750 volts (WF #3) I_L = 150 amps (WF #3) I_T = 30 amps [2]
3	Multiple Stroke – Waveform 4 and 5. Applicable to aircraft with composite skin/structure. Not applicable to an all-metal skin/structure aircraft.	Initial Stroke V_L = 300 volts (WF #4) I_T = 1000 amps (WF #5) I_L = 300 amps [2] Subsequent Strokes V_L = 75 volts (WF #2) I_T = 200 amps (WF #1) I_L = 150 amps [2]	Initial Stroke V_L = 750 volts (WF #4) I_T = 2000 amps (WF #5) I_L = 750 amps [2] Subsequent Strokes V_L = 187.5 volts (WF #2) I_T = 400 amps (WF #1) I_L = 375 amps [2]
4	Multiple Burst –Waveform 3, (apply at both 1 and 10 MHz). Applicable to all aircraft.	V_T = 360 volts (WF #3) I_L = 6 amps (WF #3) F = 1 MHz, 10 MHz	V_T = 900 volts (WF #3) I_L = 15 amps (WF #3) F = 1 MHz, 10 MHz
5	Multiple Burst –Waveform 6. Applicable to low impedance bundles only.	V_T = 600 volts (WF #6) I_L = 30 amps (WF #6)	V_T = 1500 volts (WF #6) I_L = 75 amps (WF #6)

NOTES:

1/ Amplitude Tolerance is +20%,-0% for the all waveforms, except the tolerance is relaxed to +50%,-0% for the Subsequent Strokes. V_T represents the test voltage level in Volts and I_T represents the test current level in Amperes. V_L (Volts) and I_L (Amperes) represent limits intended to prevent over-stressing the EUT beyond the requirements.

2/ Levels intended for individual power leads or low count wire bundles. When multiple leads are tested together, this current shall be increased to the full bundle level or to the number of leads multiplied by the appropriate individual current test or limit level, whichever is less.

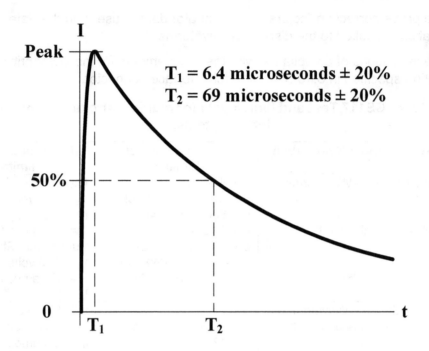

FIGURE CS117-1. Current Waveform 1.

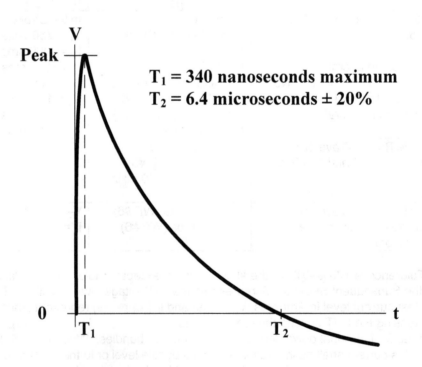

FIGURE CS117-2. Voltage Waveform 2.

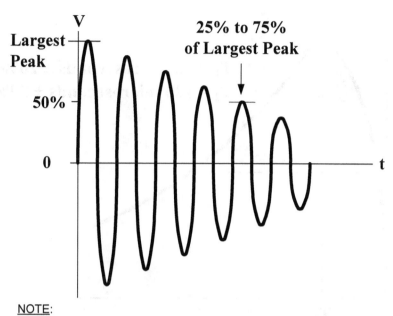

NOTE:
The waveshape may have either a damped sine or cosine waveshape.

FIGURE CS117-3. Voltage Waveform 3.

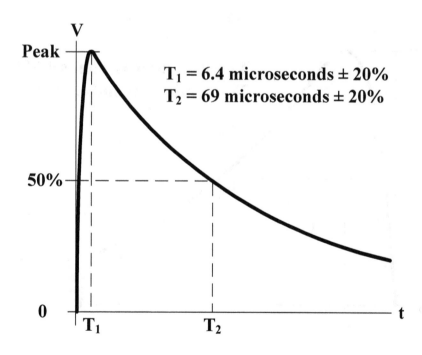

FIGURE CS117-4. Voltage Waveform 4.

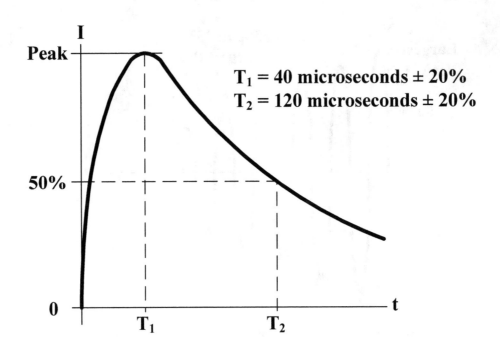

FIGURE CS117-5. Current Waveform 5A.

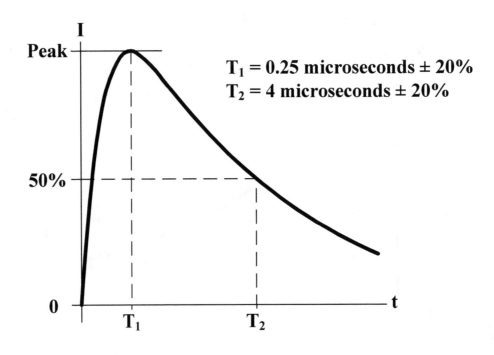

FIGURE CS117-6. Current Waveform 6.

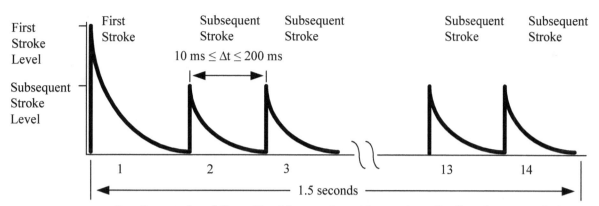

One first transient followed by thirteen subsequent transients distributed over a period of up to 1.5 seconds.

FIGURE CS117-7. Multiple stroke application.

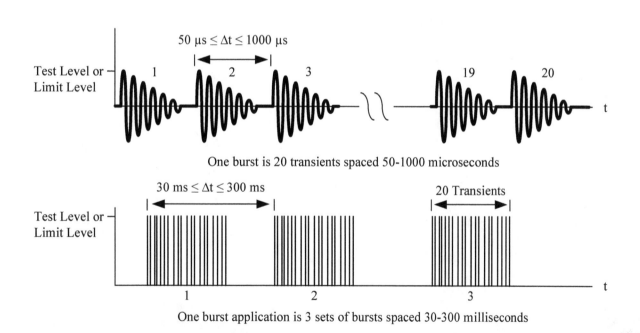

One burst is 20 transients spaced 50-1000 microseconds

One burst application is 3 sets of bursts spaced 30-300 milliseconds

FIGURE CS117-8. Multiple burst application.

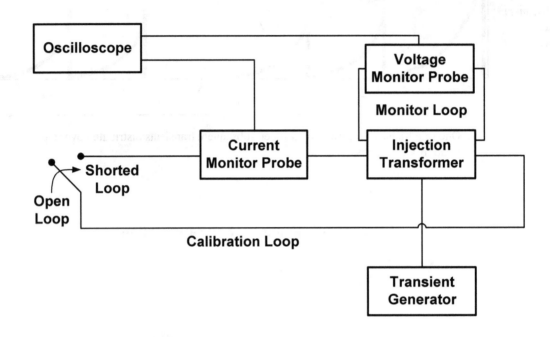

FIGURE CS117-9. Typical test setup for calibration of lightning waveforms.

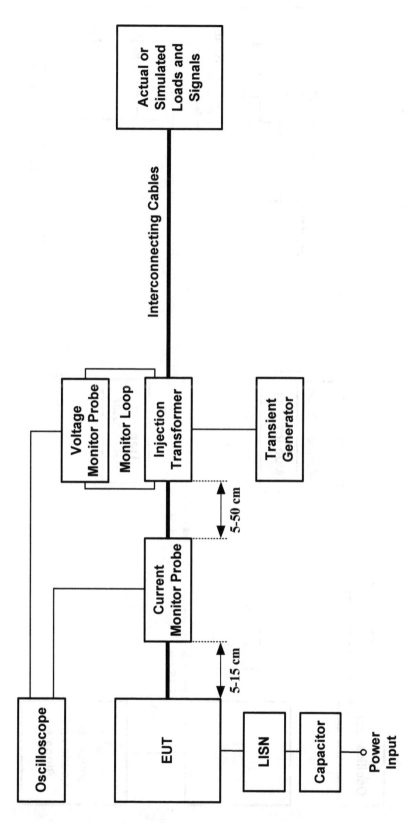

FIGURE CS117-10. Typical setup for bulk cable injection of lightning transients on complete interconnecting cable bundles.

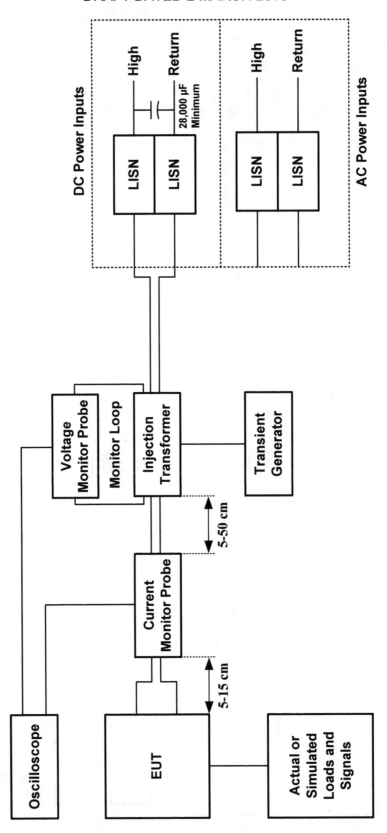

FIGURE CS117-11. Typical setup for bulk cable injection of lightning transients on complete power cables (high sides and returns).

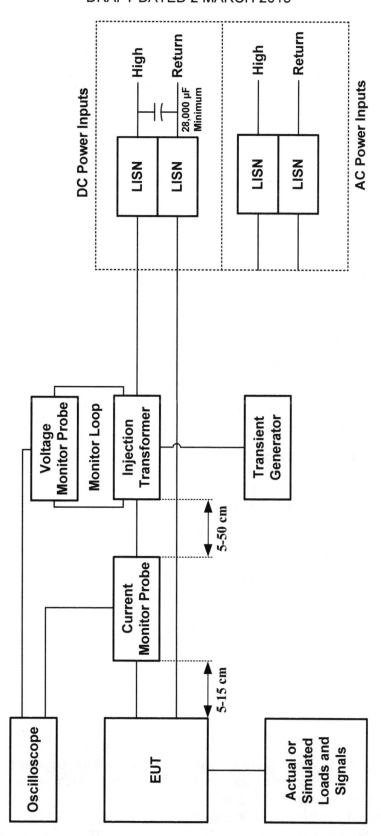

FIGURE CS117-12. Typical setup for bulk cable injection of lightning transients on power cables with power returns and chassis grounds excluded from the cable bundle.

5.16 CS118, personnel borne electrostatic discharge.

5.16.1 CS118 applicability.
This requirement is applicable to electrical, electronic, and electromechanical subsystems and equipment that have a man-machine interface. It is not applicable to equipment that interfaces with or controls ordnance items.

5.16.2 CS118 limits.
The EUT shall not exhibit any malfunction, degradation of performance, or deviation from specified indications, beyond the tolerances indicated in the individual equipment or subsystem specification, when subjected to the values shown Table CS118-1. Contact up to 8kV is the required method. Air discharges shall be required only if specified by the procuring activity.

5.16.3 CS118 test procedures

5.16.3.1 Purpose.
This test procedure is used to verify the ability of the EUT to withstand personnel borne electrostatic discharge (ESD) in a powered up configuration.

5.16.3.2 Test equipment.
The test equipment shall be as follows:

    a.   ESD Generator, adjustable from ±2kV to ±15kV (minimum range), see Figure CS118-1 and Table CS118-5 for simplified ESD generator characteristics.

    b.   ESD network, 150 picofarads (pF) capacitance, 330 ohm discharge resistance.

    c.   Contact discharge tip Figure CS118-2.

    d.   Air discharge tip Figure CS118-2.

    e.   Electrostatic voltmeter.

    f.   Oscilloscope, measurement bandwidth ≥ 1 GHz.

    g.   ESD current target, input resistance 2 ±5% ohms, Figure CS118-3.

    h.   Attenuator, 20 dB.

    i.   Coaxial cable, 50 ohm impedance, ≤ 1 meter.

    j.   Metallic ground plane.

    k.   Ionizer or one (1) megaohm resistor (1MΩ±10%).

5.16.3.3 Setup.
The test setup shall be as follows:

    a.   Maintain a basic test setup for the EUT as shown and described on Figures 2 through 5 and in 4.3.8.

    b.   Test Point Selection. The electrostatic discharges shall be applied to those points and surfaces of the EUT which are accessible to the operator/installer during normal use. Test points to be considered shall include the following locations as applicable: any conductive or non-conductive points in the control or keyboard area and any other point of human contact such as switches, knobs, buttons, indicators LEDs, seams slots, grilles, connector shells and other accessible areas. As a minimum, each face shall be included. Direct pin testing shall be required only if specified by the procuring activity.

c.   Calibration. The calibration procedures shall be as follows:

(1)   Install the 150 pF/330 ohm ESD network and air discharge tip onto the ESD generator.

(2)   Turn on the measurement equipment and allow sufficient time for stabilization.

(3)   ESD generator voltage verification:

(a)   Configure the test equipment in accordance with Figure CS118-5. Setup the electrostatic voltmeter to monitor voltage from ESD generator.

(b)   Set the ESD generator output voltage to ±2 kV.

(c)   Using the electrostatic voltmeter, verify the output voltage of the ESD generator is within +/-10% of the desired voltage level.

(d)   Repeat step 3 above for each ESD test level in Table CS118-1.

(4)   Discharge current verification. This system measurement check shall be performed prior to testing and the results recorded.

(a)   Setup the ESD current target, attenuator, and oscilloscope as shown on Figure CS118-6.

(b)   Configure the ESD simulator to use the contact discharge mode.

(c)   Place the tip of the ESD simulator in contact with the target and measure the waveform using the oscilloscope. Verify that each parameter in Table CS118-4 and on Figure CS118-4 is met.

5.16.3.4 Test procedures.
The test procedures shall be as follows:

a.   Maintain a basic test setup for the EUT as shown and described on Figures 2 through 5 and 4.3.8.

b.   The EUT shall be powered and operating during this test in a manner sufficient to verify its operation.

(1)   Set the ESD generator's tip voltage to the selected test level as specified in Table CS118-1.

(2)   Apply five (5) positive discharges and five (5) negative discharges to each EUT test point as discussed in test point selection in 5.16.3.3 (b) above.

(3)   Apply the discharges using the following techniques:

(a)   For contact discharges, place the ESD simulator tip directly on the test point and discharge the ESD simulator.

(b)   For air discharges, start at a distance from the test point where no discharge occurs as the ESD simulator is energized, and slowly move the tip towards the test point at a rate no faster than 0.3 m per second (0.3m/sec) until the discharge occurs or the tip physically contacts the test point. In between discharges, remove the residual charge from the test point by briefly grounding the test point through a one (1) MegaOhm (1MΩ ± 10%) resistor, use of ionizer, or by waiting for the charge to dissipate.

NOTE: Not all voltage levels may result in a discharge onto a dielectric surface. If the test point withstands the voltage, the requirement is met.

(4)   Monitor the EUT for degradation of performance during testing.

(5)   Repeat for each level in Table CS118-1.

5.16.3.5 Data presentation.

Data shall be presented detailing each discharge point, tip used, voltage applied to the EUT at that point (including magnitude and polarity), type of discharge (air or contact), and resulting operating behavior.

TABLE CS118-1. ESD test levels.

Level	Test Voltage (kV)	Method
1	±2	Contact
2	±4	Contact
3	±6	Contact
4	±8	Contact
5	±15	Air only

TABLE CS118-2. ESD simulator discharge current verification values.

Displayed Voltage (KV)	First Peak Current, ±15% (A)	Rise time [1] (ns)	Current I_1, ±30% (A) at t_1 = 30 ns	Current I_2 ±30% (A) at t_2 = 60 ns
±2	7.5	$0.6 \le t_r \le 1.0$	4	2
±8	30		16	8
[1]/Rise time is defined as the time from 10% to 90% of the peak value of the current waveform.				

TABLE CS118-3. ESD generator general specifications.

Parameters	Values
Output voltage, contact discharge mode (see NOTE 1)	At least ±2 kV to 8 kV, nominal
Output voltage, air discharge mode (see NOTE 1)	At least 2 kV to 15 kV, nominal
Tolerance of output voltage	±5 %
Polarity of output voltage	Positive and negative
Holding time	≥5 s
Discharge mode of operation	Single discharge (see NOTE 2)
NOTE 1: Open circuit voltage measured at the discharge electrode of the ESD generator. NOTE 2: The generator should be able to generate at the repetition rate of at least 20 discharges per second for exploratory purposes.	

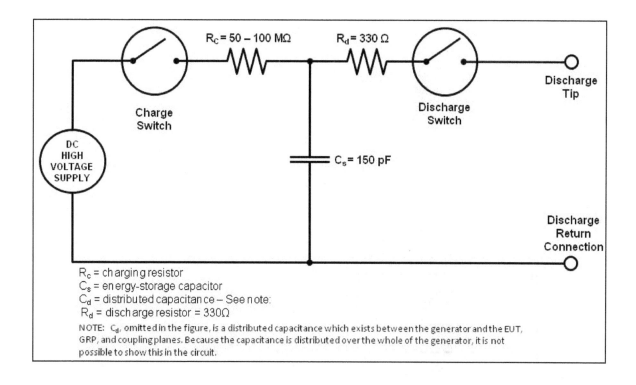

R_c = charging resistor
C_s = energy-storage capacitor
C_d = distributed capacitance – See note:
R_d = discharge resistor = 330Ω

NOTE: C_d, omitted in the figure, is a distributed capacitance which exists between the generator and the EUT, GRP, and coupling planes. Because the capacitance is distributed over the whole of the generator, it is not possible to show this in the circuit.

FIGURE CS118-1 simplified diagram of the ESD generator.

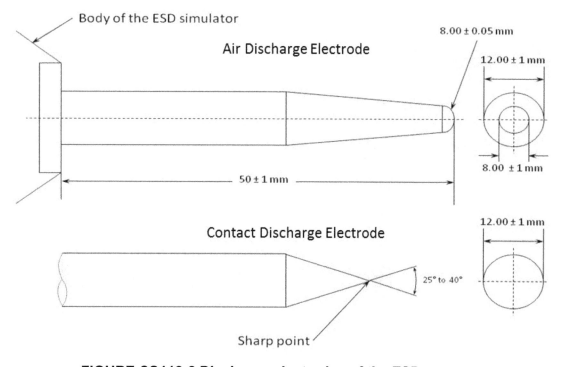

FIGURE CS118-2 Discharge electrodes of the ESD generator.

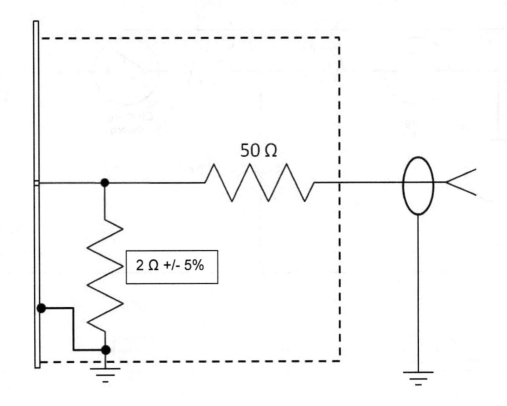

FIGURE CS118-3 Sample ESD current target schematic representation.

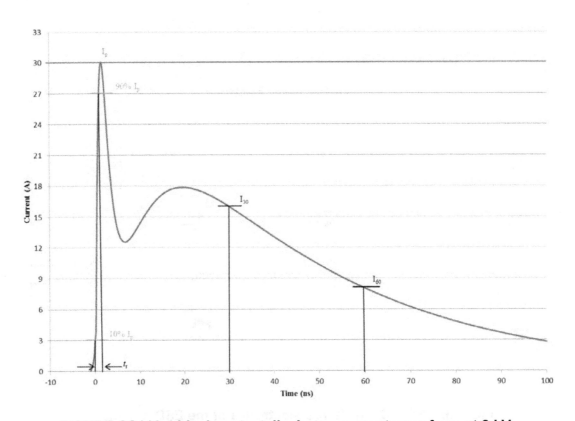

FIGURE CS118-4 Ideal contact discharge current waveform at 8 kV.

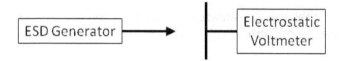

FIGURE CS118-5 Measurement system check setup, tip voltage verification.

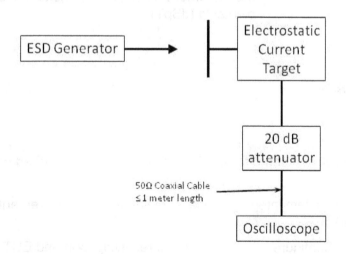

FIGURE CS118-6 Measurement system check setup, discharge current verification.

5.17 RE101, radiated emissions, magnetic field.

5.17.1 RE101 applicability.

This requirement is applicable from 30 Hz to 100 kHz for radiated emissions from equipment and subsystem enclosures, including electrical cable interfaces. The requirement does not apply to radiation from antennas. For Navy aircraft, this requirement is applicable only for aircraft with ASW equipment which operates between 30 Hz and 10 kHz such as: Acoustic (Sonobouy) Receivers or Magnetic Anomaly Detectors (MAD).

5.17.2 RE101 limit.

Magnetic field emissions shall not be radiated in excess of the levels shown on Figures RE101-1 and RE101-2 at a distance of 7 cm.

5.17.3 RE101 test procedures.

5.17.3.1 Purpose.

This test procedure is used to verify that the magnetic field emissions from the EUT and its associated electrical interfaces do not exceed specified requirements.

5.17.3.2 Test equipment.

The test equipment shall be as follows:

    a.   Measurement receivers

    b.   Data recording device

    c.   Loop sensor having the following specifications:

        (1)   Diameter: 13.3 cm

        (2)   Number of turns: 36

        (3)   Wire: DC resistance between 5 and 10 ohms

        (4)   Shielding: Electrostatic

        (5)   Correction factor: See manufacturer's data for factors to convert measurement receiver readings to decibels above one picotesla (dBpT).

    d.   LISNs

    e.   Ohmmeter

    f.   Signal generator

5.17.3.3 Setup.

The test setup shall be as follows:

    a.   Maintain a basic test setup for the EUT as shown and described on Figures 2 through 5 and 4.3.8.

    b.   Measurement system integrity check. Configure the measurement setup as shown on Figure RE101-3.

    c.   EUT testing. Configure the measurement receiving loop and EUT as shown on Figure RE101-4.

5.17.3.4 Procedures.

The test procedures shall be as follows:

a.   Turn on the measurement equipment and allow sufficient time for stabilization.

b.   Measurement system integrity check.

   (1)   Apply a calibrated signal level, which is at least 6 dB below the limit (limit minus the loop sensor correction factor), at a frequency of 50 kHz. Tune the measurement receiver to a center frequency of 50 kHz. Record the measured level.

   (2)   Verify that the measurement receiver indicates a level within ±3 dB of the injected signal level.

   (3)   If readings are obtained which deviate by more than ±3 dB, locate the source of the error and correct the deficiency prior to proceeding with the testing.

   (4)   Using an ohmmeter, verify that the resistance of the loop sensor winding is approximately 10 ohms.

c.   EUT testing.

   (1)   Turn on the EUT and allow sufficient time for stabilization.

   (2)   Locate the loop sensor 7 cm from the EUT face or electrical interface connector being probed. Orient the plane of the loop sensor parallel to the EUT faces and parallel to the axis of connectors.

   (3)   Scan the measurement receiver over the applicable frequency range to locate the frequencies of maximum radiation, using the bandwidths and minimum measurement times of Table II.

   (4)   Tune the measurement receiver to one of the frequencies or band of frequencies identified in 5.17.3.4c(3) above.

   (5)   Monitor the output of the measurement receiver while moving the loop sensor (maintaining the 7 cm spacing) over the face of the EUT or around the connector. Note the point of maximum radiation for each frequency identified in 5.17.3.4c(4).

   (6)   At 7 cm from the point of maximum radiation, orient the plane of the loop sensor to give a maximum reading on the measurement receiver and record the reading. If the measured emission exceeds the limit at the 7 cm distance, increase the measurement distance until the emission falls within the specified limit. Record the emissions and the measurement distance for assessment by the procuring activity.

   NOTE: The EUT shall comply with the applicable RE101 limit at 7 cm.

   (7)   Repeat 5.17.3.4c(4) through 5.17.3.4c(6) for at least two frequencies of maximum radiation per octave of frequencies below 200 Hz and for at least three frequencies of maximum radiation per octave above 200 Hz.

   (8)   Repeat 5.17.3.4c(2) through 5.17.3.4c(7) for each face of the EUT and for each EUT electrical connector.

5.17.3.5 Data presentation.

Data presentation shall be as follows:

a. Provide graphs of scans and tabular listings of each measurement frequency, mode of operation, measured magnetic field, and magnetic field limit level.

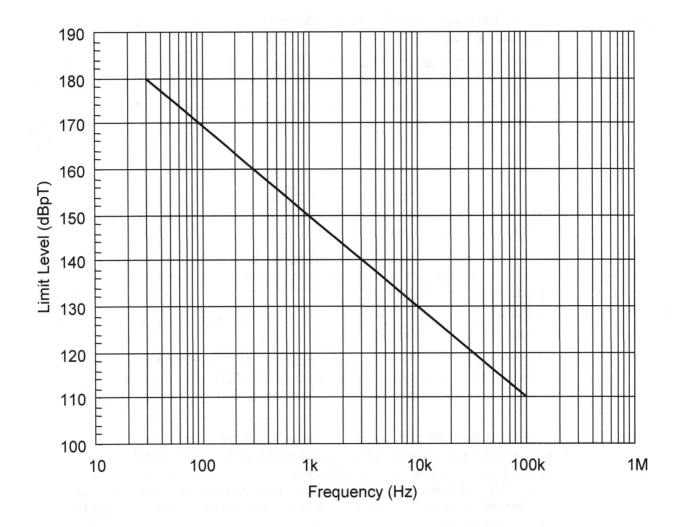

FIGURE RE101-1. RE101 limit for all Army applications.

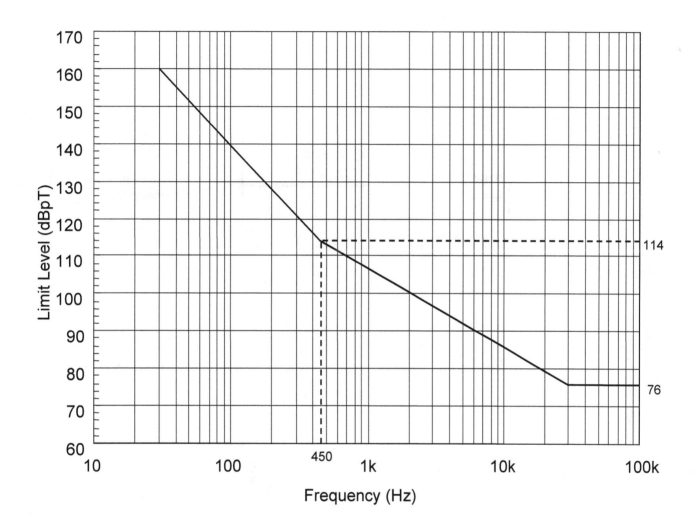

FIGURE RE101-2. RE101 limit for all Navy applications.

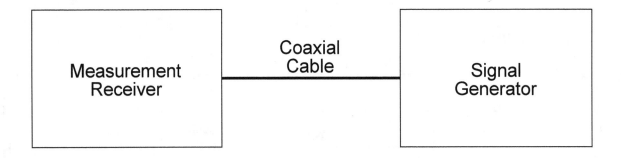

FIGURE RE101-3. Measurement system integrity check configuration.

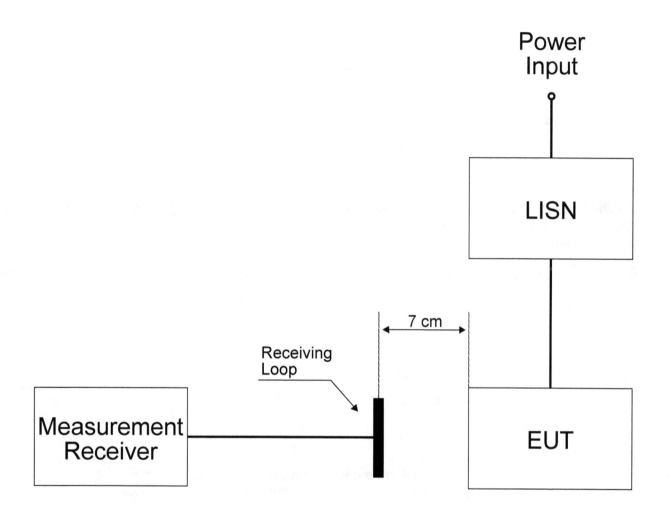

FIGURE RE101-4. Basic test setup.

5.18 RE102, radiated emissions, electric field.

5.18.1 RE102 applicability.

This requirement is applicable for radiated emissions from equipment and subsystem enclosures, and all interconnecting cables. For equipment with permanently mounted antennas this requirement does not apply at the transmitter fundamental frequencies and the necessary occupied bandwidth of the signal. The requirement is applicable as follows:

a.	Ground	2 MHz to 18 GHz
b.	Ships, surface	10 kHz to 18 GHz
c.	Submarines	10 kHz to 18 GHz
d.	Aircraft (Army and Navy)	10 kHz to 18 GHz
e.	Aircraft (Air Force)	2 MHz to 18 GHz
f.	Space	10 kHz to 18 GHz

5.18.2 RE102 limits.

Electric field emissions shall not be radiated in excess of those shown on Figures RE102-1 through RE102-4. Above 30 MHz, the limits shall be met for both horizontally and vertically polarized fields.

5.18.3 RE102 test procedures.

5.18.3.1 Purpose.

This test procedure is used to verify that electric field emissions from the EUT and its associated cabling do not exceed specified requirements.

5.18.3.2 Test equipment.

The test equipment shall be as follows:

a. Measurement receivers.

b. Data recording device.

c. Antennas:

    (1) 10 kHz to 30 MHz, 104 cm rod with impedance matching network. The signal output connector shall be bonded to the antenna matching network case.

        (a) When the impedance matching network includes a preamplifier (active rod), observe the overload precautions in 4.3.7.3.

        (b) Use a square counterpoise measuring at least 60 cm on a side.

    (2) 30 MHz to 200 MHz, Biconical, 137 cm tip to tip.

    (3) 200 MHz to 1 GHz, Double ridge horn, 69.0 by 94.5 cm opening.

    (4) 1 GHz to 18 GHz, Double ridge horn, 24.2 by 13.6 cm opening.

d. Signal generators.

e. Stub radiator.

f. Capacitor, 10 pF.

g. LISNs.

5.18.3.3 Setup.
The test setup shall be as follows:

a. Maintain a basic test setup for the EUT as shown and described on Figures 1 through 5 and in 4.3.8. Ensure that the EUT is oriented such that the surface that produces the maximum radiated emissions is toward the front edge of the test setup boundary.

b. Measurement system integrity check. Configure the test equipment as shown on Figure RE102-5.

c. EUT testing.

    (1) For rod antenna measurements, electrical bonding of the counterpoise is prohibited. The required configuration is shown on Figure RE102-6. The shield of the coaxial cable from the rod antenna matching network shall be electrically bonded to the floor in a length as short as possible (not to exceed 10 cm excess length). A ferrite sleeve with 20 to 30 ohms impedance at 20 MHz shall be placed near the center of the coaxial cable length between the antenna matching network and the floor.

    (2) Antenna positioning.

       (a) Determine the test setup boundary of the EUT and associated cabling for use in positioning of antennas.

       (b) Use the physical reference points on the antennas shown on Figure RE102-6 for measuring heights of the antennas and distances of the antennas from the test setup boundary.

          <u>1</u>. Position antennas 1 meter from the front edge of the test setup boundary for all setups.

          <u>2</u>. Position antennas 120 cm above the floor ground plane. For free standing EUTs, antenna heights shall be determined as described in 5.18.3.3.c.(2).(c).2 and 5.18.3.3.c.(2).(c).3.

          <u>3</u>. Ensure that no part of any antenna is closer than 1 meter from the walls and 0.5 meter from the ceiling of the shielded enclosure.

       (c) The number of required antenna positions depends on the size of the test setup boundary and the number of enclosures included in the setup.

          <u>1</u>. For testing below 200 MHz, use the following criteria to determine the individual antenna positions.

             <u>a</u>. For setups with the side edges of the boundary 3 meters or less, one position is required and the antenna shall be centered with respect to the side edges of the boundary.

             <u>b</u>. For setups with the side edges of the boundary greater than 3 meters, use multiple antenna positions at spacings as shown on Figure RE102-7. Determine the number of antenna positions (N) by dividing the edge-to-edge boundary distance (in meters) by 3 and rounding up to an integer.

          <u>2</u>. For testing from 200 MHz up to 1 GHz, place the antenna in a sufficient number of positions such that the entire area of each EUT enclosure

and the first 35 cm of cables and leads interfacing with the EUT enclosure are within the 3 dB beamwidth of the antenna.

3. For testing at 1 GHz and above, place the antenna in a sufficient number of positions such that the entire area of each EUT enclosure and the first 7 cm of cables and leads interfacing with the EUT enclosure are within the 3 dB beamwidth of the antenna.

5.18.3.4 Procedures.

The test procedures shall be as follows:

a. Verify that the ambient requirements specified in 4.3.4 are met. Take plots of the ambient when required by the referenced paragraph.

b. Turn on the measurement equipment and allow a sufficient time for stabilization.

c. Using the system check path of Figure RE102-5, perform the following evaluation of the overall measurement system from the coaxial cable end used at each antenna to the data output device at 10.5 kHz (only for measurements implemented between 10 kHz and 2 MHz), 2.1 MHz, 12 MHz and 29.5 MHz for active rod antennas, 197 MHz for the biconical antenna, 990 MHz for the large double ridge horn and 17.5 GHz for the small double ridge horn. For rod antennas that use passive matching networks, the evaluation shall be performed at the center frequency of each band. A check shall also be performed when the measurement path is changed for a particular antenna such as the coaxial cable, addition or removal of preamplifiers, or different ports used on the measurement receiver. System check path verification shall be performed near the upper end of the affected frequency band.

(1) Apply a calibrated signal level, which is at least 6 dB below the limit (limit minus antenna factor), to the coaxial cable at the antenna connection point.

(2) Scan the measurement receiver in the same manner as a normal data scan. Verify that the data recording device indicates a level within ±3 dB of the injected signal level.

(3) For the 104 cm rod antenna, remove the rod element and apply the signal to the antenna matching network through a capacitor connected to the rod mount as shown on Figure RE102-8. The capacitor value is nominally 10 pF, but shall be per the manufacturer's instruction. Commercial calibration jigs or injection networks shall not be used.

(4) If readings are obtained which deviate by more than ±3 dB, locate the source of the error and correct the deficiency prior to proceeding with the testing.

d. Using the measurement path of Figure RE102-5, perform the following evaluation for each antenna to demonstrate that there is electrical continuity through the antenna.

(1) Radiate a signal using an antenna or stub radiator at the highest measurement frequency of each antenna.

(2) Tune the measurement receiver to the frequency of the applied signal and verify that a received signal of appropriate amplitude is present. NOTE: This evaluation is intended to provide a coarse indication that the antenna is functioning properly. There is no requirement to accurately measure the signal level.

e. Turn on the EUT and allow sufficient time for stabilization.

f. Using the measurement path of Figure RE102-5, determine the radiated emissions from the EUT and its associated cabling.

    (1) Scan the measurement receiver for each applicable frequency range, using the bandwidths and minimum measurement times in Table II.

    (2) Above 30 MHz, orient the antennas for both horizontally and vertically polarized fields.

    (3) Take measurements for each antenna position determined under 5.18.3.3c(2)(c) above.

5.18.3.5 Data presentation.

Data presentation shall be as follows:

a. Continuously and automatically plot amplitude versus frequency profiles. Manually gathered data is not acceptable except for plot verification. Vertical and horizontal data for a particular frequency range shall be presented on separate plots or shall be clearly distinguishable in black or white format for a common plot.

b. Display the applicable limit on each plot.

c. Provide a minimum frequency resolution of 1% or twice the measurement receiver bandwidth, whichever is less stringent, and a minimum amplitude resolution of 1 dB for each plot.

d. Provide plots for both the measurement and system check portions of the procedure.

e. Provide a statement verifying the electrical continuity of the measurement antennas as determined in 5.18.3.4d.

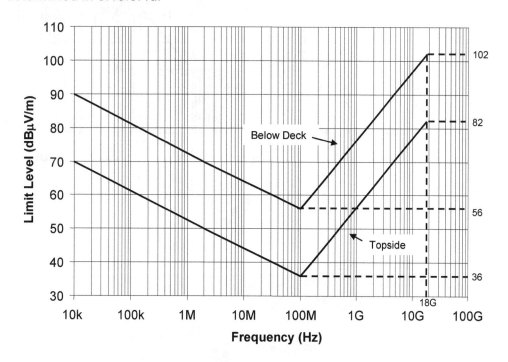

FIGURE RE102-1. RE102 limit for surface ship applications.

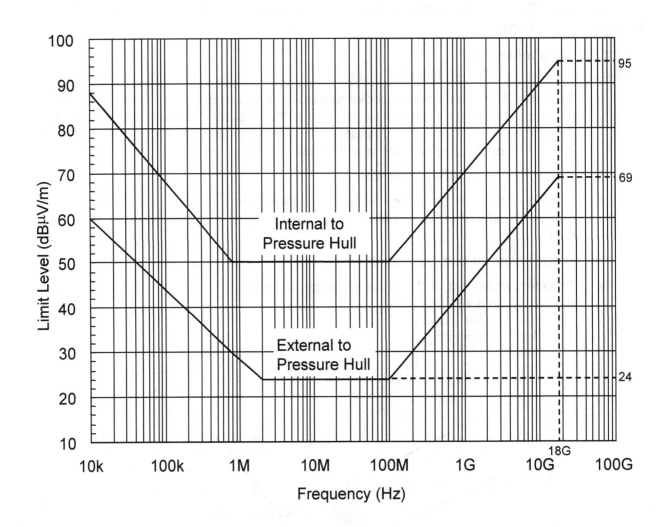

FIGURE RE102-2. RE102 limit for submarine applications.

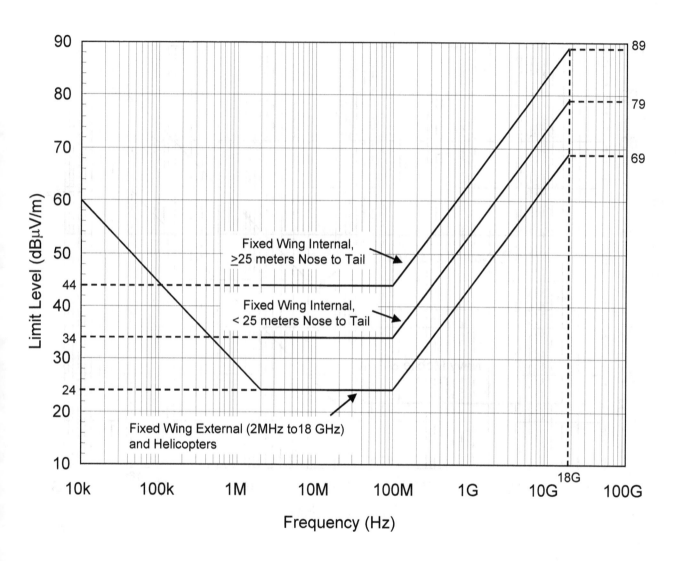

FIGURE RE102-3. RE102 limit for aircraft and space system applications.

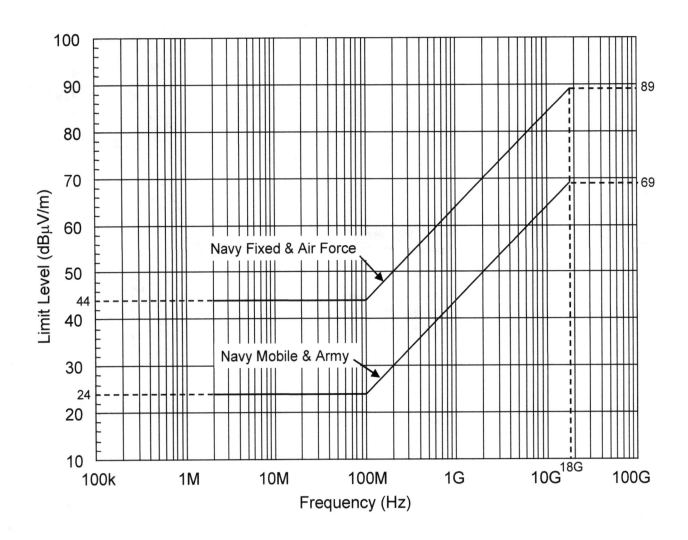

FIGURE RE102-4. RE102 limit for ground applications.

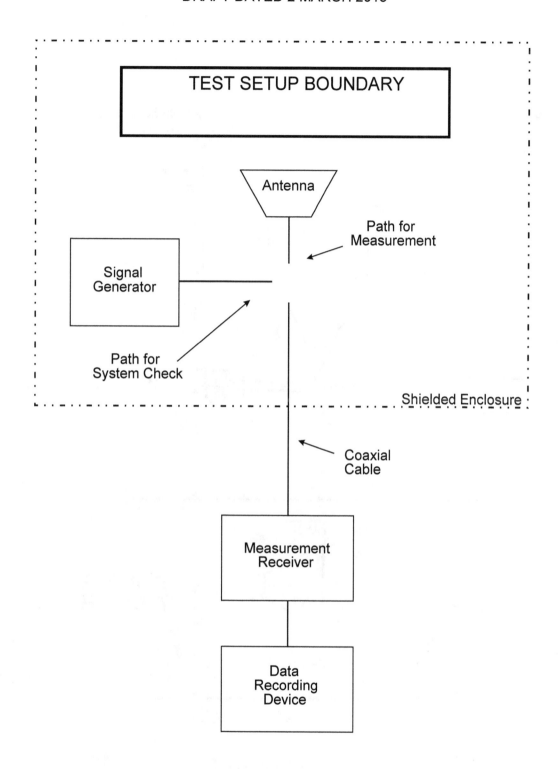

FIGURE RE102-5. Basic test setup.

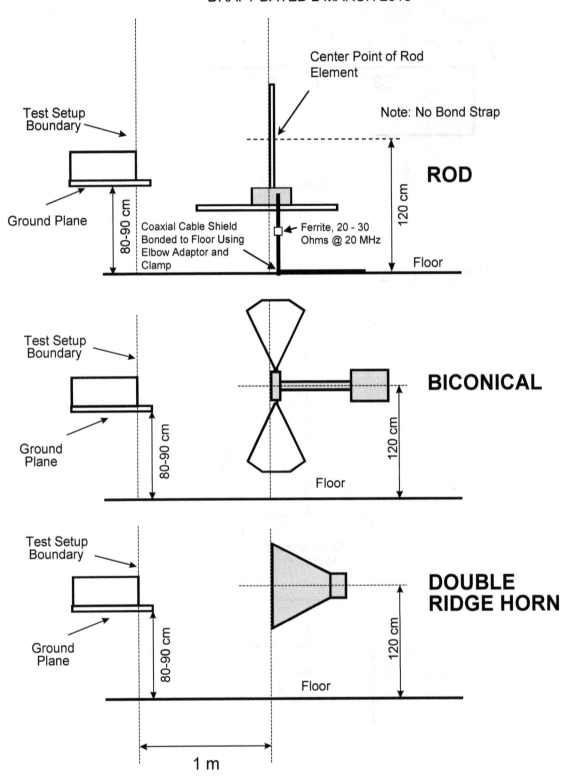

FIGURE RE102-6. Antenna positioning.

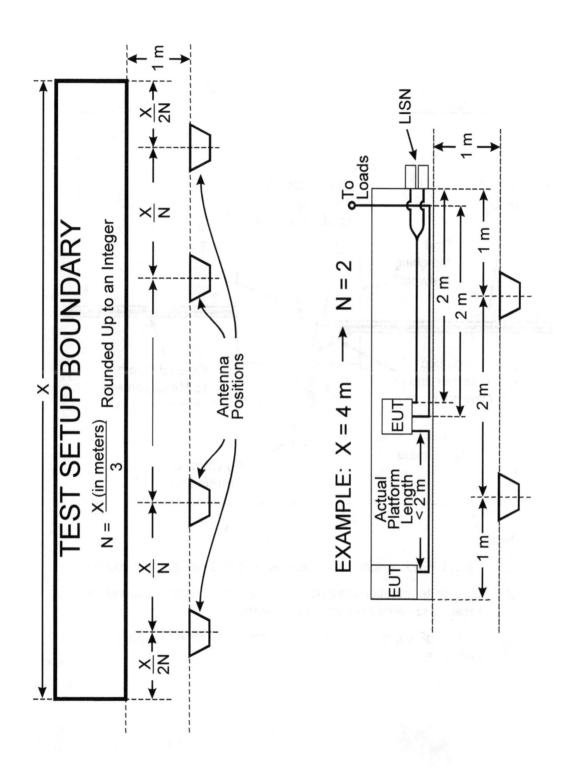

FIGURE RE102-7. Multiple antenna positions.

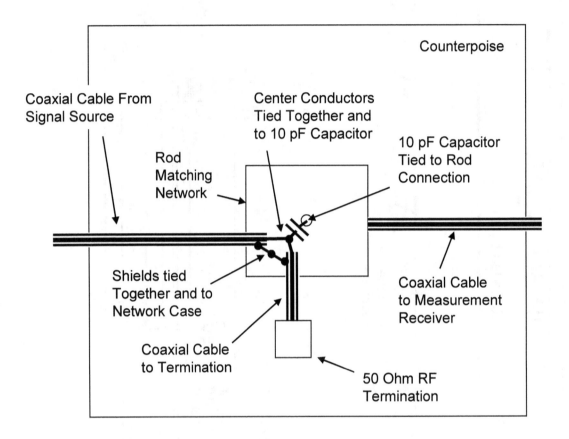

FIGURE RE102-8. Rod antenna system check.

Notes:

1. Each individual wire connection limited to 5 cm length maximum.

2. 50 ohm termination may be replaced with 50 ohm measurement receiver to verify level of injected signal.

3. The 10 pF capacitor may be built into some antenna matching networks.

5.19 RE103, radiated emissions, antenna spurious and harmonic outputs.

5.19.1 RE103 applicability.

This requirement may be used as an alternative for CE106 when testing transmitters with their intended antennas. This requirement is met if the emissions do not exceed the applicable RE102 limit in transmit mode. CE106 is the preferred requirement unless the equipment or subsystem design characteristics preclude its use. RE103 should be the preferred method for systems using active antenna or when the antenna impedance has a non-standard impedance curve. The requirement is applicable from 10 kHz to 40 GHz and not applicable within the bandwidth of the EUT transmitted signal or within ±5 percent of the fundamental frequency, whichever is larger. For Navy shipboard applications with peak transmitter power greater than 1 kW, the 5% frequency exclusion will be increased by an additional 0.1% of the fundamental frequency for each dB above 1 kW of peak power.

Frequency Exclusion = $\pm f * (0.05 + (0.001/dB) * (P_{tPk} [dBm] - 60 [dBm]))$

Depending on the operating frequency range of the EUT, the start frequency of the test is as follows:

Operating Frequency Range (EUT)	Start Frequency of Test
10 kHz to 3 MHz	10 kHz
3 MHz to 300 MHz	100 kHz
300 MHz to 3 GHz	1 MHz
3 GHz to 40 GHz	10 MHz

The equipment will be tested to an upper frequency limit based on the highest frequency generated or received by the EUT. For systems with the frequencies generated or received less than 1 GHz, the upper frequency limit will be 20 times the highest frequency or 18 GHz whichever is greater. For systems with frequencies generated or received greater than or equal to 1 GHz, the upper frequency limit will be 10 times the highest frequency or 40 GHz whichever is less. For equipment using waveguide, the requirement does not apply below eight-tenths of the waveguide's cutoff frequency.

5.19.2 RE103 limits.

Harmonics, except the second and third, and all other spurious emissions shall be at least 80 dB down from the level at the fundamental. The second and third harmonics shall be suppressed to a level of -20 dBm or 80 dB below the fundamental, whichever requires less suppression. For Navy shipboard applications, the second and third harmonics will be suppressed to a level of -20 dBm and all other harmonics and spurious emissions shall be suppressed to -40 dBm, except if the duty cycle of the emissions are less than 0.2%, then the limit may be relaxed to 0 dBm.

5.19.3 RE103 test procedures.

5.19.3.1 Purpose.

This test procedure is used to verify that radiated spurious and harmonic emissions from transmitters do not exceed the specified requirements.

5.19.3.2 Test equipment.

The test equipment shall be as follows:

    a.   Measurement receiver

    b.   Attenuators, 50 ohm

    c.   Antennas

    d.   Rejection networks

    e.   Signal generators

    f.   Power monitor

5.19.3.3 Setup.

It is not necessary to maintain the basic test setup for the EUT as shown and described on Figures 1 through 5 and in 4.3.8. The test setup shall be as follows:

    a.   Measurement system integrity check. Configure the test setup for the signal check path shown on Figure RE103-1 or RE103-2, as applicable.

    b.   EUT testing. Configure the test setup for the measurement path shown on Figure RE103-1 or RE103-2, as applicable.

5.19.3.4 Procedures.

The test procedures shall be as follows:

    a.   The measurements must be performed in the far-field of the transmitting frequency. Consequently, the far-field test distance must be calculated prior to performing the test using the relationships below:

         R = distance between transmitter antenna and receiver antenna.

         D = maximum physical dimension of transmitter antenna.

         d = maximum physical dimension of receiver antenna.

         λ = wavelength of frequency of the transmitter.

All dimensions are in meters.

For transmitter frequencies less than or equal to 1.24 GHz, the greater distance of the following relationships shall be used:

         $R = 2D^2/\lambda$ $R = 3\lambda$

For transmitter frequencies greater than 1.24 GHz, the separation distance shall be calculated as follows:

         For $2.5\,D < d$ use $R = 2D^2/\lambda$

         For $2.5\,D \geq d$ use $R = (D+d)^2/\lambda$

    b.   Turn on the measurement equipment and allow sufficient time for stabilization.

    c.   Measurement system integrity check.

         (1)   Apply a known calibrated signal level from the signal generator through the system check path at a midband fundamental frequency (f_o).

(2)   Scan the measurement receiver in the same manner as a normal data scan. Verify the measurement receiver detects a level within ±3 dB of the expected signal.

(3)   If readings are obtained which deviate by more than ±3 dB, locate the source of the error and correct the deficiency prior to proceeding with the test.

(4)   Repeat 5.19.3.4c(1) through 5.19.3.4c(3) for two other frequencies over the frequency range of test.

d.   EUT testing.

(1)   Turn on the EUT and allow a sufficient time for stabilization.

(2)   Tune the EUT to the desired test frequency and use the measurement path to complete the rest of this procedure.

(3)   Tune the test equipment to the measurement frequency (f_o) of the EUT and adjust for maximum indication.

(4)   For transmitters where a power monitor can be inserted, measure the modulated transmitter power output P, using a power monitor while keying the transmitter. Convert this power level to units of dB relative to 1 watt (dBW). Calculate the Effective Radiated Power (ERP) by adding the EUT antenna gain to this value. Record the resulting level for comparison with that obtained in 5.19.3.4d(6).

(5)   Key the transmitter with desired modulation. Tune the measurement receiver for maximum output indication at the transmitted frequency. If either or both of the antennas have directivity, align both in elevation and azimuth for maximum indication. Verbal communication between sites via radiotelephone will facilitate this process. Record the resulting maximum receiver meter reading and the measurement receiver bandwidth.

(6)   Calculate the transmitter ERP in dBW, based on the receiver meter reading V, using the following equation:

ERP = V + 20 log R + AF - 135

where:

V =   reading on the measurement receiver in dBμV

R =   distance between transmitter and receiver antennas in meters

AF =   antenna factor of receiver antenna in dB (1/m)

Compare this calculated level to the measured level recorded in 5.19.3.4d(4). The compared results should agree within ±3 dB. If the difference exceeds ±3 dB, check the test setup for errors in measurement distance, amplitude calibration, power monitoring of the transmitter, frequency tuning or drift and antenna boresight alignment. Assuming that the results are within the ±3 dB tolerance, the ERP becomes the reference for which amplitudes of spurious and harmonics will be compared to determine compliance with standard limits.

(7)   With the rejection network filter connected and tuned to f_o, scan the measurement receiver over the frequency range of test to locate spurious and harmonic transmitted outputs. It may be necessary to move the measuring system antenna in elevation and azimuth at each spurious and harmonic output

to assure maximum levels are recorded. Maintain the same measurement receiver bandwidth used to measure the fundamental frequency in 5.19.3.4d(5).

    (8)   Verify that spurious outputs are from the EUT and not spurious responses of the measurement system or the test site ambient.

    (9)   Calculate the ERP of each spurious output. Include all correction factors for cable loss, amplifier gains, filter loss, and attenuator factors.

    (10)   Repeat 5.19.3.4d(2) through 5.19.3.4d(9) for other f_o of the EUT.

5.19.3.5 Data presentation.

Data presentation shall be as follows:

    a.   Provide tabular data showing fundamental frequency (f_o) and frequency of all harmonics and spurious emissions measured, the measured power monitor level and the calculated ERP of the fundamental frequency, the ERP of all spurious and harmonics emissions measured, dB down levels, and all correction factors including cable loss, attenuator pads, amplifier gains, insertion loss of rejection networks and antenna gains.

        The relative dB down level is determined by subtracting the level in 5.19.3.4d(6) from that recorded in 5.19.3.4d(9).

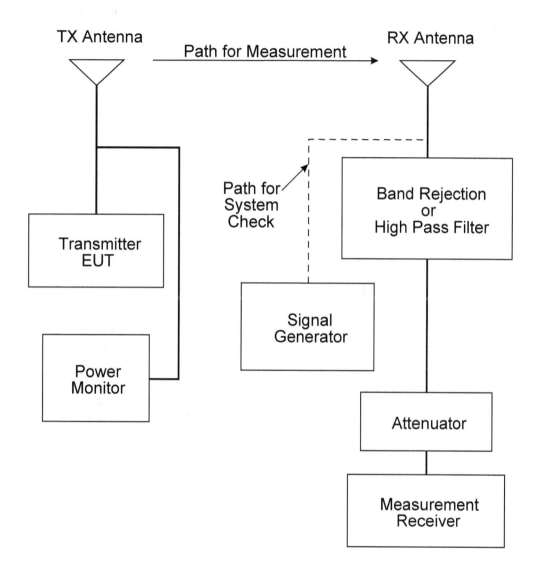

FIGURE RE103-1. Measurement system integrity check and test setup for radiated harmonics and spurious emissions, 10 kHz to 1 GHz.

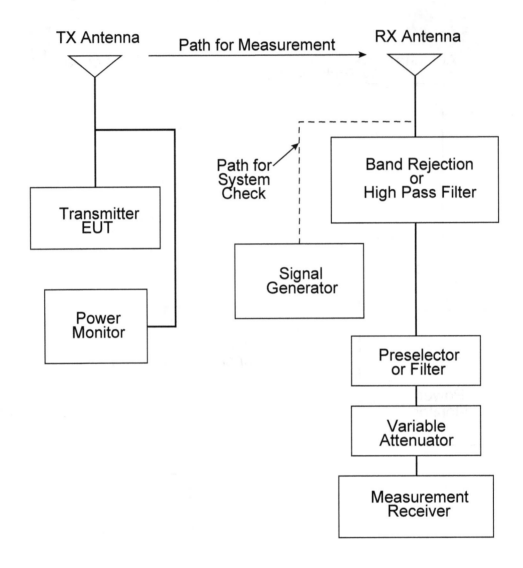

FIGURE RE103-2. Measurement system integrity check and test setup for radiated harmonics and spurious emissions, 1 GHz to 40 GHz.

5.20 RS101, radiated susceptibility, magnetic field.

5.20.1 RS101 applicability.

This requirement is applicable from 30 Hz to 100 kHz for equipment and subsystem enclosures, including electrical cable interfaces. The requirement is not applicable for electromagnetic coupling via antennas. For Army ground equipment, the requirement is applicable only to vehicles having a minesweeping or mine detection capability. For submarines, this requirement is applicable only to equipment and subsystems that have an operating frequency of 100 kHz or less and an operating sensitivity of 1 µV or better (such as 0.5 µV). For equipment intended to be installed on Navy aircraft, the requirement is applicable only as specified by the procuring activity.

5.20.2 RS101 limit.

The EUT shall not exhibit any malfunction, degradation of performance, or deviation from specified indications, beyond the tolerances indicated in the individual equipment or subsystem specification, when subjected to the magnetic fields shown on Figures RS101-1 and RS101-2.

5.20.3 RS101 test procedures.

5.20.3.1 Purpose.

This test procedure is used to verify the ability of the EUT to withstand radiated magnetic fields.

5.20.3.2 Test equipment.

The test equipment shall be as follows:

    a.   Signal source

    b.   Radiating loop having the following specifications:

        (1)   Diameter: 12 cm

        (2)   Number of turns: 20

        (3)   Wire: No. 12 insulated copper

        (4)   Magnetic flux density: 9.5×10^7 pT/ampere of applied current at a distance of 5 cm from the plane of the loop.

    c.   Loop sensor having the following specifications:

        (1)   Diameter: 4 cm

        (2)   Number of turns: 51

        (3)   Wire: 7-41 Litz wire (7 Strand, No. 41 AWG)

        (4)   Shielding: Electrostatic

        (5)   Correction Factor: See manufacturer's data for factors to convert measurement receiver readings to decibels above one picotesla (dBpT).

    d   Measurement receiver or narrowband voltmeter

    e.   Current probe

    f.   LISNs

5.20.3.3 Setup.

The test setup shall be as follows:

    a.   Maintain a basic test setup for the EUT as shown and described on Figures 2 through 5 and 4.3.8.

    b.   Calibration. Configure the measurement equipment, radiating loop, and loop sensor as shown on Figure RS101-3.

    c.   EUT testing. Configure the test as shown on Figure RS101-4.

5.20.3.4 Procedures.

The test procedures shall be as follows:

    a.   Turn on the measurement equipment and allow sufficient time for stabilization.

    b.   Calibration.

        (1)   Set the signal source to a frequency of 1 kHz and adjust the output to provide a magnetic flux density of 110 dB above one picotesla as determined by the reading obtained on measurement receiver A and the relationship given in 5.20.3.2b(4).

        (2)   Measure the voltage output from the loop sensor using measurement receiver B.

        (3)   Verify that the output on measurement receiver B is within ±3 dB of the expected value based on the antenna factor and record this value.

    c.   EUT testing.

        (1)   Turn on the EUT and allow sufficient time for stabilization.

        (2)   Select test frequencies as follows:

            (a)   Locate the loop sensor 5 cm from the EUT face or electrical interface connector being probed. Orient the plane of the loop sensor parallel to the EUT faces and parallel to the axis of connectors.

            (b)   Supply the loop with sufficient current to produce magnetic field strengths at least 10 dB greater than the applicable limit but not to exceed 15 amps (183 dBpT).

            (c)   Scan the applicable frequency range using the scan rates in Table III.

            (d)   If susceptibility is noted, select no less than three test frequencies per octave at those frequencies where the maximum indications of susceptibility are present.

            (e)   Reposition the loop successively to a location in each 30 by 30 cm area on each face of the EUT and at each electrical interface connector, and repeat 5.20.3.4c(2)(c) and 5.20.3.4c(2)(d) to determine locations and frequencies of susceptibility.

            (f)   From the total frequency data where susceptibility was noted in 5.20.3.4c(2)(c) through 5.20.3.4c(2)(e), select three frequencies per octave over the applicable frequency range.

(3) At each frequency determined in 5.20.3.4c(2)(f), apply a current to the radiating loop that corresponds to the applicable limit. Move the loop to search for possible locations of susceptibility with particular attention given to the locations determined in 5.20.3.4c(2)(e) while maintaining the loop 5 cm from the EUT surface or connector. Verify that susceptibility is not present.

5.20.3.5 Data presentation.

Data presentation shall be as follows:

a. Provide tabular data showing verification of the calibration of the radiating loop in 5.20.3.4b.

b. Provide tabular data, diagrams, or photographs showing the applicable test frequencies and locations determined in 5.20.3.4c(2)(e) and 5.20.3.4c(2)(f).

c. Provide graphical or tabular data showing frequencies and threshold levels of susceptibility.

5.20.4 RS101 alternative test procedures – AC Helmholtz coil.

This test procedure may be substituted for the 5.20.3 procedures, provided that the EUT size versus coil size constraints of 5.20.4.3b can be satisfied.

5.20.4.1 Purpose.

This test procedure is an alternative technique used to verify the ability of the EUT to withstand radiated magnetic fields.

5.20.4.2 Test equipment.

The test equipment shall be as follows:

a. Signal source

b. Series-wound AC Helmholtz coil

c. Loop sensor having the following specifications (same as RE101 loop):

    (1) Diameter: 13.3 cm

    (2) Number of turns: 36

    (3) Wire: DC resistance between 5 and 10 ohms

    (4) Shielding: Electrostatic

    (5) Correction factor: See manufacturer's data for factors to convert measurement receiver readings to decibels above one picotesla (dBpT).

d   Measurement receiver or narrowband voltmeter

e.   Current probe

f.   LISNs

5.20.4.3 Setup.

The test setup shall be as follows:

a. Maintain a basic test setup for the EUT as shown and described on Figures 2 through 5 and 4.3.8.

b. Calibration.

    (1)   Configure the radiating system as shown on Figure RS101-5. Select coil spacing based on the physical dimensions of the EUT enclosure.

    (2)   For an EUT with dimensions less than one coil radius, use a standard Helmholtz configuration (coils separated by one coil radius). Place the field monitoring loop in the center of the test volume.

    (3)   For an EUT with dimensions greater than one coil radius, use the optional configuration. Select a coil separation such that the plane of the EUT face is at least 5 cm from the plane of the coils and such that the separation between the coils does not exceed 1.5 radii. Place the field monitoring probe in the plane of either coil at its center.

  c.   EUT testing.

    (1)   Configure the test as shown on Figure RS101-6, using the same coil spacing arrangement as determined for calibration under 5.20.4.3b.

    (2)   Position the coils such that the plane of the EUT faces is in parallel with the plane of the coils.

5.20.4.4 Procedures.

The test procedures shall be as follows:

  a.   Turn on the measurement equipment and allow sufficient time for stabilization.

  b.   Calibration.

    (1)   Set the signal source to a frequency of 1 kHz and adjust the output current to generate a magnetic flux density of 110 dB above one picotesla as determined by the reading obtained on measurement receiver A.

    (2)   Measure the voltage output from the loop sensor using measurement receiver B.

    (3)   Verify that the output on measurement receiver B is within ±3 dB of the expected value based on the antenna factor and record this value.

  c.   EUT testing.

    (1)   Turn on the EUT and allow sufficient time for stabilization.

    (2)   Select test frequencies as follows:

      (a) Supply the Helmholtz coil with sufficient current to produce magnetic field strengths at least 6 dB greater than the applicable limit.

      (b) Scan the applicable frequency range using the scan rates in Table III.

      (c) If susceptibility is noted, select no less than three test frequencies per octave at those frequencies where the maximum indications of susceptibility are present.

      (d) Reposition the Helmholtz coils successively over all areas on each face of the EUT (in all three axes), including exposure of any electrical interface connectors, and repeat 5.20.4.4c(2)(b) and 5.20.4.4c(2)(c) to determine locations and frequencies of susceptibility.

(e) From the total frequency data where susceptibility was noted in 5.20.4.4c(2)(b) through 5.20.4.4c(2)(d), select three frequencies per octave over the applicable frequency range.

(3) At each frequency determined in 5.20.4.4c(2)(e), apply a current to the Helmholtz coil that corresponds to the applicable RS101 limit. Move the coils to search for possible locations of susceptibility with particular attention given to the locations determined in 5.20.4.4c(2)(d). Ensure the EUT remains centered between the coils, or the coils remain 5 cm from the EUT surface, as applicable. Verify that susceptibility is not present.

5.20.4.5 Data presentation.

Data presentation shall be as follows:

a. Provide tabular data showing verification of the calibration of the Helmholtz coils in 5.20.4.4b.

b. Provide tabular data, diagrams, or photographs showing the applicable test frequencies and locations determined in 5.20.4.4c(2)(d) and 5.20.4.4c(2)(e).

c. Provide graphical or tabular data showing frequencies and threshold levels of susceptibility.

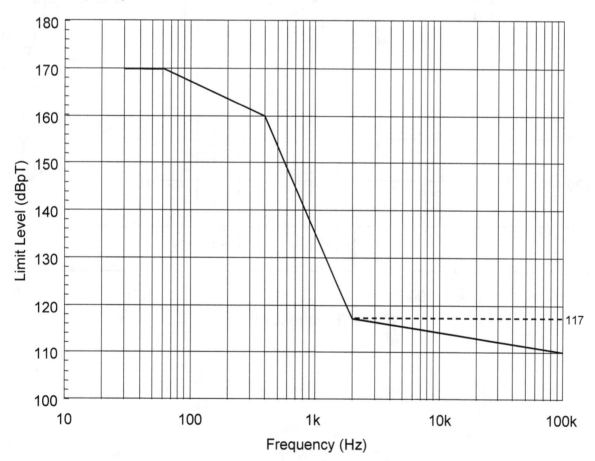

FIGURE RS101-1. RS101 limit for all Navy applications.

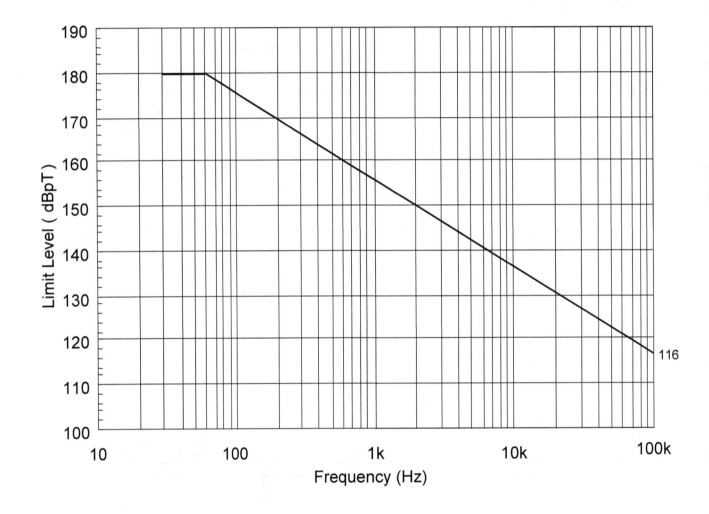

FIGURE RS101-2. RS101 limit for all Army applications.

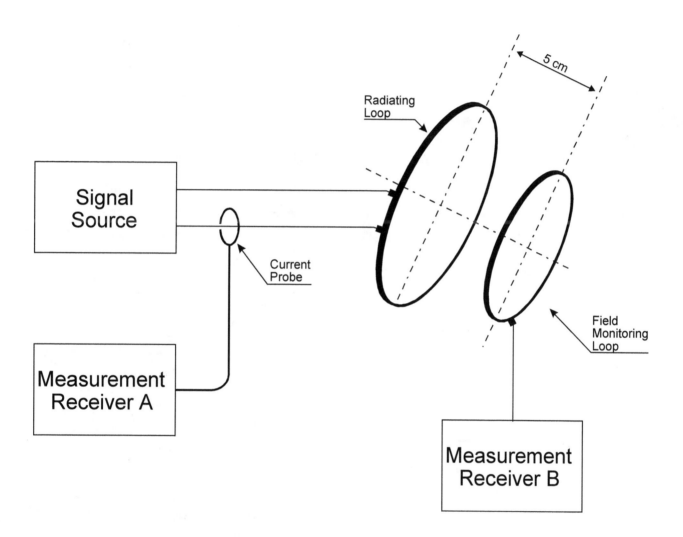

FIGURE RS101-3. Calibration of the radiating system.

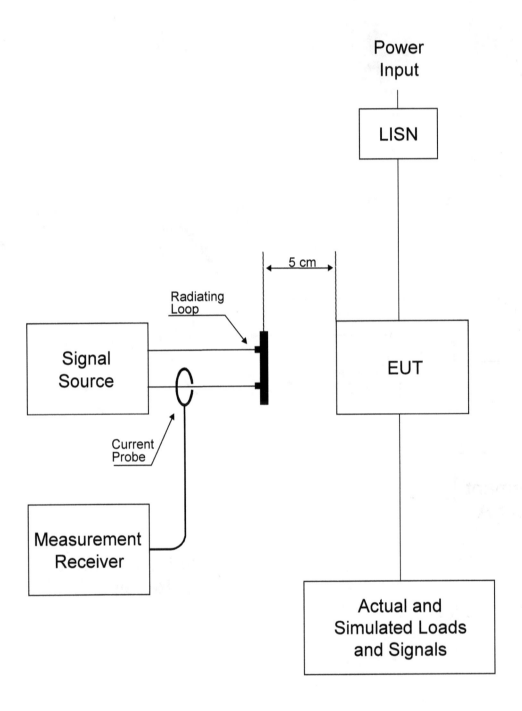

FIGURE RS101-4. Basic test setup.

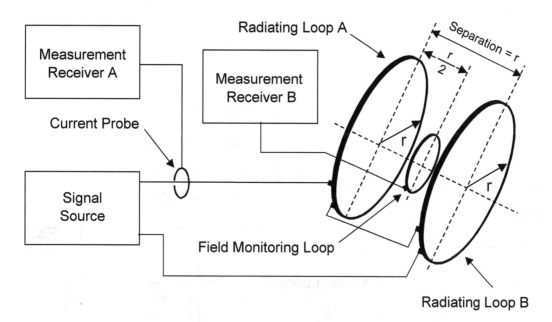

Standard Configuration

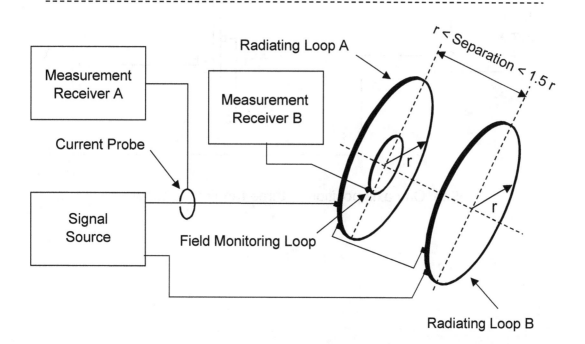

Optional Configuration

FIGURE RS101-5. Calibration of Helmholtz coils.

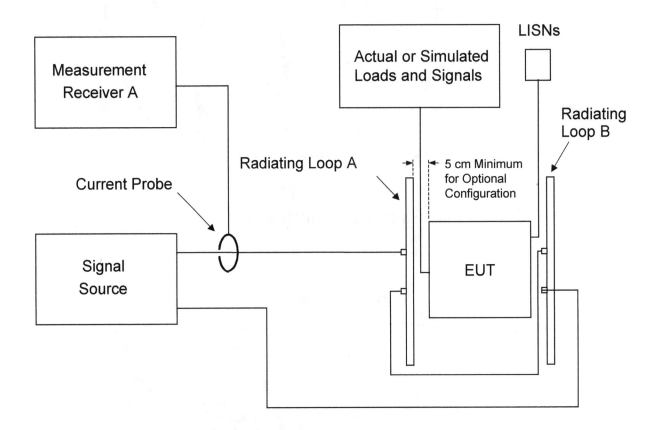

Note: One axis position of three required is shown

FIGURE RS101-6. Test setup for Helmholtz coils.

5.21 RS103, radiated susceptibility, electric field.

5.21.1 RS103 applicability.

This requirement is applicable for equipment and subsystem enclosures and all interconnecting cables. The requirement is applicable as follows:

a. 2 MHz to 30 MHz   Army ships; Army aircraft, including flight line; Navy; and optional* for all others

b. 30 MHz to 18 GHz   All

c. 18 GHz to 40 GHz   Optional* for all

*Required only if specified in the procurement specification

For Air Force only: There is no requirement at the tuned frequency of antenna-connected receivers.

5.21.2 RS103 limit.

The EUT shall not exhibit any malfunction, degradation of performance, or deviation from specified indications, beyond the tolerances indicated in the individual equipment or subsystem specification, when subjected to the radiated electric fields listed in Table VII and modulated as specified below. For receiver EUTs having permanently attached antennas ONLY, unless otherwise stated in the system specification, reduce performance over the intended receiver band of operation is allowed. The receiver shall meet its performance requirements after in-band exposure to the radiated field. Up to 30 MHz, the requirement shall be met for vertically polarized fields. Above 30 MHz, the requirement shall be met for both horizontally and vertically polarized fields. Circular polarized fields are not acceptable.

5.21.3 RS103 test procedures.

5.21.3.1 Purpose.

This test procedure is used to verify the ability of the EUT and associated cabling to withstand electric fields.

5.21.3.2 Test equipment.

The test equipment shall be as follows:

a. Signal generators

b. Power amplifiers

c. Transmit antennas

d. Electric field sensors (physically small - electrically short)

e. Measurement receiver

f. Power meter

g. Directional coupler

h. Attenuator

i. Data recording device

j. LISNs

5.21.3.3 Setup.

The test setup shall be as follows:

a. Maintain a basic test setup for the EUT as shown and described on Figures 1 through 5 and 4.3.8.

b. For electric field calibration, electric field sensors are required.

c. Configure test equipment as shown on Figure RS103-1.

d. Calibration.

    (1) Placement of electric field sensors (see 5.21.3.3b). Position sensors at same distance as the EUT is located from the transmit antenna, directly opposite the transmit antenna as shown on Figures RS103-2 and RS103-3, and a minimum of 30 cm above the ground plane at or below 1 GHz. Above 1 GHz, place the sensors at height corresponding to the area of the EUT being illuminated. Do not place sensors directly at corners or edges of EUT components.

e. EUT testing.

    (1) Placement of transmit antennas. Antennas shall be placed 1 meter or greater from the test setup boundary as follows:

        (a) 2 MHz to 200 MHz

            <u>1</u> Test setup boundaries $\leq$ 3 meters. Center the antenna between the edges of the test setup boundary. The boundary includes all enclosures of the EUT and the 2 meters of exposed interconnecting and power leads required in 4.3.8.6. Interconnecting leads shorter than 2 meters are acceptable when they represent the actual platform installation.

            <u>2</u> Test setup boundaries > 3 meters. Use multiple antenna positions (N) at spacings as shown on Figure RS103-3. The number of antenna positions (N) shall be determined by dividing the edge-to-edge boundary distance (in meters) by 3 and rounding up to an integer.

        (b) 200 MHz and above. Multiple antenna positions may be required as shown on Figure RS103-2. Determine the number of antenna positions (N) as follows:

            <u>1</u> For testing from 200 MHz up to 1 GHz, place the antenna in a sufficient number of positions such that the entire area of each EUT enclosure and the first 35 cm of cables and leads interfacing with the EUT enclosure are within the 3 dB beamwidth of the antenna.

            <u>2</u> For testing at 1 GHz and above, place the antenna in a sufficient number of positions such that the entire area of each EUT enclosure and the first 7 cm of cables and leads interfacing with the EUT enclosure are within the 3 dB beamwidth of the antenna.

    (2) Maintain the placement of electric field sensors as specified in 5.21.3.3d(1) above.

5.21.3.4 Procedures.

The test procedures shall be as follows:

a. Turn on the measurement equipment and EUT and allow a sufficient time for stabilization.

b. Assess the test area for potential RF hazards and take necessary precautionary steps to assure safety of test personnel.

c. Calibration:

   (1) Electric field sensor procedure. Record the amplitude shown on the electric field sensor display unit due to EUT ambient. Reposition the sensor, as necessary, until this level is < 10% of the applicable field strength to be used for testing.

d. EUT testing:

   (1) E-field sensor procedure:

       (a) Set the signal source to 1 kHz pulse modulation, 50% duty cycle. Verify that the modulation is present on the drive signal for each signal generator/modulation source combination. Ensure that the modulation frequency, waveform and depth (40 dB minimum from peak to baseline) are correct. Using appropriate amplifier and transmit antenna, establish an electric field at the test start frequency. Gradually increase the electric field level until it reaches the applicable limit.

       (b) Scan the required frequency ranges in accordance with the rates and durations specified in Table III. Maintain field strength levels in accordance with the applicable limit. Monitor EUT performance for susceptibility effects.

       (c) Ensure that the E-field sensor is indicating the field from the fundamental frequency and not from the harmonics.

   (2) If susceptibility is noted, determine the threshold level in accordance with 4.3.10.4.3.

   (3) Perform testing over the required frequency range with the transmit antenna vertically polarized. Repeat the testing above 30 MHz with the transmit antenna horizontally polarized.

   (4) Repeat 5.21.3.4d for each transmit antenna position required by 5.21.3.3e.

5.21.3.5 Data presentation.

Data presentation shall be as follows:

a. Provide graphical or tabular data showing frequency ranges and field strength levels tested.

b. Provide graphical or tabular data listing (antenna procedure only) all calibration data collected to include input power requirements used versus frequency, and results of system check in 5.21.3.4c(2)(c) and 5.21.3.4c(2)(d).

c. Provide the correction factors necessary to adjust sensor output readings for equivalent peak detection of modulated waveforms.

d. Provide graphs or tables listing any susceptibility thresholds that were determined along with their associated frequencies.

e. Provide diagrams or photographs showing actual equipment setup and the associated dimensions.

5.21.4 RS103 alternative test procedures – reverberation chamber (mode-tuned).
These procedures may be substituted for the 5.21.3 procedures over the frequency range of 200 MHz to 40 GHz. The lower frequency limit is dependent on chamber size. To determine the lower frequency limit for a given chamber, use the following formula to determine the number of possible modes (N) which can exist at a given frequency. If, for a given frequency, N is less than 100 then the chamber should not be used at or below that frequency.

$$N = \frac{8\pi}{3} abd \frac{f^3}{c^3}$$

where: a, b, and d are the chamber internal dimensions in meters

f is the operation frequency in Hz

c is the speed of propagation (3×10^8 m/s)

5.21.4.1 Purpose.
This test procedure is an alternative technique used to verify the ability of the EUT and associated cabling to withstand electric fields.

5.21.4.2 Test equipment.
The test equipment shall be as follows:

a. Signal generators

b. Power amplifiers

c. Receive antennas

    (1) 200 MHz to 1 GHz, log periodic or double ridge horns.

    (2) 1 GHz to 18 GHz, double ridge horns.

    (3) 18 GHz to 40 GHz, other antennas as approved by the procuring activity.

d. Transmit antennas

e. Electric field sensors (physically small - electrically short), each axis independently displayed

f. Measurement receiver

g. Power meter

h. Directional coupler

i. Attenuator, 50 ohm

j. Data recording device

k. LISNs

5.21.4.3 Setup.

The test setup shall be as follows:

a. Install the EUT in a reverberation chamber using the basic test setup for the EUT as shown and described on Figures 2 through 5 and 4.3.8. The EUT shall be at least 1.0 meter from the chamber walls, the tuner, and antennas.

b. For electric field calibration, electric field sensors (5.21.4.2e) are required from 200 MHz to 1 GHz. Either field sensors or receive antennas may be used above 1 GHz.

c. Configure the test equipment as shown on Figures RS103-4 and RS103-5. The same configuration is used for both calibration and EUT testing. The transmit and receive antennas shall be present in the chamber for all calibration and EUT testing, including for the electric-field probe technique. Unused receive antennas shall be terminated in 50 ohms.

5.21.4.4 Procedure.

The test procedures shall be as follows:

a. Calibration. Use the following procedure to determine the electric field strength that will be created inside the chamber when a fixed amount of RF energy is injected into the chamber.

(1) Receive antenna procedure.

(a) Adjust the RF source to inject an appropriate forward power (unmodulated) into the chamber at the start frequency of the test.

(b) Measure the level at the receive antenna using the measurement receiver.

(c) Rotate the tuner 360 degrees using the minimum number of steps required from Table VIII. Allow the paddle wheel to dwell at each position for a period corresponding to a minimum of 1.5 times the response time of the measurement receiver.

(d) Record the maximum amplitude of the signal received and use the following formula to derive a calibration factor for the field strength created inside the chamber. (P_{r-max} and $P_{forward}$ in watts; λ in meters).

$$\text{Calibration factor} = \frac{8\pi}{\lambda}\sqrt{5(\frac{P_{r-max}}{P_{forward}})} \quad \text{V/m (for one watt)}$$

(e) Repeat the procedure in frequency steps no greater than 2% of the preceding frequency until 1.1 times the start frequency is reached. Continue the procedure in frequency steps no greater than 10% of the preceding frequency, thereafter.

(2) Electric field probe procedure.

(a) Adjust the RF source to inject an appropriate forward power ($P_{forward}$) (unmodulated) into the chamber at the start frequency of the test.

(b) Rotate the tuner 360 degrees using the minimum number of steps required from Table VIII. Allow the tuner to dwell at each position for a period corresponding to a minimum of 1.5 times the probe response time.

(c) Record the maximum amplitude from the receive antenna ($P_{r\text{-max}}$) and from each element of the probe and use the following formula to derive a calibration factor for the field strength created inside the chamber. (Probe reading in V/m and $P_{forward}$ in watts).

$$\text{Calibration factor} = \sqrt{\left(\frac{E_{x\text{-max}} + E_{y\text{-max}} + E_{z\text{-max}}}{3}\right)^2 \bigg/ P_{forward}} \quad \text{V/m (for one watt)}$$

(d) Repeat the procedure in frequency steps no greater than 2% of the preceding frequency until 1.1 times the start frequency is reached. Continue the procedure in frequency steps no greater than 10% of the preceding frequency, thereafter.

b. EUT testing. The same antennas used for calibration shall be used for EUT testing.

(1) Turn on the measurement equipment and allow a sufficient time for stabilization.

(2) Set the RF source to the start frequency of the test with 1 kHz pulse modulation, 50 % duty cycle.

(3) Calculate the amount of RF power needed to create the desired field strength by determining the difference (in dB - decibel differences are the same for both field strength and power, there is a square law relationship between field strength and power in real numbers) between the desired field strength and the field strength obtained during the calibration. Adjust the chamber peak forward power to this value. Interpolation between calibration points is required.

(4) Adjust the measurement receiver to display the received signal at the receive antenna to verify that an electric field is present.

(5) Rotate the tuner 360 degrees using the minimum of steps shown in Table VIII. Allow the tuner to dwell at each position for the duration specified in Table III. As the tuner rotates, maintain the forward power required to produce field levels at the applicable limit as determined from the calibration.

(6) Scan the required frequency range in accordance with the maximum frequency step sizes and durations specified in Table III. Monitor EUT performance for susceptibility effects.

(7) If susceptibility is noted, determine the threshold level in accordance with 4.3.10.4.3.

5.21.4.5 Data presentation.

Data presentation shall be as follows:

a. Provide graphical or tabular data showing frequency ranges and field strength levels tested.

b. Provide graphical or tabular data listing of all calibration data collected to include input power requirements used versus frequency and results of calibration in 5.21.4.4a(1)(d) and 5.21.4.4a(2)(c).

c. Provide the correction factors necessary to adjust sensor output readings for equivalent peak detection of modulated waveforms.

d. Provide graphs or tables listing any susceptibility thresholds that were determined along with their associated frequencies.

e. Provide diagrams or photographs showing the actual equipment setup and the associated dimensions.

f. Provide the data certifying the baseline performance of the shielded room as a properly functioning reverberation chamber over a defined frequency range.

TABLE VII. RS103 limits.

PLATFORM / FREQ. RANGE		AIRCRAFT (EXTERNAL OR SAFETY CRITICAL)	AIRCRAFT INTERNAL	ALL SHIPS (ABOVE DECKS) AND SUBMARINES (EXTERNAL)*	SHIPS (METALLIC) (BELOW DECKS)	SHIPS (NON-METALLIC) (BELOW DECKS)**	SUBMARINES (INTERNAL)	GROUND	SPACE
2 MHz → 30 MHz	A	200	200	200	10	50	5	50	20
	N	200	200	200	10	50	5	10	20
	AF	200	20	-	-	-	-	10	20
30 MHz → 1 GHz	A	200	200	200	10	10	10	50	20
	N	200	200	200	10	10	10	10	20
	AF	200	20	-	-	-	-	10	20
1 GHz → 18 GHz	A	200	200	200	10	10	10	50	20
	N	200	200	200	10	10	10	50	20
	AF	200	60	-	-	-	-	50	20
18 GHz → 40 GHz	A	200	200	200	10	10	10	50	20
	N	200	200	200	10	10	10	50	20
	AF	200	60	-	-	-	-	50	20

Column group heading: LIMIT LEVEL (VOLTS/METER)

* For equipment located external to the pressure hull of a submarine but within the superstructure, use SHIPS (METALLIC)(BELOW DECKS)

** Equipment located in the hanger deck of Aircraft Carriers

KEY: A = Army
      N = Navy
      AF = Air Force

138

TABLE VIII. Required number of tuner positions for a reverberation chamber.

Frequency Range (MHz)	Tuner Positions
200 - 300	50
300 - 400	20
400 - 600	16
Above 600	12

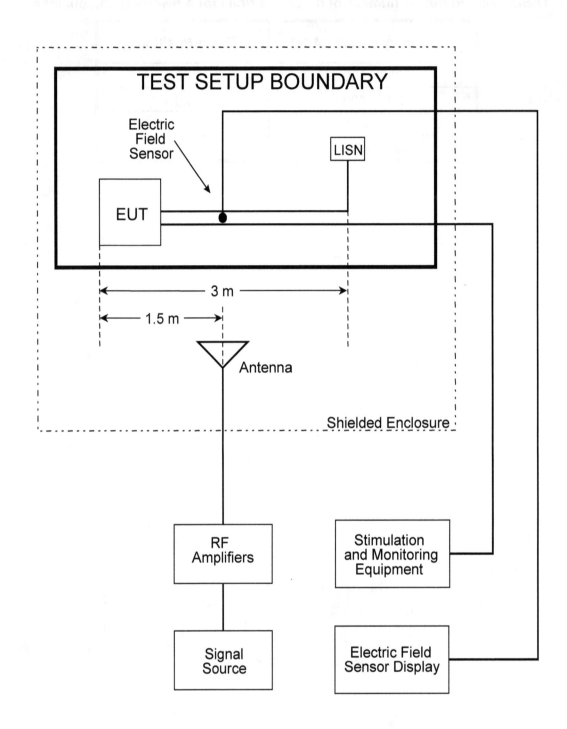

FIGURE RS103-1. Test equipment configuration.

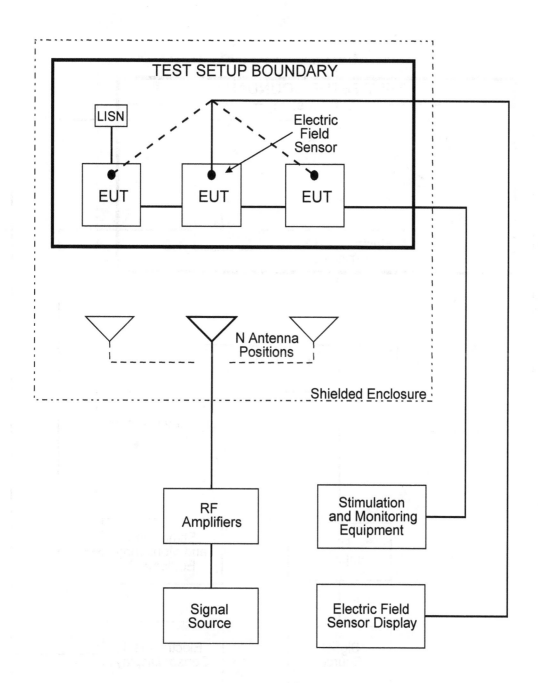

FIGURE RS103-2. Multiple test antenna locations for frequency > 200 MHz.

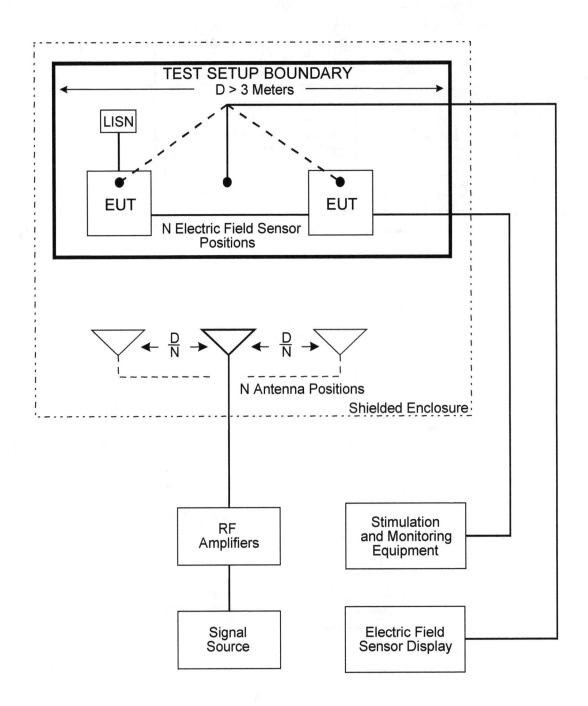

FIGURE RS103-3. Multiple test antenna locations for N positions, D > 3 meters.

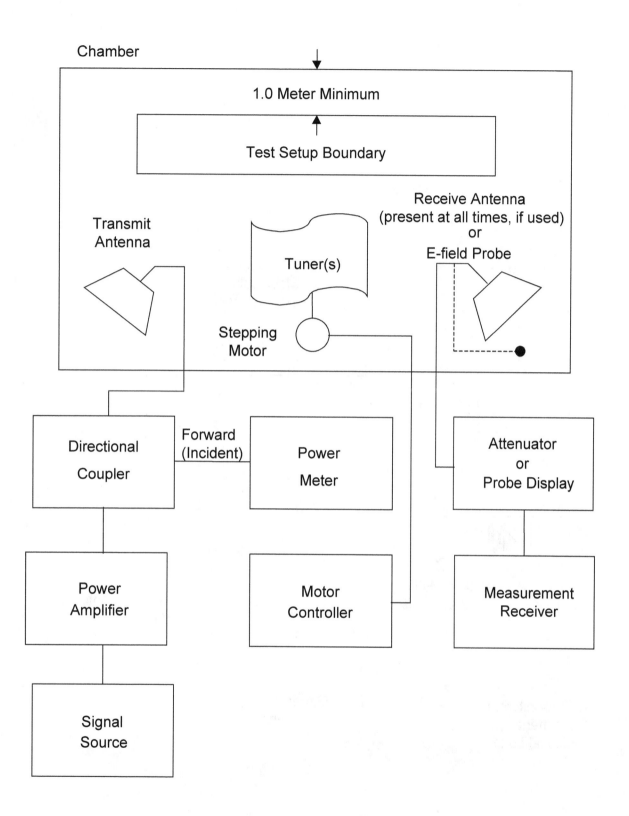

FIGURE RS103-4. Reverberation chamber setup.

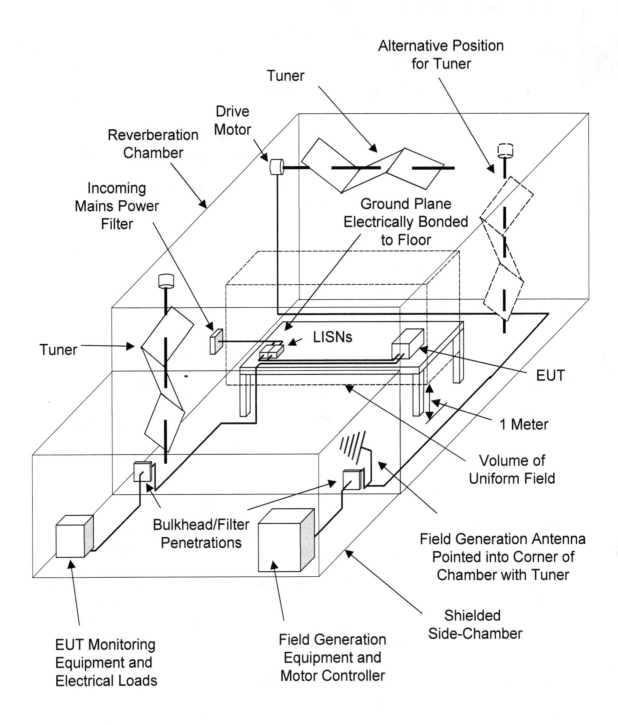

FIGURE RS103-5. Reverberation chamber overview.

5.22 RS105, radiated susceptibility, transient electromagnetic field.

5.22.1 RS105 applicability.

This requirement is applicable to equipment and subsystem enclosures which are exposed to the external electromagnetic environment. For surface ships, this includes external, above deck and exposed below deck installations. The requirement is applicable to Army aircraft for safety critical equipment and subsystems located in an external installation.

5.22.2 RS105 limit.

The EUT shall not exhibit any malfunction, degradation of performance, or deviation from specified indications, beyond the tolerances indicated in the individual equipment or subsystem specification, when subjected to a test signal having the waveform and amplitude shown on Figure RS105-1. At least five pulses shall be applied at the rate of not more than one pulse per minute.

5.22.3 RS105 test procedures.

5.22.3.1 Purpose.

This test procedure is used to verify the ability of the EUT enclosure to withstand a transient electromagnetic field.

5.22.3.2 Test equipment.

The test equipment shall be as follows:

    a.   Transverse electromagnetic (TEM) cell, parallel plate transmission line or equivalent

    b.   Transient pulse generator, monopulse output, plus and minus polarity

    c.   Storage oscilloscope, 500 MHz, single-shot bandwidth (minimum), variable sampling rate up to 1gigasample per second (GSa/s)

    d.   Terminal protection devices

    e.   High-voltage probe, 1 GHz bandwidth (minimum)

    f.   B-dot sensor probe

    g.   D-dot sensor probe

    h.   LISNs

    i.   Integrator, time constant ten times the overall pulse width

5.22.3.3 Setup.

Set up the EUT as described below. CAUTION: Exercise extreme care if an open radiator is used for this test.

    a.   Calibration. Configure the test equipment in accordance with Figure RS105-2.

        (1)   Before installing the EUT in the test volume, place the B-dot or D-dot sensor probe in the center position of the five point grid in the vertical plane where the front face of the EUT will be located (see Figure RS105-2).

        (2)   Place the high-voltage probe across the input to the radiation system at the output of the transient pulse generator. Connect the probe to a storage oscilloscope.

    b.   EUT testing. Configure the test equipment as shown on Figure RS105-3 for testing of the EUT.

(1) Place the EUT centerline on the centerline of the working volume of the radiation system in such a manner that it does not exceed the usable volume of the radiation system (h/3, B/2, A/2)/(x,y,z) as shown on Figure RS105-3 (h is the maximum vertical separation of the plates). If the EUT is mounted on a ground plane in the actual installation, the EUT shall be placed on the radiating system ground plane. The EUT shall be bonded to the ground plane in a manner that duplicates the actual installation. Otherwise, the EUT shall be supported by dielectric material that produces a minimum distortion of the EM fields.

(2) The EUT orientation shall be such that the maximum coupling of electric and or magnetic fields is simulated. This may require more than one test orientation.

(3) Cables for EUT operation and monitoring shall be oriented to minimize induced currents and voltages on the cables. Cabling shall be oriented normal to the electric field vector and in a manner that minimizes the loop area normal to the magnetic field vector. Cables extending out of the parallel plate working volume should remain normal to the electric field vector for a minimum distance equal to 2 times h.

(4) Bond the bottom plate of the radiation system to an earth reference.

(5) Keep the top plate of the radiation system at least 2 times h from the closest metallic ground, including ceiling, building structural beams, metallic air ducts, shielded room walls, and so forth.

(6) Place the EUT actual or simulated loads and signals for electrical interfaces in a shielded enclosure when an open radiator is used.

(7) Place transient protection devices (TPDs) in the EUT power lines near the power source to protect the power source.

(8) Connect the transient pulse generator to the radiation system.

5.22.3.4 Procedures.
The test procedures shall be as follows:

a. Turn on the measurement equipment and allow a sufficient time for stabilization.

b. Calibration. Perform the following procedures using the calibration setup:

(1) Generate a pulse and adjust the pulse generator to produce a pulsed field, as measured with the B-dot or D-dot probes, which meets the peak amplitude, rise time, and pulse width requirements. CAUTION: High voltages are used which are potentially lethal. Record the drive pulse waveform as displayed on the oscilloscope.

(2) Tolerances and characteristics of the RS105 limit shall be as follows:

(a) Rise time (between 10% and 90% points) between 1.8 ns and 2.8 ns (electric field continuously increasing).

(b) Full width half maximum (FWHM) pulse width equal to 23 ns ± 5 ns.

(c) Peak value of the electric or magnetic field for each grid position:

0 dB ≤ magnitude ≤ 6 dB above limit.

(3) Repeat steps (1) and (2) above for the other four test points on Figure RS105-2.

(4)　Determine the pulse generator settings and associated pulse drive amplitude which simultaneously satisfies the field requirements for all five grid positions.

c.　EUT testing.　Perform the following procedures using the test setup:

(1)　Turn on the EUT and allow sufficient time for stabilization.

(2)　Test the EUT in its orthogonal orientations whenever possible.

(3)　Apply the pulse starting at 10% of the pulse peak amplitude determined in 5.22.3.4b(4) with the specified waveshape where practical.　Increase the pulse amplitude in step sizes of 2 or 3 until the required level is reached.

(4)　Ensure that the drive pulse waveform characteristics at the required test level are consistent with those noted in 5.22.3.4b(2).

(5)　Apply the required number of pulses at a rate of not more than 1 pulse per minute.

(6)　Monitor the EUT during and after each pulse for signs of susceptibility or degradation of performance.

(7)　If an EUT malfunction occurs at a level less than the specified peak level, terminate the test and record the level.

(8)　If susceptibility is noted, determine the threshold level in accordance with 4.3.10.4.3.

5.22.3.5　Data presentation.

Data presentation shall be as follows:

a.　Provide photographs of EUT orientation including cables.

b.　Provide a detailed written description of the EUT configuration.

c.　Provide oscilloscope recordings that show peak value, rise time, and pulse width of one applied pulse for each EUT orientation.

d.　Provide the pulse number, with the first pulse being Number 1, for each recorded waveshape.

e.　Record the time-to-recovery for each EUT failure, if applicable.

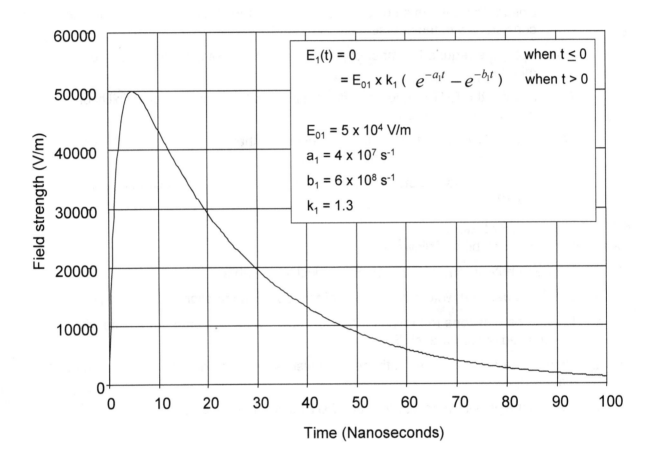

FIGURE RS105-1. RS105 limit for all applications.

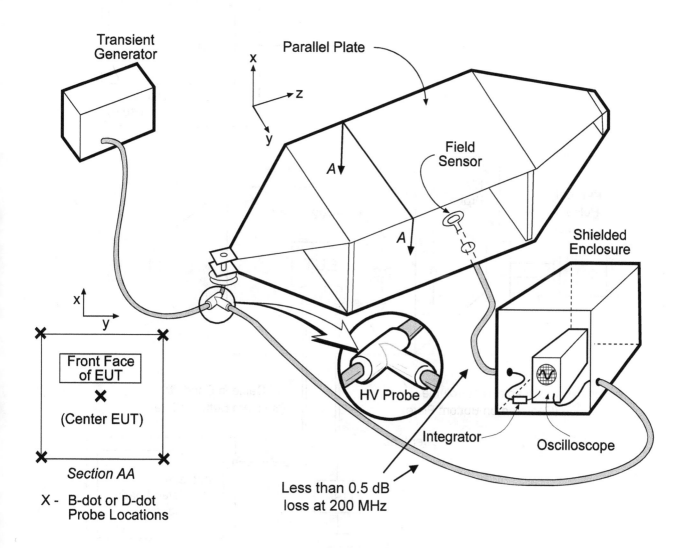

FIGURE RS105-2. Typical calibration setup using parallel plate radiation system.

TOP VIEW

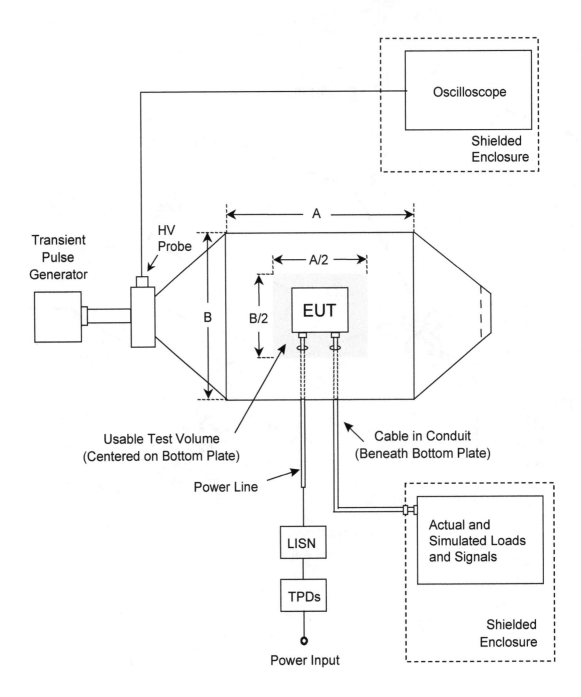

FIGURE RS105-3. Typical test setup using parallel plate radiation system.

6. NOTES

(This section contains information of a general or explanatory nature that may be helpful, but is not mandatory.)

6.1 Intended use.

This standard is intended for use in the acquisition cycle of equipment and subsystems to specify the electromagnetic emission and susceptibility requirements for the control of EMI.

6.2 Acquisition requirements.

Acquisition documents should specify the following:

a. Title, number, and date of this standard.

6.3 Associated Data Item Descriptions (DIDs).

This standard has been assigned an Acquisition Management Systems Control (ASMC) number authorizing it as the source document for the following DIDs. When it is necessary to obtain the data, the applicable DIDs must be listed on the Contract Data Requirements List (DD Form 1423).

DID Number	DID Title
DI-EMCS-80199	Electromagnetic Interference Control Procedures (EMICP)
DI-EMCS-80201	Electromagnetic Interference Test Procedures (EMITP)
DI-EMCS-80200	Electromagnetic Interference Test Report (EMITR)

The above DIDs were current as of the date of this standard. The ASSIST database should be researched at http://quicksearch.dla.mil to ensure that only current and approved DIDs are cited on the DD Form 1423.

6.4 Tailoring guidance.

Application specific criteria may be derived from operational and engineering analyses on the equipment or subsystem being procured for use in specific environments. When analyses reveal that a requirement in this standard is not appropriate or adequate for that procurement, the requirement should be tailored and incorporated into the appropriate documentation, prior to contract award or through contractual modification early in the developmental phase. The appendix of this standard provides guidance for tailoring.

6.5 Subject term (key word) listing.

EMC
EMI
Electromagnetic compatibility
Electromagnetic emission
Electromagnetic susceptibility
Test Limits, EMI

6.6 International standardization agreement implementation.

This standard implements STANAG 3516, *Electromagnetic Interference, Test Methods for Aircraft Electrical and Electronic Equipment*, and STANAG 4370, *Environmental Testing*. When changes to, revision, or cancellation of this standard are proposed, the preparing activity must coordinate the action with the U.S. National Point of Contact for the international standardization agreement, as identified in the ASSIST database at https://assist.dla.mil.

6.7 Technical points of contact.

Requests for additional information or assistance on this standard can be obtained from the following:

a. Commander, U.S. Army, AMCOM
    AMSRD-AMR-AE-S
    Building 4488
    Redstone Arsenal, AL 35898
    Mr. Duane Driver
    DSN 897-8447; Commercial (256) 313-8447
    E-mail: duane.e.driver.civ@mail.mil

b. Naval Air Systems Command
    Code: 4.1.13
    28187 Standley Road
    Building 4010
    Patuxent River, MD 20670
    Mr. Craig Simmons
    DSN 342-4907; Commercial (301) 342-4907
    E-mail: craig.simmons@navy.mil

c. AFLCMC/EZAC, Building 28
    2145 Monahan Way
    Wright Patterson AFB, OH 45433-7017
    Mr. Joseph DeBoy
    DSN 785-6957; Commercial (937) 255-6957
    E-mail: joseph.deboy@us.af.mil

Any information relating to Government contracts must be obtained through contracting officers.

6.8 Changes from previous issue.

Marginal notations are not used in the revision to identify changes with respect to the previous issue due to the extensiveness of the changes.

APPENDIX A

APPLICATION GUIDE

A.1 GENERAL

A.1.1 Scope.
This appendix provides background information for each emission and susceptibility and associated test requirement in the main body of the standard. This information includes rationale for requirements, guidance in applying the requirements, and lessons learned from platform and laboratory experience. This information should help users understand the intent behind the requirements, should aid the procuring activity in tailoring emission and susceptibility requirements as necessary for particular applications, and should help users develop detailed test procedures in the EMITP based on the general test procedures in this document. This appendix is not a mandatory part of the standard. The information contained herein is intended for guidance only.

A.1.2 Structure.
This appendix follows the same general format as the main body of the standard. Section 4 general requirements from the main body are repeated in this appendix and are in italics. Main body paragraph numbers corresponding to each requirement are included in parentheses. A "Discussion" paragraph is provided for each requirement. Though section 5 detailed requirements from the main body are not repeated, discussion paragraphs on "Applicability and limits" and "Test procedure" are included.

A.2 APPLICABLE DOCUMENTS

A.2.1 General.
The documents listed in this section are specified within this appendix.

A.2.2 Government documents.
A.2.2.1 Specifications, standards, and handbooks.
The following specifications, standards, and handbooks specified herein are referenced solely to provide supplemental technical data. These documents are for informational purposes only.

DEPARTMENT OF DEFENSE STANDARDS

MIL-STD-188-125-1	High-Altitude Electromagnetic Pulse (HEMP) Protection for Ground-Based C^{4}I Facilities Performing Critical, Time-Urgent Missions Part 1 Fixed Facilities
MIL-STD-464	Electromagnetic Environmental Effects Requirements for Systems
MIL-STD-704	Aircraft Electric Power Characteristics
MIL-STD-1275	Characteristics of 28 Volt DC Input Power to Utilization Equipment in Military Vehicles
MIL-STD-1399	Interface Standard for Shipboard Systems
MIL-STD-1399-300	Section 300B, Electric Power, Alternating Current
MIL-STD-1539	Electrical Power, Direct Current, Space Vehicle Design Requirements (Inactive for New Design)

DEPARTMENT OF DEFENSE HANDBOOKS

MIL-HDBK-235-1   Military Operational Electromagnetic Environment Profiles, Part 1C, General Guidance

MIL-HDBK-237   Electromagnetic Environmental Effects and Spectrum Supportability Guidance for the Acquisition Process

MIL-HDBK-423   High-Altitude Electromagnetic Pulse (HEMP) Protection for Fixed and Transportable Ground-Based C^4I Facilities, Volume 1, Fixed Facilities

(Copies of these documents are available online at http://quicksearch.dla.mil For copies of MIL-HDBK-423 call DLA Document Services at 215-697-6396 or DSN 442-6396 for additional information.)

A.2.2.2 Other Government documents, drawings, and publications.

The following other Government documents, drawings, and publications specified herein are referenced solely to provide supplemental technical data. These documents are for informational purposes only.

ARMY PUBLICATIONS

ARMY REGULATION (AR)

AR 40-61   Medical Logistics Policies

AR 70-62   Airworthiness Qualification of Aircraft Systems

(Copies of Army Regulations and Pamphlets are available online at http://armypubs.army.mil/epubs.)

ARMY MATERIEL COMMAND PAMPHLET (AMCP)

AMCP 706-410   Engineering Design Handbook, EMC

(Copies of these documents are available online at www.dtic.mil.)

ARMY AERONAUTICAL DESIGN STANDARD

ADS-37-PRF   Electromagnetic Environmental Effects (E^3) Performance and Verification Requirements

(Copies of this document are available online at http://www.amrdec.army.mil/amrdec/rdmr-se/tdmd/StandardAero.html.)

NAVY PUBLICATIONS

NAVAL SEA SYSTEMS COMMAND

NAVSEA OD 30393   Design Principles and Practices for Controlling Hazards of Electromagnetic Radiation to Ordnance (HERO Design Guide)

(Copies of this document are available online at https://acc.dau.mil/adl/en-

US/122635/file/25365/OD%2030393pdf.)

AIR FORCE PUBLICATIONS

AIR FORCE INSTRUCTIONS (AFI)

AFI 11-202V3   General Flight Rules

(Copies of this document are available online at http://www.e-publishing.af.mil/.)

AIR FORCE DOCUMENTS

AIR FORCE SYSTEMS COMMAND DESIGN HANDBOOK (AFSC DH)

AFSC DH 1-4   Air Force Systems Command Design Handbook, Electromagnetic Compatibility

(Copies of this document are available from AFLCMC/ENRS, Engineering.Standards@us.af.mil.)

CODE OF FEDERAL REGULATIONS (CFR)

47 CFR 2   Frequency Allocations and Radio Treaty Matters; General Rules and Regulations

47 CFR 15   Radio Frequency Devices

47 CFR 18   Industrial, Scientific, and Medical Equipment

(Copies of these documents are available online at http://www.gpo.gov or http://www.ntia.doc.gov.)

NATIONAL BUREAU OF STANDARDS (NBS)

Technical Note 1092   Design, Evaluation, and Use of a Reverberation Chamber for Performing Electromagnetic Susceptibility/Vulnerability Measurements

(Copies of this document are available online at https://archive.org/details/designevaluation1092craw.

NATIONAL INSTITUTE OF STANDARDS AND TECHNOLOGY (NIST)

Technical Note 1508   Evaluation of the NASA Langley Research Center Mode-Stirred Chamber Facility

(Copies of this document are available online at http://www/nist.gov/.)

NATIONAL TELECOMMUNICATONS AND INFORMATION ADMINISTRATION (NTIA)

NTIA Manual of Regulations and Procedures for Federal Radio Frequency Management (Redbook)

(Copies of this document are available online at http://www.ntia.doc.gov/.)

A.2.3 Non-Government publications.
The following non-government documents specified herein are referenced solely to provide supplemental technical data. These documents are for informational purposes only.

AMERICAN NATIONAL STANDARDS INSTITUTE (ANSI)

ANSI C63.4	American National Standard for Methods of Measurement of Radio-Noise Emissions from Low-Voltage Electrical and Electronic Equipment in the Range of 9 kHz to 40 GHz
ANSI C63.12	American National Standard Recommended Practice for Electromagnetic Compatibility Limits

(Copies of these documents are available online at http://www.ieee.org or http://www.ansi.org.)

INTERNATIONAL ELECTROTECHNICAL COMMISSION (IEC)

IEC 61000-4-2	Electromagnetic compatibility (EMC) Part 4-2: Testing and measurement techniques – Electrostatic discharge immunity test
IEC 61000-4-21	Electromagnetic compatibility (EMC) Part 4-21: Testing and measurement techniques – Reverberation chamber test methods

(Copies of this document are available online at http://www.iec.ch/ or http://www.ansi.org.)

NATIONAL FIRE PROTECTION ASSOCIATION (NFPA)

NFPA 70	National Electrical Code (DoD Adopted)

(Copies of this document are available online at http://www.nfpa.org.)

RADIO TECHNICAL COMMISSION FOR AERONAUTICS (RTCA) INC.

DO-160	Environmental Conditions and Test Procedures for Airborne Equipment

(Copies of these documents are available online at http://www.rtca.org.)

SAE INTERNATIONAL

AEROSPACE RECOMMENDED PRACTICE

ARP 5412	(R) Aircraft Lightning Environment and Related Test Waveforms
ARP 5414	Aircraft Lightning Zone

ARP 5415   User's Manual for Certification of Aircraft Electrical/Electronic
                Systems for the Indirect Effects of Lightning

ARP5416   Aircraft Lightning Test Methods

(Copies of this document are available online at http://www.sae.org.)

A.3 DEFINITIONS

A.3.1 General.
The terms used in this appendix are defined in ANSI C63.14. In addition, the following definitions are applicable for the purpose of this appendix.

A.3.2 Acronyms used in this appendix.

AM	Amplitude Modulation
BCI	Bulk Cable Injection
CW	Continuous Wave
E3	Electromagnetic Environmental Effects
EID	Electrically Initiated Device
EMP	Electromagnetic Pulse
GPI	Ground Plane Interference
HF	High Frequency
LRU	Line-Replaceable Unit
NOE	Nap-of-the-earth
RF	Radio Frequency
UPS	Uninterruptible Power Supplies
VFR	Visual Flight Rules
VSWR	Voltage Standing Wave Ratio

A.4 GENERAL REQUIREMENTS

A.4.1 (4.1) General.
Electronic, electrical, and electromechanical equipment and subsystems shall comply with the applicable general interface requirements in 4.2. General requirements for verification shall be in accordance with 4.3. These general requirements are in addition to the applicable detailed emission and susceptibility requirements and associated test procedures defined in 5.

Discussion: The requirements in this paragraph are universally applicable to all subsystems and equipment. Separate emission and susceptibility requirements that are structured to address specific concerns with various classes of subsystems and equipment are contained in other portions of this standard.

This document is concerned only with specifying technical requirements for controlling electromagnetic interference (EMI) emissions and susceptibility at the subsystem-level and equipment-level. The requirements in this document are not intended to be directly applied to subassemblies of equipment such as modules or circuit cards. The basic concepts can be implemented at the subassembly level; however, significant tailoring needs to be accomplished for the particular application. The requirements included herein are intended to be used as a baseline. Placement of the limits is based on demonstrated performance typically required for use on existing platforms in order to achieve electromagnetic compatibility. System-level requirements dealing with integration of subsystems and equipment are contained in documents such as MIL-STD-464 and MIL-STD-188-125-1. MIL-STD-464 requirements include intra-system compatibility within the system, inter-system compatibility with external radio frequency environments, lightning protection, and hazards of electromagnetic radiation to ordnance, fuel and personnel. The procuring activity and system contractors should review the requirements contained herein for possible tailoring based on system design and expected operational environments. NTIA Manual provides requirements for complying with laws governing use of the radio frequency spectrum by federal agencies.

Guidance and techniques which are helpful in meeting the requirements of this standard are contained in MIL-HDBK-423, AFSC DH 1-4, and AMCP 706-410. MIL-HDBK-237 provides guidance for management of Electromagnetic Environmental Effects (E3) efforts. ADS-37-PRF provides additional guidance for Army equipment located or operated on fixed-wing aircraft and helicopters. MIL-HDBK-235-1 provides information on land, air, and sea based RF emitters, both hostile and friendly, which contribute to the overall EME.

The qualification status of equipment and subsystems becomes uncertain when hardware or software changes are incorporated due to equipment updates or test failures, including failures from testing to requirements other than EMI. To maintain certification to MIL-STD-461 after changes are implemented, either an analysis showing no substantive impact needs to be issued or continued compliance needs to be demonstrated by limited testing deemed to be appropriate to evaluate the changes. The approach used to maintain continued certification and the results of analysis and testing are normally subject to procuring activity approval.

A.4.2 (4.2) Interface requirements.

A.4.2.1 (4.2.1) Joint procurement.
Equipment or subsystems procured by one DoD activity for multi-agency use shall comply with the requirements of the user agencies.

Discussion: When the government procures equipment that will be used by more than one service or agency, a particular activity is assigned responsibility for overall procurement. The responsible activity must address the concerns of all the users. Conflicts may exist among the parties concerned. Also, imposition of more severe design requirements by one party may adversely affect other performance characteristics required by the second party. For example, severe radiated susceptibility levels on an electro-optical sensor may require aperture protection measures which compromise sensitivity. It is important that these issues be resolved to the satisfaction of all parties and that all genuine requirements be included.

A.4.2.2 (4.2.2) Filtering (Navy only).
The use of line-to-ground filters for EMI control shall be minimized. Such filters establish low impedance paths for structure (common-mode) currents through the ground plane and can be a major cause of interference in systems, platforms, or installations because the currents can couple into other equipment using the same ground plane. If such a filter must be employed, the line-to-ground capacitance for each line shall not exceed 0.1 microfarads (μF) for 60 Hertz (Hz) equipment or 0.02 μF for 400 Hz equipment. For submarine DC-powered equipment and

aircraft DC-powered equipment, the filter capacitance from each line-to-ground at the user interface shall not exceed 0.075 µF/kW of connected load. For DC loads less than 0.5 kW, the filter capacitance shall not exceed 0.03 µF. The filtering employed shall be fully described in the equipment or subsystem technical manual and the Electromagnetic Interference Control Procedures (EMICP) (see 6.3).

Discussion: The power systems for Navy ships and submarines are ungrounded. The capacitance-to-ground of power line filters provides a path for conducting current into the hull structure. The Navy uses very sensitive low frequency radio and sonar receivers. At low frequencies, currents flowing through the installation structure and across surfaces of electronic enclosures will penetrate to the inside of the enclosure. The magnetic fields created by these currents can couple into critical circuits and degrade performance. At higher frequencies (greater than 100 kHz), the combination of power line filter capacitance-to-ground limitation, skin effect of equipment enclosures, and reduced harmonic currents tend to minimize the problems associated with structure currents.

The total line-to-ground capacitance is limited to 0.1 µf for 60 Hz equipment and 0.02 µf for 400 Hz equipment. This will, in turn, limit the power line current to 5 mA which is consistent with leakage current (safety) requirements. The filtering employed should be fully described in the Electromagnetic Interference Control Procedures.

A.4.2.3 (4.2.3) Self-compatibility.
The operational performance of an equipment or subsystem shall not be degraded, nor shall it malfunction, when all of the units or devices in the equipment or subsystem are operating together at their designed levels of efficiency or their design capability.

Discussion: The EMI controls imposed by this standard apply to subsystem-level hardware with the purpose of insuring compatibility when various subsystems are integrated into a system platform. In a parallel sense, a subsystem can be considered to be an integration of various assemblies, circuit cards, and electronics boxes. While specific requirements could be imposed to control the interference characteristics of these individual items, this standard is concerned only with the overall performance characteristics of the subsystem after integration. Therefore, the subsystem itself must exhibit compatibility among its various component parts and assemblies.

A.4.2.4 (4.2.4) Non-developmental items (NDI).
In accordance with the guidance provided by SD-2, the requirements of this standard shall be met when applicable and warranted by the intended installation and platform requirements.

Discussion: NDI refers to any equipment that is already developed and ready for use including both commercial and military items. The SD-2 provides guidance on EMC integration issues relating to the use of NDI. The SD-2 states concerns with proper operation in the mission environment and the need for compatibility with existing operational equipment. The document includes cautions that acceptance in the commercial marketplace does not mean that EMC requirements are met, that modifications to correct EMC problems can be costly and time consuming, and that EMC problems can be potentially hazardous. The SD-2 states that quantitative EMC requirements should be developed and that valid data needs to be gathered during a market investigation for performance of analysis to determine the suitability of the NDI. Testing may be required if there is insufficient data. An EMC advisory board is recommended to provide alternatives to decision makers.

It is common for the DoD to use commercially available medical devices onboard aeromedical evacuation aircraft. This equipment needs to undergo a suitability assessment which involves determining the environmental and EMI characteristics of the equipment for review by flight certification personnel. A basic methodology has been established as described below for the EMI portion of this assessment for Army and Air Force applications. Contractual compliance with MIL-STD-461 is not imposed on the procurements. The MIL-STD-461 requirements that are evaluated are CE102, CS101, CS114, CS115, CS116, RE102, and RS103 for both Services and the addition of CE101 for the Army. Depending on whether aircraft power or battery operation is used and the type of electrical interfaces, if any, will influence whether CE101, CE102, CS101, CS114, CS115, and CS116 are necessary, as is the case with any equipment. CS114 Curve 3 and the Air Force RS103 requirement of 20 V/m from 2 to 1000 MHz and 60 V/m levels from 1 to 18 GHz are treated as anticipated nominal performance levels. Thresholding of any response is accomplished for these levels and the other susceptibility evaluations. CS114 Curve 5 and 200 V/m measurements for RS103 are performed for severe Army helicopter evaluations; however, the results are assessed using risk analysis oriented toward patient safety, absolute performance is not expected and often does not result across the frequency range of interest. Thresholding is not performed at these levels, only the results are reported. Also, only the standard 1 kHz pulse modulation, 50% duty cycle, specified in MIL-STD-461 is used. The other types of modulation sometimes used by Army aviation are not applied.

A.4.2.4.1 (4.2.4.1) Commercial items (CI).

Discussion: The use of CI presents a dilemma between the need for EMI control with appropriate design measures implemented and the desire to take advantage of existing designs which may exhibit undesirable EMI characteristics. Paragraphs 4.2.4.1.1 and 4.2.4.1.2 address the specific requirements for the two separate cases of contractor selection versus procuring activity specification of commercial equipment.

For some applications of commercially developed products, such as commercial transport aircraft, EMI requirements similar to those in this standard are usually imposed on equipment. Most commercial aircraft equipment is required to meet the EMI requirements in RTCA DO-160 or an equivalent contractor in-house document. Recent revisions to RTCA DO-160 are making the document more compatible with this standard. Equipment qualified to revisions C, D, or E of RTCA DO-160 is often suitable for military aircraft applications. However, the procuring activity must obtain the test reports to ensure the equipment meets the applicable requirements.

EMI requirements on most commercial equipment are more varied and sometimes nonexistent. The Federal Communication Commission (FCC) is responsible for regulating "Non-Licensed Radio Frequency Devices" in the commercial and residential environment to control interference to radio reception. Requirements are imposed in FCC CFR Title 47, Parts 2, 15, and 18. The FCC does not control susceptibility (referred to as immunity in the commercial community) characteristics of equipment. The most widely applied requirement is Part 15 which requires that any "digital device" comply with the following conducted and radiated emission limits for commercial environments (Class A) and residential environments (Class B).

CONDUCTED EMISSIONS

FREQUENCY (MHz)	CLASS A (dBμV)	CLASS B (dBμV)
0.45 - 1.705	60	48
1.705 – 30	70	48

RADIATED EMISSIONS

FREQUENCY (MHz)	CLASS A (dBμV/m at 10 meters)	CLASS B (dBμV/m at 3 meters)
30 – 88	39	40
88 – 216	44	44
216 – 960	46	46
above 960	50	54

These requirements are typically less stringent than military requirements of a similar type. Also, there is difficulty in comparing levels between commercial and military testing due to differences in measurement distances, different types of antennas, and near-field conditions.

The commercial community is moving toward immunity standards. The basis for immunity requirements is given in ANSI C63.12. There is also activity in the international area. The European Union is imposing mandatory standards and the International Electrotechnical Commission is working on standards.

A.4.2.4.1.1 (4.2.4.1.1) Selected by contractor.

When it is demonstrated that a commercial item selected by the contractor is responsible for equipment or subsystems failing to meet the contractual EMI requirements, either the commercial item shall be modified or replaced or interference suppression measures shall be employed, so that the equipment or subsystems meet the contractual EMI requirements.

Discussion: The contractor retains responsibility for complying with EMI requirements regardless of the contractor's choice of commercial off-the-shelf items. The contractor can treat selected commercial items as necessary provided required performance is demonstrated.

A.4.2.4.1.2 (4.2.4.1.2) Specified by procuring activity.

When it is demonstrated by the contractor that a commercial item specified by the procuring activity for use in an equipment or subsystem is responsible for failure of the equipment or subsystem to meet its contractual EMI requirements, the data indicating such failure shall be included in the Electromagnetic Interference Test Report (EMITR) (see 6.3). No modification or replacement shall be made unless authorized by the procuring activity.

Discussion: The procuring activity retains responsibility for EMI characteristics of commercial items that the procuring activity specifies to be used as part of a subsystem or equipment. The procuring activity will typically study trade-offs between the potential for system-level problems and the benefits of retaining unmodified commercial equipment. The procuring activity needs to provide specific contractual direction when modifications are considered to be necessary.

A.4.2.4.2. (4.2.4.2) Procurement of equipment or subsystems having met other EMI requirements.

Procurement of equipment and subsystems electrically and mechanically identical to those previously procured by activities of DoD or other Federal agencies, or their contractors, shall meet the EMI requirements and associated limits, as applicable in the earlier procurement, unless otherwise specified by the Command or agency concerned.

Discussion: In general, the government expects configuration controls to be exercised in the manufacturing process of equipment and subsystems to ensure that produced items continue to meet the particular EMI requirements to which the design was qualified. This standard reflects the most up-to-date environments and concerns. Since the original EMI requirements may be substantially different than those in this standard, they may not be adequate to assess the suitability of the item in a particular installation. This situation most often occurs for equipment susceptibility tests related to the radiated electromagnetic environment. Procuring activities need to consider imposing additional test requirements on the contractor to gather additional data to permit adequate evaluation.

Testing of production items has shown degraded performance of the equipment from that previously demonstrated during development. One problem area is engineering changes implemented for ease of manufacturing which are not adequately reviewed for potential effects on EMI control design measures. Specific problems have been related to treatment of cable and enclosure shields, electrical grounding and bonding, and substitution of new component parts due to obsolescence.

A.4.2.5 (4.2.5) Government furnished equipment (GFE).

When it is demonstrated by the contractor that a GFE is responsible for failure of an equipment or subsystem to meet its contractual EMI requirements, the data indicating such failure shall be included in the EMITR. No modification shall be made unless authorized by the procuring activity.

Discussion: GFE is treated the same as commercial items specified by the procuring activity.

A.4.2.6 (4.2.6) Switching transients.

Switching transient emissions that result at the moment of operation of manually actuated switching functions are exempt from the requirements of this standard. Other transient type conditions, such as automatic sequencing following initiation by a manual switching function, shall meet the emissions requirements of this standard.

Discussion: Proper treatment of manually actuated switching functions has long been a dilemma. Platform experience has shown that switching of electronics equipment subjected to EMI requirements rarely causes electromagnetic compatibility problems. On this basis, there are no requirements included in this standard. "On-off" switching has been of particular interest. "On-off" switching has occasionally caused power quality type problems. These problems are associated with voltage regulation difficulties from a large load being switched on a power bus; however, such power quality issues are not addressed by this standard.

Platform problems have also been observed from switching of items not normally subjected to EMI requirements such as unsuppressed inductors (valves, relays, etc.), motors, and high current resistive loads. These types of problems are more related to coupling of transients onto platform wiring through electric and magnetic fields than direct conduction of the interference. There are substantial requirements included in the standard to protect against susceptibility to transients. This statement is not intended to imply that inductive devices and other transient producers should not be suppressed as a normal good design practice. For example, some integrating contractors routinely require vendors to provide diode suppression on inductors.

In earlier versions of EMI standards, manually actuated functions were measured using frequency domain techniques. Although measured emission levels were often 40-70 dB above the limit, no platform problems were observed. This technique was largely abandoned in later versions of the standards in favor of a time domain requirement on power leads (CE07). Except for some above limit conditions associated with on-off functions, equipment rarely have had any problems with the requirement. Testing of on-off functions has often been controversial because of the need to often use a switch external to the equipment. A number of issues arise regarding placement of the switch, where the transient should be measured, whether the switch or the equipment causes the transient, and whether the switch can be suppressed.

The exemption is applicable only for transient effects occurring at the moment of manual switch operation. Many other transient type effects occur during the operation of electronics. An argument could be made that the operation of microprocessor controlled electronics produces continuous transients with every change of state. There are certain transient effects that occur infrequently which could be presented to the procuring activity as events similar to the action of a manual switch with a request for an exemption. An example is a heater circuit that functions intermittently dependent upon a sensed temperature.

Other documents such as MIL-STD-704, MIL-STD-464, and MIL-STD-1399-300 impose transient controls at the system-level.

A.4.2.7 (4.2.7) Interchangeable modular equipment.
The requirements of this standard are verified at the Shop Replaceable Unit, Line Replaceable Unit, or Integrated Equipment Rack assembly level. When modular equipment such as line replaceable modules are replaced or interchanged within the assembly additional testing or a similarity assessment is required and shall be approved by the procuring activity.

Discussion: Different equipment with the same form, fit and function characteristics may have the potential for different EMI profiles, thus resulting in interchangeability issues. Additionally, more subsystems and equipment are being designed and built by more than one manufacturer. Different manufacturer's unique designs such as filter placement on the motherboard or module, general board design/circuit layout, compatibilities of Inputs/Outputs at higher frequencies, component tolerances, board proximity, etc., will affect the electromagnetic interference characteristics of the equipment. Therefore, testing of all possible configurations or a detailed analysis assessing the design configuration changes is required.

A.4.3 (4.3) Verification requirements.
The general requirements related to test procedures, test facilities, and equipment stated below, together with the detailed test procedures included in 5, shall be used to determine compliance with the applicable emission and susceptibility requirements of this standard. Any procuring activity approved exceptions or deviations from these general requirements shall be documented in the Electromagnetic Interference Test Procedures (EMITP) (see 6.3). Equipment that is intended to be operated as a subsystem shall be tested as such to the applicable emission and susceptibility requirements whenever practical. Formal testing is not to commence without approval of the EMITP by the Command or agency concerned. Data gathered as a result of performing tests in one electromagnetic discipline might be sufficient to satisfy requirements in another. Therefore, to avoid unnecessary duplication, a single test

program should be established with tests for similar requirements conducted concurrently whenever possible.

Discussion: This portion of the document specifies general requirements that are applicable to a variety of test procedures applicable for individual emissions and susceptibility requirements. The detailed test procedures for each emissions and susceptibility requirement include procedures that are unique to that requirement. Other sources of information dealing with electromagnetic interference testing are available in industry documents such as RTCA DO-160.

Electromagnetic disciplines [EMC, electromagnetic pulse (EMP), lightning, RF compatibility, frequency allocation, etc.] are integrated to differing levels in various government and contractor organizations. There is often a common base of requirements among the disciplines. It is more efficient to have unified requirements and complete and concise testing. For example, the EMC, EMP and lightning areas all pertain to electronic hardness to transients. The transient requirements in this standard should satisfy most concerns or should be adapted as necessary to do so.

Testing integrated equipment at the subsystem-level is advantageous because the actual electrical interfaces are in place rather than electrical load or test equipment simulations. When simulations are used, there is always doubt regarding the integrity of the simulation and questions arise whether emission and susceptibility problems are due to the equipment under test or the simulation.

Contractor generated test procedures provide a mechanism to interpret and adapt MIL-STD-461 as it is applicable to a particular subsystem or equipment and to detail the test agency's facilities and instrumentation and their use. It is important that the procedures are available to the procuring activity early so that the procuring activity can approve the test procedures prior to the start of testing. Agreement needs to exist between the procuring activity and the contractor on the interpretation of test requirements and procedures, thereby minimizing the possible need for retesting.

When testing large equipment, equipment that requires special handling provision or high power equipment, deviations from the standard testing procedures may be required. Large equipment may not fit through the typical shielded room door or may be so heavy that it would crush the floor. Other equipment has large movable arms or turrets or equipment that requires special heating or cooling facilities. This equipment may have to be tested at the manufacturer's facilities or at the final installation. The following examples are for guidance. Sound engineering practices should be used and explained in detail in the EMITP when deviating from the standard test procedures due to EUT characteristics. The design of the tests is of primary importance and the data recorded during the testing must reflect the final installation characteristics as closely as possible.

For equipment which requires high input current (for example: > 200 A), commercial LISNs may not be available. Since LISNs are ineffective below 10 kHz, they may be deleted for CE101 testing. For CE102, the "voltage probe" called out in ANSI C63.4 may be substituted. The construction of the probe is shown on Figure A-1. A direct connection to the power lines is required and care must be taken to establish a reference ground for the measurements. It may be necessary to perform repeated measurements over a suitable period of time to determine the variation in the power line impedance and the impact on the measured emissions from the EUT.

The measurements are made between each current-carrying conductor in the supply mains and the ground conductor with a blocking capacitor C and resistor R, as shown on Figure A-1, so that the total resistance between the line under test and ground is 1500 ohm. The probe attenuates the voltage so calibration factors are required. The measurement point (probe's position on the cables) must be identified in all test setups.

When equipment is too large or requires special provisions (loads, drives, water, emission of toxic fumes and such), testing in a typical semi-anechoic room may not be feasible. Temporary screen rooms consisting of hardware cloth can be built around the test area to reduce the ambient for radiated emission testing and to contain the RF field during radiated susceptibility testing. Since the room may be highly reflective, care must be taken to identify any resonances. Several antenna positions may be required in order to reduce the effect of the resonances.

Equipment which produces high power RF output may be required to be tested on an open area test site. Additionally, equipment that needs to have a communication link to the outside world must be tested in the open. FCC approval may be required in order to generate the RF fields for the RS103 test requirement. If the communication link can be simulated, then the test can be performed in a shielded room. In this case, special dummy loads may be required, since the high power RF radiation could damage the anechoic material due to heating.

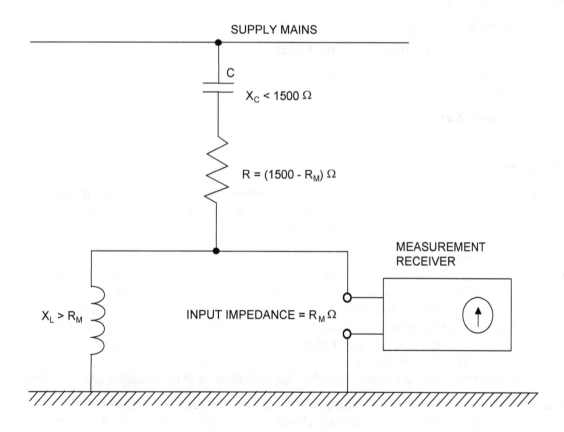

FIGURE A-1. Voltage probe for tests at user's installation.

Imposition of EMI requirements on large equipment has become essential to prevent EMI problems. Therefore, EMI requirements should not be waived simply because of special handling problems or equipment size. Typical equipment and subsystems for which these special provisions have been applied are as follows:

Air handling units (heating, ventilating, and air conditioning)

Large uninterruptible power supplies (UPS)

Equipment vans/motorized vehicles

Desalinization units

Large motors/generators/drives/power distribution systems

Large radars

Rail guns and their power sources

Catapults and their power sources

Multiple console subsystems

A.4.3.1 (4.3.1) Measurement tolerances.
Unless otherwise stated for a particular measurement, the tolerance shall be as follows:

a. *Distance: ±5%*

b. *Frequency: ±2%*

c. *Amplitude, measurement receiver: ±2 dB*

d. *Amplitude, measurement system (includes measurement receivers, transducers, cables, and so forth): ±3 dB*

e. *Time (waveforms): ±5%*

f. *Resistors: ±5%*

g. *Capacitors: ±20%*

Discussion: Tolerances are necessary to maintain reasonable controls for obtaining consistent measurements. Paragraphs 4.3.1b through 4.3.1d are in agreement with ANSI C63.2 for electromagnetic noise instrumentation.

A.4.3.2 (4.3.2) Shielded enclosures.
To prevent interaction between the EUT and the outside environment, shielded enclosures will usually be required for testing. These enclosures prevent external environment signals from contaminating emission measurements and susceptibility test signals from interfering with electrical and electronic items in the vicinity of the test facility. Shielded enclosures must have adequate attenuation such that the ambient requirements of 4.3.4 are satisfied. The enclosures must be sufficiently large such that the EUT arrangement requirements of paragraph 4.3.8 and antenna positioning requirements described in the individual test procedures are satisfied.

Discussion: Potential accuracy problems introduced by shielded enclosure resonances are well documented and recognized; however, shielded enclosures are usually a necessity for testing of military equipment to the requirements of this standard. Most test agencies are at locations where ambient levels outside of the enclosures are significantly above the limits in this standard and would interfere with the ability to obtain meaningful data.

Electrical interfaces with military equipment are often complex and require sophisticated test equipment to simulate and evaluate the interface. This equipment usually must be located outside of the shielded enclosure to achieve sufficient isolation and prevent it from contaminating the ambient and responding to susceptibility signals.

The shielded enclosure also prevents radiation of applied susceptibility signals from interfering with local antenna-connected receivers. The most obvious potential offender is the RS103 test. However, other susceptibility tests can result in substantial radiated energy that may violate Federal Communication Commission (FCC) rules.

A.4.3.2.1 (4.3.2.1) Radio frequency (RF) absorber material.

RF absorber material (carbon impregnated foam pyramids, ferrite tiles, and so forth) shall be used when performing electric field radiated emissions or radiated susceptibility testing inside a shielded enclosure to reduce reflections of electromagnetic energy and to improve accuracy and repeatability. The RF absorber shall be placed above, behind, and on both sides of the EUT, and behind the radiating or receiving antenna as shown in Figure 1. Minimum performance of the material shall be as specified in Table I. The manufacturer's certification of their RF absorber material (basic material only, not installed) is acceptable.

TABLE I. *Absorption at normal incidence.*

Frequency	Minimum absorption
80 MHz – 250 MHz	6 dB
above 250 MHz	10 dB

Discussion: Accuracy problems with making measurements in untreated shielded enclosures due to reflections of electromagnetic energy have been widely recognized and documented. The values of RF absorption required by Table I are considered to be sufficient to substantially improve the integrity of the measurements without unduly impacting test facilities. The minimum placement provisions for the material are specified to handle the predominant reflections. The use of additional material is desirable, where possible. It is intended that the values in Table I can be met with available ferrite tile material or standard 24 inch (0.61 meters) pyramidal absorber material.

A.4.3.3 (4.3.3) Other test sites.

If other test sites are used, the ambient requirements of paragraph 4.3.4 shall be met.

Discussion: For certain types of EUTs, testing in a shielded enclosure may not be practical. Examples are EUTs which are extremely large, require high electrical power levels or motor drives to function, emit toxic fumes, or are too heavy for normal floor loading (see A.4.3 discussion for additional information). There is a serious concern with ambient levels contaminating data when testing is performed outside of a shielded enclosure. Therefore, special attention is given to this testing under 4.3.4, "Ambient electromagnetic level." All cases where testing is performed outside a shielded enclosure shall be justified in detail in the EMITP, including typical profiles of expected ambient levels.

If it is necessary to operate EUTs that include RF transmitters outside of a shielded enclosure, spectrum certification and a frequency assignment must first be obtained through the spectrum management process.

An option in emission testing is the use of an open area test site (OATS) in accordance with ANSI C63.4. These sites are specifically designed to enhance accuracy and repeatability. Due to differences between ANSI C63.4 and this standard in areas such as antenna selection, measurement distances, and specified frequency ranges, the EMITP shall detail the techniques for using the OATS and relating the test results to the requirements of this standard.

A.4.3.4 (4.3.4) Ambient electromagnetic level.

During testing, the ambient electromagnetic level measured with the EUT de-energized and all auxiliary equipment turned on shall be at least 6 dB below the allowable specified limits when the tests are performed in a shielded enclosure. Ambient conducted levels on power leads shall be measured with the leads disconnected from the EUT and connected to a resistive load which draws the same rated current as the EUT. When tests are performed in a shielded enclosure and the EUT is in compliance with required limits, the ambient profile need not be recorded in the EMITR. When measurements are made outside a shielded enclosure, the tests shall be performed during times and conditions when the ambient is at its lowest level. The ambient shall be recorded in the EMITR and shall not compromise the test results.

Discussion: Controlling ambient levels is critical to maintaining the integrity of the gathered data. High ambients present difficulties distinguishing between EUT emissions and ambient levels. Even when specific signals are known to be ambient related, they may mask EUT emissions that are above the limits of this standard.

The requirement that the ambient be at least 6 dB below the limit ensures that the combination of the EUT emissions and ambient does not unduly affect the indicated magnitude of the emission. If a sinusoidal noise signal is at the limit and the ambient is 6 dB below the limit, the indicated level would be approximately 3 dB above the limit. Similarly, if the ambient were allowed to be equal to the limit for the same true emission level, the indicated level would be approximately 5 dB above the limit.

A resistive load is specified to be used for conducted ambients on power leads. However, under certain conditions actual ambient levels may be higher than indicated with a resistive load. The most likely reason is the presence of capacitance at the power interface of the EUT that will lower the input impedance at higher frequencies and increase the current. This capacitance should be determined and ambient measurements repeated with the capacitance in place. There is also the possibility of resonance conditions with shielded room filtering, EUT filtering, and power line inductance. These types of conditions may need to be investigated if unexpected emission levels are observed.

Testing outside of a shielded enclosure often must be performed at night to minimize influences of the ambient. A prevalent problem with the ambient is that it continuously changes with time as various emitters are turned on and off and as amplitudes fluctuate. A useful tool for improving the flow of testing is to thoroughly analyze the EUT circuitry prior to testing and identify frequencies where emissions may be expected to be present.

An option to improve overall measurement accuracy is to make preliminary measurements inside a shielded enclosure and accurately determine frequencies where emissions are present. Testing can be continued outside the shielded enclosure with measurements being repeated at the selected frequencies. The 6 dB margin between the ambient and limits must then be observed only at the selected frequencies.

A.4.3.5 (4.3.5) Ground plane.

The EUT shall be installed on a ground plane that simulates the actual installation. If the actual installation is unknown or multiple installations are expected, then a metallic ground plane shall be used. Unless otherwise specified below, ground planes shall be 2.25 square meters or larger in area with the smaller side no less than 76 cm. When a ground plane is not present in the EUT installation, the EUT shall be placed on a non-conductive table.

Discussion: Generally, the radiated emissions and radiated susceptibilities of equipment are due to coupling from and to the interconnecting cables and not via the case of the EUT. Emissions and susceptibility levels are directly related to the placement of the cable with respect to the ground plane and to the electrical conductivity of the ground plane. Thus, the ground plane plays an important role in obtaining the most realistic test results.

When the EUT is too large to be installed on a conventional ground plane on a bench, the actual installation should be duplicated. For example, a large radar antenna may need to be installed on a test stand and the test stand bonded to the floor of the shielded enclosure. Ground planes need to be placed on the floor of shielded rooms with floor surfaces such as tiles that are not electrically conductive.

The use of ground planes is also applicable for testing outside of a shielded enclosure. These ground planes will need to be referenced to earth as necessary to meet the electrical safety requirements of the National Electrical Code (NFPA 70). Where possible, these ground planes should be electrically bonded to other accessible grounded reference surfaces such as the outside structure of a shielded enclosure.

The minimum dimensions for a ground plane of 2.25 square meters with 76 cm on the smallest side will be adequate only for setups involving a limited number of EUT enclosures with few electrical interfaces. The ground plane must be large enough to allow for the requirements included in paragraph 4.3.8 on positioning and arrangement of the EUT and associated cables to be met.

A.4.3.5.1 (4.3.5.1) Metallic ground plane.

When the EUT is installed on a metallic ground plane, the ground plane shall have a surface resistance no greater than 0.1 milliohms per square. The DC resistance between metallic ground planes and the shielded enclosure shall be 2.5 milliohms or less. The metallic ground planes shown on Figures 2 through 5 shall be electrically bonded to the floor or wall of the basic shielded room structure at least once every 1 meter. The metallic bond straps shall be solid and maintain a five-to-one ratio or less in length to width. Metallic ground planes used outside a shielded enclosure shall extend at least 1.5 meters beyond the test setup boundary in each direction.

Discussion: For the metallic ground plane, a copper ground plane with a thickness of 0.25 millimeters has been commonly used and satisfies the surface resistance requirements. Other metallic materials of the proper size and thickness needed to achieve the resistivity can be substituted.

For metallic ground planes, the surface resistance can be calculated by dividing the bulk resistivity by the thickness. For example, copper has a bulk resistivity of 1.75×10^{-8} ohm-meters. For a 0.25 millimeter thick ground plane as noted above, the surface resistance is $1.7 \times 10^{-8} / 2.5 \times 10^{-4} = 6.8 \times 10^{-5}$ ohms per square = 0.068 milliohms per square. The requirement is 0.1 milliohms per square.

A.4.3.5.2 (4.3.5.2) Composite ground plane.

When the EUT is installed on a conductive composite ground plane, the surface resistivity of the typical installation shall be used. Composite ground planes shall be electrically bonded to the enclosure with means suitable to the material.

Discussion: A copper ground plane has typically been used for all testing in the past. For most instances, this has been adequate. However, with the increasing use of composites, the appropriate ground plane will play a bigger role in the test results. Limited testing on both copper and conductive composite ground planes has shown some differences in electromagnetic coupling test results, thus the need exists to duplicate the actual installation, if possible. In some cases, it may be necessary to include several ground planes in the same test setup if different units of the same EUT are installed on different materials in the installation.

With the numerous different composite materials being used in installations, it is not possible to specify a general resistivity value. The typical resistivity of carbon composite is about 2000 times that of aluminum. The actual resistivity needs to be obtained from the installation contractor and used for testing.

A.4.3.6 (4.3.6) Power source impedance.

The impedance of power sources providing input power to the EUT shall be controlled by Line Impedance Stabilization Networks (LISNs) for all measurement procedures of this document unless otherwise stated in a particular test procedure. LISNs shall not be used on output power leads. The LISNs shall be located at the power source end of the exposed length of power leads specified in paragraph 4.3.8.6.2. The LISN circuit shall be in accordance with the schematic shown on Figure 6. The LISN impedance characteristics shall be in accordance with Figure 7. The LISN impedance shall be measured at least annually under the following conditions:

    a.   *The impedance shall be measured between the power output lead on the load side of the LISN and the metal enclosure of the LISN.*

    b.   *The signal output port of the LISN shall be terminated in fifty ohms.*

    c.   *The power input terminal on the power source side of the LISN shall be unterminated.*

The impedance measurement results shall be provided in the EMITR.

Discussion: The impedance is standardized to represent expected impedances in actual installations and to ensure consistent results between different test agencies. Versions of MIL-STD-462 (previously contained test procedures for MIL-STD-461 requirements) in the past used 10 µF feedthrough capacitors on the power leads. The intent of these devices was to determine the current generator portion of a Norton current source model. If the impedance of the interference source was also known, the interference potential of the source could be analytically determined for particular circumstances in the installation. A requirement was never established for measuring the impedance portion of the source model. More importantly, concerns arose over the test configuration influencing the design of power line filtering. Optimized filters are designed based on knowledge of both source and load impedances. Significantly different filter designs will result for the 10 µF capacitor loading versus the impedance loading shown on Figure 7 of the main body.

LISNs are not used on output power leads. Emission measurements using LISNs are performed on input power leads because the EUT is using a power source common to many other equipment items and the EUT must not degrade the quality of the power. When the EUT is the source of power, the issue is completely different since the electrical characteristics of the power required are controlled by the defined power quality requirements. Output power leads should be terminated with appropriate electrical loading that produces potentially worst case emission and susceptibility characteristics.

The particular configuration of the LISN is specified for several reasons. A number of experiments were performed to evaluate typical power line impedances present in a shielded room on various power input types both with and without power line filters and to assess the possible methods of controlling the impedance. An approach was considered for the standard to simply specify an impedance curve from 30 Hz to 100 MHz and to allow the test agency to meet the impedance using whatever means the agency found suitable. The experiments showed that there were no straightforward techniques to maintain desired controls over the entire frequency range.

A specific 50 µH LISN (see ANSI C63.4) was selected to maintain a standardized control on the impedance as low as 10 kHz. Five µH LISNs used commonly in the past provide little control below 100 kHz. Impedance control below 10 kHz is difficult. From evaluations of several 50 µH LISN configurations, the one specified demonstrated the best overall performance for various shielded room filtering variations. Near 10 kHz, the reactances of the 50 µH inductor and 8 µF capacitor cancel and the LISN is effectively a 5 ohm resistive load across the power line.

Using a common LISN is important for standardization reasons. However, the use of alternative LISNs may be desirable in certain application where the characteristics of the LISN may not be representative of the actual installation and the design of EUT circuitry is being adversely affected. For example, there are issues with switching power supply stability and the power source impedance seen by the power supply. The 50 µH inductor in the LISN represents the inductance of power distribution wiring running for approximately 50 meters. For a large platform, such as a ship or cargo aircraft, this value is quite representative of the actual installation. However, for smaller platforms such as fighter aircraft, inductance values may be substantially lower than 50 µH. If alternative LISN designs are used, certain issues need to be addressed such as the frequency range over which effective impedance control is present and where voltage versus current measurements are appropriate.

Caution needs to be exercised in using the LISN for 400 Hz power systems. Some existing LISNs may not have components sufficient to handle the power dissipation requirements. At 115 volts, 400 Hz, the 8 µF capacitor and 5 ohm resistor will pass approximately 2.3 amperes which results in 26.5 watts being dissipated in the resistor.

Under CE101 and CE102 discussions, the use of a 5 µH LISN is suggested as a possible alternative under certain circumstances. Figures A-2 and A-3 below show design and impedance characteristics of an appropriate LISN. Refer to those sections in this appendix for further details.

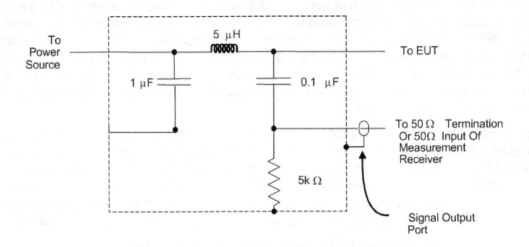

FIGURE A-2. 5 µH LISN schematic.

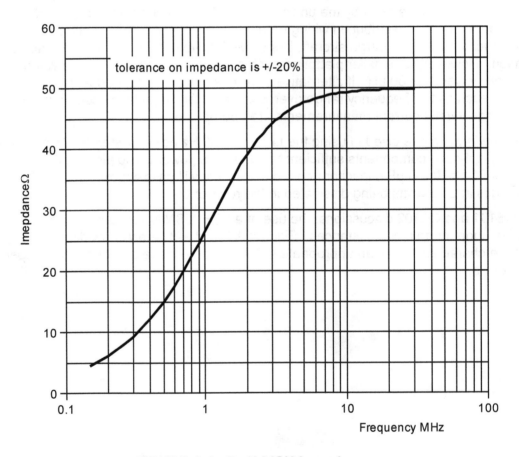

FIGURE A-3. 5 µH LISN impedance.

A.4.3.7 (4.3.7) General test precautions.
Discussion: The requirements included in paragraph 4.3.7 cover important areas related to improving test integrity and safety that need special attention. There are many other areas where test difficulties may develop. Some are described here.

It is common for shields to become loose or broken at connectors on coaxial cables resulting in incorrect readings. There also are cases where center conductors of coaxial cables break or separate. Periodic tests should be performed to ensure cable integrity. Special low loss cables may be required when testing at higher frequencies.

Caution needs to be exercised when performing emission testing at frequencies below approximately 10 kHz to avoid ground loops in the instrumentation which may introduce faulty readings. A single-point ground often needs to be maintained. It is usually necessary to use isolation transformers at the measurement receiver and accessory equipment. The single-point ground is normally established at the access (feedthrough) panel for the shielded enclosure. However, if a transducer is being used which requires an electrical bond to the enclosure (such as the rod antenna counterpoise), the coaxial cable will need to be routed through the enclosure access panel without being grounded. Since the shielded room integrity will then be compromised, a normal multiple point grounded setup needs to be re-established as low in frequency as possible.

Rather than routing the coaxial cable through the enclosure access panel without grounding it to the enclosure, a 50-ohm video isolation transformer may be connected to the grounded RF connector at the access panel inside the room. Normal connection of the measuring receiver is made to the grounded connector at the panel outside the room. This technique effectively breaks the ground loop without sacrificing the room's shielding integrity. The losses of the video isolation transformer must be accounted for in the measurement data. These devices are typically useful up to approximately 10 MHz.

If isolation transformers are found to be necessary in certain setups, problems may exist with items powered by switching power supplies. A solution is to use transformers that are rated at approximately five times the current rating of the item.

Solid state instrumentation power sources have been found to be susceptible to radiated fields even to the extent of being shut down. It is best to keep these items outside of the shielded enclosure.

A.4.3.7.1 (4.3.7.1) Accessory equipment.
Accessory equipment used in conjunction with measurement receivers shall not degrade measurement integrity.

Discussion: Measurement receivers are generally designed to meet the limits of this standard so they do not contaminate the ambient for emission testing when they are used inside the shielded enclosure. However, accessory equipment such as computers, oscilloscopes, plotters, or other instruments used to control the receiver or monitor its outputs can cause problems. They may compromise the integrity of the receiver by radiating signals conducted out of the receiver from improperly treated electrical interfaces or may produce interference themselves and raise the ambient. Even passive devices such as headsets have been known to impact the test results.

It is best to locate all of the test equipment outside of the shielded enclosure with the obvious exception of the transducer (antenna or current probe). Proper equipment location will ensure that the emissions being measured are being generated in the EUT only and will help ensure that the ambient requirements of 4.3.4 are met. If the equipment must be used inside the enclosure or if testing is being conducted outside of an enclosure, the measurement receiver and accessory equipment should be located as far away from the transducers as practical to minimize any impact.

A.4.3.7.2 (4.3.7.2) Excess personnel and equipment.

The test area shall be kept free of unnecessary personnel, equipment, cable racks, and desks. Only the equipment essential to the test being performed shall be in the test area or enclosure. Only personnel actively involved in the test shall be permitted in the enclosure.

Discussion: Excess personnel and both electronic and mechanical equipment such as desks or cable racks in the enclosure can affect the test results. During radiated emission testing in particular, all nonessential personnel and equipment should be removed from the test site. Any object in the enclosure can significantly influence or introduce standing waves in the enclosure and thus alter the test results. The requirement to use RF absorber material will help to mitigate these effects. However, material performance is not defined below 80 MHz for practical reasons and standing waves continue to be a concern.

A.4.3.7.3 (4.3.7.3) Overload precautions.

Measurement receivers and transducers are subject to overload, especially receivers without preselectors and active transducers. Periodic checks shall be performed to assure that an overload condition does not exist. Instrumentation changes shall be implemented to correct any overload condition.

Discussion: Overloads can easily go unnoticed if there is not an awareness of the possibility of an overload or active monitoring for the condition. The usual result is a leveling of the output indication of the receiver.

Two types of overloads are possible. A narrowband signal such as a sinusoid can saturate any receiver or active transducer. Typical procedures for selecting attenuation settings for measurement receivers place detected voltages corresponding to emission limits well within the dynamic range of the receiver. Saturation problems for narrowband type signals will normally only appear for a properly configured receiver if emissions are significantly above the limits. Saturation can occur more readily when receivers are used to monitor susceptibility signals due to the larger voltages involved.

Overload from impulsive type signals with broad frequency content can be much more deceptive. This condition is most likely to occur with devices without a tunable bandpass feature in the first stage of the signal input. Examples are preamplified rod antennas and spectrum analyzers without preselectors. The input circuitry is exposed to energy over a large portion of the frequency spectrum. Preselectors include a tunable tracking filter which bandwidth limits the energy applied to the receiver front end circuitry.

Measurement receiver overload to both narrowband and impulsive type signals can be evaluated by applying a 10 dB additional attenuation in the first stage of the receiver (before mixer circuitry) or external to the receiver. If overload is not present, the observed output will uniformly decrease by 10 dB.

Overload conditions for active antennas are normally published as part of the literature supplied with the antenna. For narrowband signals, the indicated level in the data can be reviewed with respect to the literature to evaluate overload. Levels are also published for impulsive type signals; however, these levels are not very useful since they usually assume that a flat field exists across the useable range of the antenna. In reality, the impulsive field will vary significantly with frequency and the antenna circuitry sees the integration of the spectral content of this field over its bandpass. The primary active antenna used is an active rod antenna. Overload can be evaluated by collapsing the rod and observing the change in indication. If overload is not present, the indicated level should drop approximately 8 dB (rod at 30% of its original height). The actual change for any particular manufacturer's product will depend on the telescoping design and can be determined by radiating a signal to the antenna that is within its linear range.

A.4.3.7.4 (4.3.7.4) RF hazards.

Some tests in this standard will result in electromagnetic fields that are potentially dangerous to personnel. The permissible exposure levels in DoDI 6055.11 shall not be exceeded in areas where personnel are present. Safety procedures and devices shall be used to prevent accidental exposure of personnel to RF hazards.

Discussion: During some radiated susceptibility and radiated emission testing, RS103, RS105 and RE103 in particular, fields may exceed the permissible exposure levels in DoDI 6055.11. During these tests, precautions must be implemented to avoid inadvertent exposure of personnel. Monitoring of the EUT during testing may require special techniques such as remotely connected displays external to the enclosure or closed circuit television to adequately protect personnel.

A.4.3.7.5 (4.3.7.5) Shock hazard.

Some of the tests require potentially hazardous voltages to be present. Extreme caution must be taken by all personnel to assure that all safety precautions are observed.

Discussion: A safety plan and training of test personnel are normally required to assure that accidents are minimized. Test equipment manufacturers' precautions need to be followed, if specified. If these are not available, the test laboratory should establish adequate safety precautions and train all test personnel. Special attention should be observed for CS109 since electronic enclosures are intentionally isolated from the ground plane for test purposes.

A.4.3.7.6 (4.3.7.6) Federal Communications Commission (FCC) restrictions.

Some of the tests require high level signals to be generated that could interfere with normal FCC approved frequency assignments. All such testing should be conducted in a shielded enclosure. Some open site testing may be feasible if prior FCC coordination is accomplished.

Discussion: Radiated susceptibility RS103 testing and possibly other tests will produce signals above FCC authorizations. This situation is one of the reasons that shielded enclosures are normally required.

A.4.3.8 (4.3.8) EUT test configurations.

The EUT shall be configured as shown in the general test setups of Figures 1 through 5 as applicable. These setups shall be maintained during all testing unless other direction is given for a particular test procedure.

Discussion: Emphasis is placed on "maintaining" the specified setup for all testing unless a particular test procedure directs otherwise. Confusion has resulted from previous versions of the standard regarding consistency of setups between individual requirements in areas such as lead lengths and placement of 10 µF capacitors on power leads. In this version of the standard, any changes from the general test setup are specifically stated in the individual test procedure.

A.4.3.8.1 (4.3.8.1) EUT design status.

EUT hardware and software shall be representative of production. Software may be supplemented with additional code that provides diagnostic capability to assess performance.

Discussion: It is important that the hardware and software being tested is the same as the equipment that is being fielded. Sometimes equipment is tested which is pre-production and contains circuit boards that do not include the final layout or software that is not the final version. Questions inevitably arise concerning the effects of the differences between the tested equipment and production configurations on the qualification status of the equipment. Analytically determining the impact is usually difficult.

A.4.3.8.2 (4.3.8.2) Bonding of EUT.

Only the provisions included in the design of the EUT shall be used to bond units such as equipment case and mounting bases together, or to the ground plane. When bonding straps are required, they shall be identical to those specified in the installation drawings.

Discussion: Electrical bonding provisions for equipment are an important aspect of platform installation design. Adequacy of bonding is usually one of the first areas reviewed when platform problems develop. Electrical bonding controls common mode voltages that develop between the equipment enclosures and the ground plane. Voltages potentially affecting the equipment will appear across the bonding interface when RF stresses are applied during susceptibility testing. Voltages will also develop due to internal circuit operation and will contribute to radiated emission profiles. Therefore, it is important that the test setup use actual bonding provisions so that test results are representative of the intended installation.

Revision G of this standard adds verification of bonding in the setup. This verification should be performed prior to testing to ensure test repeatability and representation of actual installation requirements. Bonding measurements should be taken from bonding points identified in EUT documentation to the ground plane using a milliohm meter to the nearest 10th of a milliohm. The test report should identify test locations and measurements obtained. EUT documentation should specify the bonding requirements; otherwise, MIL-STD-464 provides default requirements.

A.4.3.8.3 (4.3.8.3) Shock and vibration isolators.

EUTs shall be secured to mounting bases having shock or vibration isolators if such mounting bases are used in the installation. The bonding straps furnished with the mounting base shall be connected to the ground plane. When mounting bases do not have bonding straps, bonding straps shall not be used in the test setup.

Discussion: Including shock and vibration isolators in the setup when they represent the platform installation is important. The discussion above for 4.3.8.2 is also applicable to shock and vibration isolators; however, the potential effect on test results is even greater. Hard mounting of the equipment enclosures to the ground plane can produce a low impedance path across the bonding interface over most of the frequency range of interest. The bonding straps associated with isolators will typically represent significant impedances at frequencies as low as tens of kilohertz. The common mode voltages associated with these impedances will generally be greater than the hard mounted situation. Therefore, the influence on test results can be substantial.

A.4.3.8.4 (4.3.8.4) Safety grounds.

When external terminals, connector pins, or equipment grounding conductors are available for safety ground connections and are used in the actual installation, they shall be connected to the ground plane. Arrangement and length shall be in accordance with 4.3.8.6.1. Shorter lengths shall be used if they are specified in the installation instructions.

Discussion: Safety grounds used in equipment enclosures have been the source of problems during EMI testing. Since they are connected to the equipment enclosure, they would be expected to be at a very low potential with respect to the ground plane and a non-contributor to test results. However, the wire lengths within enclosures are often sufficiently long that coupling to them results from noisy circuits. Also, safety grounds can conduct induced signals from external sources and reradiate within the equipment enclosure. Therefore, they must be treated similarly to other wiring.

A.4.3.8.5 (4.3.8.5) Orientation of EUTs.

EUTs shall be oriented such that surfaces which produce maximum radiated emissions and respond most readily to radiated signals face the measurement antennas. Bench mounted EUTs shall be located 10 ±2 cm from the front edge of the ground plane subject to allowances for providing adequate room for cable arrangement as specified below.

Discussion: Determination of appropriate surfaces is usually straightforward. Seams on enclosures that have metal-to-metal contact or contain EMI gaskets rarely contribute and should be considered low priority items. Prime candidates are displays such as video screens, ventilation openings, and cable penetrations. In some cases, it may be necessary to probe the surfaces with a sensor and measurement receiver to decide on EUT orientation.

MIL-STD-462 (superseded by this standard) specifically required probing with a loop antenna to determine localized areas producing maximum emissions or susceptibility for radiated electric field testing. The test antennas were to be placed one meter from the identified areas. The requirement was not included in this standard due to difficulties in applying the requirement and the result that probing was often not performed. Probing implies both scanning in frequency and physical movement of the probe. These two actions cannot be performed in a manner to cover all physical locations at all frequencies. A complete frequency scan can be performed at particular probe locations and movement of the probe over the entire test setup can be performed at particular frequencies. The detailed requirements on the use of multiple antenna positions and specific requirements on the placement of the antennas in test procedures for RE102 and RS103 minimize concerns with the need to probe.

A.4.3.8.6 (4.3.8.6) Construction and arrangement of EUT cables.

Electrical cable assemblies shall simulate actual installation and usage. Shielded cables or shielded leads within cables shall be used only if they have been specified in installation requirements. Input (primary) power leads, returns, and wire grounds shall not be shielded. Cables shall be checked against installation requirements to verify proper construction techniques such as use of twisted pairs, shielding, and shield terminations. Details on the cable construction used for testing shall be included in the EMITP.

Discussion: For most EUTs, electrical interface requirements are covered in interface control or similar documents. Coordination between equipment manufacturers and system integration organizations is necessary to ensure a compatible installation from both functional and electromagnetic interference standpoints. For general purpose EUTs, which may be used in many different installations, either the equipment specifications cover the interface requirements or the manufacturers publish recommendations in the documentation associated with the equipment.

Equipment manufacturers sometimes contend that failures during EMI testing are not due to their equipment and can be cured simply by placing overall shields on the interface cabling. High level emissions are often caused by electronic circuits within EUT enclosures coupling onto cables simulating the installation which interface with the EUT. Overall shielding of the cabling is certainly permissible if it is present in the installation. However, the use of overall shielding that is not representative of the installation would result in test data that is useless.

Also, overall shielding of cabling in some installations is not a feasible option due to weight and maintenance penalties. The presence of platform structure between cabling and antennas on a platform is not an acceptable reason for using overall shields on cables for testing in accordance with this standard. The presence of some platform shielding is a basic assumption.

An issue that arises with power leads concerns the use of shielding. It is unusual for power leads to be shielded in the actual installation. If they come directly off a prime power bus, shielding can only be effective if the entire bus is shielded end-to-end. Since buses normally distribute power to many locations, it is not practical to shield them. An exception to this situation is when power is derived from an intermediate source that contains filtering. Shielding between the intermediate source and the EUT will then be effective. When it is proposed that shielded power leads be used in the test setup, the configuration needs to be researched to ensure that it is correct. There may be instances when published interface information is not available. In this case, overall shielding is not to be used. Individual circuits are to be treated as they typically would for that type of interface with shielding not used in questionable cases.

For some testing performed in the past using bulk cable drive techniques, overall cable shields were routinely removed and the injected signal was applied to the core wiring within the shield. The intent of this standard is to test cables as they are configured in the installation. If the cable uses an overall shield, the test signal is applied to the overall shielded cable. If the procuring agency desires that the test be performed on the core wiring, specific wording needs to be included in contractual documentation.

In some instances, Navy surface ship applications specify shielded power leads for a particular length of run. The shielded arrangement may be simulated in the test setup. Since unshielded power distribution wiring will be present at some point in the installation, an additional length of unshielded power leads (not less than 2 meters) should normally be added and routed parallel to the front plane of the test setup boundary during radiated testing. Approval of the procuring activity is required for using power leads that are entirely shielded. The additional unshielded cable should not be used during conducted emissions testing.

A.4.3.8.6.1 (4.3.8.6.1) Interconnecting leads and cables.
Individual leads shall be grouped into cables in the same manner as in the actual installation. Total interconnecting cable lengths in the setup shall be the same as in the actual platform installation. If a cable is longer than 10 meters, at least 10 meters shall be included. When cable lengths are not specified for the installation, cables shall be sufficiently long to satisfy the conditions specified below. At least the first 2 meters (except for cables which are shorter in the actual installation) of each interconnecting cable associated with each enclosure of the EUT shall be run parallel to the front boundary of the setup. Remaining cable lengths shall be routed to the back of the setup and shall be placed in a zig-zagged arrangement. When the setup includes more than one cable, individual cables shall be separated by 2 cm measured from their outer circumference. For bench top setups using ground planes, the cable closest to the front boundary shall be placed 10 cm from the front edge of the ground plane. All cables shall be supported 5 cm above the ground plane.

Discussion: Actual lengths of cables used in installations are necessary for several reasons. At frequencies below resonance, coupling is generally proportional to cable length. Resonance conditions will be representative of the actual installation. Also, distortion and attenuation of intentional signals due strictly to cable characteristics will be present and potential susceptibility of interface circuits to induced signals will therefore be similar to the actual installation.

Zig-zagging of long cables is accomplished by first placing a length of cable in an open area and then reversing the direction of the cable run by 180 degrees each time a change of direction is required. Each subsequent segment is farther from the first. Individual segments of the cable are parallel and should be kept 2 cm apart. The zig-zagging of long cables rather than coiling is to control excess inductance. A 2 cm spacing between cables is required to expose all cabling to the test antennas and limit coupling of signals between cables. The 10 cm dimension for cables from the front edge of the ground plane ensures that there is sufficient ground plane surface below the first cable to be effective. The 5 cm standoffs standardize loop areas available for coupling and capacitance to the ground plane. The standoffs represent routing and clamping of cables in actual installations a fixed distance from structure.

The requirement that the first 2 meters of each interconnecting cable associated with each enclosure of the EUT be routed parallel to the front boundary of the setup is intended to ensure that radiated emissions and susceptibility testing properly assesses the performance of the EUT. Noise signals developed within the EUT and conducted outside on electrical interfaces will tend to be attenuated as they travel along interconnecting cables, particularly at frequencies where the associated wavelength is becoming short compared with the cable length. Similarly, induced signals on interconnecting cables from radiated susceptibility fields will be attenuated as they travel along the cable. Requiring that the first 2 meters of the cabling be exposed therefore maximizes the effects of potential radiated coupling.

In some military applications, there can be over 2000 cables associated with a subsystem. In most cases where large numbers of cables are involved, there will be many identical cable interfaces connected to identical circuitry. Testing of every cable interface is not necessary in this situation. The EMITP should document instances where these circumstances exist and should propose which cables are to be included in the setup and to be tested.

A.4.3.8.6.2 (4.3.8.6.2) Input (primary) power leads.
Two meters of input power leads (including neutrals and returns) shall be routed parallel to the front edge of the setup in the same manner as the interconnecting leads. Each input power lead, including neutrals and returns, shall be connected to a LISN (see 4.3.6). Power leads that are bundled as part of an interconnecting cable in the actual installation shall be separated from the bundle and routed to the LISNs (outside the shield of shielded cables). After the 2 meters exposed length, the power leads shall be terminated at the LISNs in as short a distance as possible. The total length of power lead from the EUT electrical connector to the LISNs shall not exceed 2.5 meters. All power leads shall be supported 5 cm above the ground plane. If the power leads are twisted in the actual installation, they shall be twisted up to the LISNs.

Discussion: Appropriate power lead length is a trade-off between ensuring sufficient length for efficient coupling of radiated signals and maintaining the impedance of the LISNs. To keep a constant setup, it is undesirable to change the power lead length for different test procedures. Requiring a 2 meters exposed length is consistent with treatment of interconnecting leads for radiated concerns. Wiring inductance 5 cm from a ground plane is approximately 1 µH/m. At 1 MHz this inductance has an impedance of approximately 13 ohms which is significant with respect to the LISN requirement.

While it is common to require that neutrals and returns be isolated from equipment chassis within equipment enclosures, there are some cases where the neutral or return is tied directly to chassis. If the equipment is electrically bonded to metallic system structure in the installation and the system power source neutral or return is also tied to system structure, power return currents will flow primarily through system structure rather than through wiring. For this case, a LISN should normally be used only on the high side of the power. There are other installations, such as many types of aircraft, where returns and neutrals are isolated within the equipment, but they are often connected to system structure outside of the equipment enclosure. This practice allows for the flexibility of using a wired return, if necessary. For this situation, LISNs should normally be used on neutrals and returns to test for the wired return configuration.

The LISN requirement standardizes impedance for power leads. While signal and control circuits are usually terminated in specified impedances, power circuit impedances are not usually well defined. The LISN requirement applies to all input prime power leads. The LISN requirement does not apply to output power leads. These leads should be terminated after the 2 meters exposed length in a load representing worst-case conditions. This load would normally draw the maximum current allowed for the power source.

The construction of the power cable between the EUT and the LISNs must be in accordance with the requirements of 4.3.8.6. For example, if a twisted triplet is used to distribute three phase ungrounded power in the actual installation, the same construction should be used in the test setup. The normal construction must be interrupted over a sufficient length to permit connection to the LISNs.

A.4.3.8.7 (4.3.8.7) Electrical and mechanical interfaces.

All electrical input and output interfaces shall be terminated with either the actual equipment from the platform installation or loads which simulate the electrical properties (impedance, grounding, balance, and so forth) present in the actual installation. Signal inputs shall be applied to all applicable electrical interfaces to exercise EUT circuitry. EUTs with mechanical outputs shall be suitably loaded. When variable electrical or mechanical loading is present in the actual installation, testing shall be performed under expected worst case conditions. When active electrical loading (such as a test set) is used, precautions shall be taken to insure the active load meets the ambient requirements of 4.3.4 when connected to the setup, and that the active load does not respond to susceptibility signals. Antenna ports on the EUT shall be terminated with shielded, matched loads.

Discussion: The application of signals to exercise the electrical interface is necessary to effectively evaluate performance. Most electronic subsystems on platforms are highly integrated with large amounts of digital and analog data being transferred between equipment. The use of actual platform equipment for the interfacing eliminates concerns regarding proper simulation of the interface. The interfaces must function properly in the presence of induced levels from susceptibility signals. Required isolation may be obtained by filtering the interface leads at the active load and either shielding the load or placing it outside of the shielded enclosure. The filtering should be selected to minimize the influence on the interface electrical properties specified above. For proper simulation, filtering at the loads should be outside the necessary bandwidth of the interface circuitry.

Antenna ports are terminated in loads for general setup conditions. Specific test procedures address electromagnetic characteristics of antenna ports and required modifications to the test setup.

A.4.3.9 (4.3.9) Operation of EUT.

During emission measurements, the EUT shall be placed in an operating mode which produces maximum emissions. During susceptibility testing, the EUT shall be placed in its most susceptible operating mode. For EUTs with several available modes (including software controlled operational modes), a sufficient number of modes shall be tested for emissions and susceptibility such that all circuitry is evaluated. The rationale for modes selected shall be included in the EMITP.

Discussion: The particular modes selected may vary for different test procedures. Considerations for maximum emissions include conditions which cause the EUT to draw maximum prime power current, result in greatest activity in interface circuit operation, and generate the largest current drain on internal digital clock signals. Settings for a radar could be adjusted such that an output waveform results which has the highest available average power. Data bus interfaces could be queried frequently to cause constant bus traffic flow. Any modes of the EUT that are considered mission critical in the installation should be evaluated during susceptibility testing.

A primary consideration for maximum susceptibility is placing the EUT in its most sensitive state for reception of intentional signals (maximum gain). An imaging sensor would normally be evaluated with a scene meeting the most stringent specifications for the sensor. RF receivers are normally evaluated using an input signal at the minimum signal to noise specification of the receiver. An additional consideration is ensuring that all electrical interfaces that intentionally receive data are exercised frequently to monitor for potential responses.

A.4.3.9.1 (4.3.9.1) Operating frequencies for tunable RF equipment.
Measurements shall be performed with the EUT tuned to not less than three frequencies within each tuning band, tuning unit, or range of fixed channels, consisting of one mid-band frequency and a frequency within ±5 percent from each end of each band or range of channels.

Discussion: Tuned circuits and frequency synthesis circuitry inside RF equipment typically vary in characteristics such as response, rejection, and spectral content of emissions as they are set to different frequencies. Several test frequencies are required simply to obtain a sampling of the performance of the EUT across its operating range.

RF equipment that operates in several frequency bands or performs multiple functions is becoming more common. One example is a radio transceiver with VHF-FM, VHF-AM, and UHF-AM capability. Other devices are adaptive over large frequency ranges and can be programmed to perform different functions as the need arises. To meet the intent of the requirement to perform measurements at three frequencies within each tuning band, tuning unit, or range of fixed channels, each of the three functions of the radio in the example should be treated as separate bands, even if they are adjacent in frequency. Similarly, each function of adaptive RF equipment needs to be separately assessed.

The "value added" of performing all required tests at three frequencies within each band needs to be weighed against the added cost and schedule. The specific equipment design and intended function needs to be evaluated for each case.

For example, performing CS101 on a VHF-FM, VHF-AM, and UHF-AM combined receiver–transmitter would require that the test be performed a minimum of 18 times (3 frequencies * 3 bands * 2 modes). Since CS101 performance generally is related to the power supply design and load rather than the specific tuned frequency, doing the test for more than a few conditions may not add much value. If there is a problem, a typical result is "hum" on the secondary power outputs that is transmitted with the RF or that appears on the output audio of the receiver portion of the equipment. An appropriate approach for this particular requirement might be to test at one mid-band frequency for each of the three functions for both transmit and receive (6 tests – 3 frequencies * 2 modes).

Other requirements need to be evaluated similarly. Since CE102 emissions are mainly caused by power supply characteristics, testing at a mid-band frequency for each band just in the transmit mode might be adequate. For requirements with frequency coverage that extends into the operating frequency range of the equipment, such as RE102, CE106, and RS103, testing at three frequencies per band may be necessary.

A.4.3.9.2 (4.3.9.2) Operating frequencies for spread spectrum equipment.

Operating frequency requirements for two major types of spread spectrum equipment shall be as follows:

    a. *Frequency hopping. Measurements shall be performed with the EUT utilizing a hop set which contains a minimum of 30% of the total possible frequencies. This hop set shall be divided equally into three segments at the low, mid, and high end of the EUTs operational frequency range.*

    b. *Direct sequence. Measurements shall be performed with the EUT processing data at the highest possible data transfer rate.*

Discussion: During testing it is necessary to operate equipment at levels that they will experience during normal field operations to allow for a realistic representation of the emission profile of the EUT during radiated and conducted testing and to provide realistic loading and simulation of the EUT during radiated and conducted susceptibility testing.

Frequency hopping: Utilization of a hopset that is distributed across the entire operational spectrum of the EUT will help assure that internal circuitry dependent on the exact EUT transmit frequency being used is active intermittently during processing of the entire pseudo random stream. The fast operating times of hopping receivers/transmitters versus the allowable measurement times of the measurement receivers being used (4.3.10.3) will allow a representative EUT emission signature to be captured.

Direct sequence: Requiring the utilization of the highest data transfer rate used in actual operation of the EUT should provide a representative worst-case radiated and conducted emission profile. Internal circuitry will operate at its highest processing rate when integrating the data entering the transmitter, and then resolving (disintegrating) the data back once again on the receiver end. Additionally, the data rate will need to be an area of concentration during all susceptibility testing.

A.4.3.9.3 (4.3.9.3) Susceptibility monitoring.

The EUT shall be monitored during susceptibility testing for indications of degradation or malfunction. This monitoring is normally accomplished through the use of built-in-test (BIT), visual displays, aural outputs, and other measurements of signal outputs and interfaces. Monitoring of EUT performance through installation of special circuitry in the EUT is permissible; however, these modifications shall not influence test results.

Discussion: Most EUTs can be adequately monitored through normal visual and aural outputs, self-diagnostics, and electrical interfaces. The addition of special circuitry for monitoring can present questions related to its influence on the validity of the test results and may serve as an entry or exit point for electromagnetic energy.

The monitoring procedure needs to be specified in the EMITP and needs to include allowances for possible weaknesses in the monitoring process to assure the highest probability of finding regions of susceptibility.

If the unit contains or controls an electrically initiated device (EID), then special monitoring may be required and described in the EMITP. This is intended as part of risk mitigation, not in lieu of HERO Test/Certification.

A.4.3.10 (4.3.10) Use of measurement equipment.

Measurement equipment shall be as specified in the individual test procedures of this standard. Any frequency selective measurement receiver may be used for performing the testing described in this standard provided that the receiver characteristics (that is, sensitivity, selection of bandwidths, detector functions, dynamic range, and frequency of operation) meet the constraints specified in this standard and are sufficient to demonstrate compliance with the applicable limits. Typical instrumentation characteristics may be found in ANSI C63.2.

Discussion: Questions frequently arise concerning the acceptability for use of measurement receivers other than instruments that are specifically designated "field intensity meters" or "EMI receivers." Most questions are directed toward the use of spectrum analyzers. These instruments are generally acceptable for use. However, depending on the type, they can present difficulties that are not usually encountered with the other receivers. Sensitivity may not be adequate in some frequency bands requiring that a low noise preamplifier be inserted before the analyzer input. Impulse type signals from the EUT with broad spectral content may overload the basic receiver or preamplifier. The precautions of 4.3.7.3 must be observed. Both of these concerns can usually be adequately addressed by the use of a preselector with the analyzer. These devices typically consist of a tunable filter which tracks the analyzer followed by a preamplifier.

ANSI C63.2 represents a coordinated position from industry on required characteristics of instrumentation receivers. This document can be consulted when assessing the performance of a particular receiver.

Many of the test procedures require non-specialized instrumentation that is used for many other purposes. The test facility is responsible for selecting instrumentation that has characteristics capable of satisfying the requirements of a particular test procedure.

Current probes used for EMI testing are more specialized instrumentation. These devices are current transformers with the circuit under test forming a single turn primary. They are designed to be terminated in 50 ohms. Current probes are calibrated using transfer impedance that is the ratio of the voltage output of the probe across 50 ohms to the current through the probe. Probes with higher transfer impedance provide better sensitivity. However, these probes also result in more series impedance added to the circuit with a greater potential to affect the electrical current level. The series impedance added by the probe is the transfer impedance divided by the number of turns in the secondary winding on the probe. Typical transfer impedances are 5 ohms or less. Typical added series impedance is 1 ohm or less.

FFT receivers time samples a portion of the frequency spectrum and use digital signal processing techniques to display frequency data in a manner similar to conventional spectrum analyzers. The dwell times specified in Table II apply to the overall sampling time and must not include any processing time.

A.4.3.10.1 (4.3.10.1) Detector.

A peak detector shall be used for all frequency domain emission and susceptibility measurements. This device detects the peak value of the modulation envelope in the receiver bandpass. Measurement receivers are calibrated in terms of an equivalent Root Mean Square (RMS) value of a sine wave that produces the same peak value. When other measurement devices such as oscilloscopes, non-selective voltmeters, or broadband field strength sensors are used for susceptibility testing, correction factors shall be applied for test signals to adjust the reading to equivalent RMS values under the peak of the modulation envelope.

Discussion: The function of the peak detector and the meaning of the output indication on the measurement receiver are often confusing. Although there may appear to be an inherent discrepancy in the use of the terms "peak" and "RMS" together, there is no contradiction. All detector functions (that is peak, carrier, field intensity, and quasi-peak) process the envelope of the signal present in the receiver intermediate frequency (IF) section. All outputs are calibrated in terms of an equivalent RMS value. For a sine wave input to the receiver, the signal envelope in the IF section is a DC level and all detectors produce the same indicated RMS output. Calibration in terms of RMS is necessary for consistency. Signal sources are calibrated in terms of RMS. If a 0 dBm (107 dBμV) unmodulated signal is applied to the receiver, the receiver must indicate 0 dBm (107 dBμV).

If there is modulation present on the signal applied to the receiver, the detectors respond differently. The IF section of the receiver sees the portion of the applied signal within the bandwidth limits of the IF. The peak detector senses the largest level of the signal envelope in the IF and displays an output equal to the RMS value of a sine wave with the same peak. The specification of a peak detector ensures that the worst case condition for emission data is obtained. A carrier detector averages the modulation envelope based on selected charge and discharge time constants.

Figure A-4 shows the peak detector output for several modulation waveforms. An item of interest is that for a square wave modulated signal, which can be considered a pulse type modulation, the receiver can be considered to be displaying the RMS value of the pulse when it is on. Pulsed signals are often specified in terms of peak power. The RMS value of a signal is derived from the concept of power, and a receiver using a peak detector correctly displays the peak power.

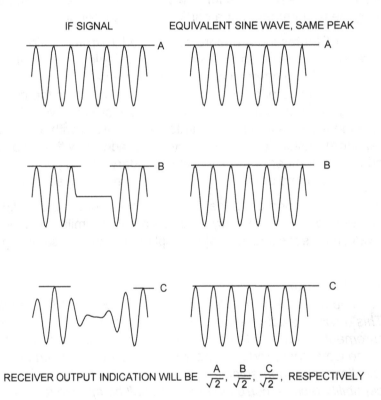

FIGURE A-4. **Peak detector response.**

All frequency domain measurements are standardized with respect to the response that a measurement receiver using a peak detector would provide. Therefore, when instrumentation is used which does not use peak detection, correction factors must be applied for certain signals. For an oscilloscope, the maximum amplitude of the modulated sine wave measured from the DC level is divided by 1.414 (square root of 2) to determine the RMS value at the peak of the modulation envelope.

Correction factors for other devices are determined by evaluating the response of the instrumentation to signals with the same peak level with and without modulation. For example, a correction factor for a broadband field sensor can be determined as follows. Place the sensor in an unmodulated field and note the reading. Apply the required modulation to the field ensuring that the peak value of the field is the same as the unmodulated field. For pulse type modulation, most signal sources will output the same peak value when modulation is applied. Amplitude modulation increases the peak amplitude of the signal and caution must be observed. Note the new reading. The correction factor is simply the reading with the unmodulated field divided by the reading with the modulated field. If the meter read 10 V/m without modulation and 5 V/m with modulation, the correction factor is 2. The evaluation should be tried at several frequencies and levels to ensure that a consistent value is obtained. When subsequently using the sensor for measurements with the evaluated modulation, the indicated reading is multiplied by the correction factor to obtain the correct reading for peak detection.

A.4.3.10.2 (4.3.10.2) Computer-controlled instrumentation.
A description of the operations being directed by software for computer-controlled instrumentation shall be included in the EMITP. Verification techniques used to demonstrate proper performance of the software shall also be included. If commercial software is being used then, as a minimum, the manufacturer, model and revision of the software needs to be provided. If the software is developed in-house, then documentation needs to be included that describes the methodology being used for the control of the test instrumentation and how the software revisions are handled.

Discussion: Computer software obviously provides excellent opportunities for automating testing. However, it also can lead to errors in testing if not properly used or if incorrect code is present. It is essential that users of the software understand the functions it is executing, know how to modify parameters (such as transducer or sweep variables) as necessary, and perform sanity checks to ensure that the overall system performs as expected. As a minimum, the following data should be included in the EMITP: sweep times, how correction factors are handled, how final data are determined and presented, and an audit trail that provides details on what part of the software controls which functions.

A.4.3.10.3 (4.3.10.3) Emission testing.
A.4.3.10.3.1 (4.3.10.3.1) Bandwidths.
The measurement receiver bandwidths listed in Table II shall be used for emission testing. These bandwidths are specified at the 6 dB down points for the overall selectivity curve of the receivers. Video filtering shall not be used to bandwidth limit the receiver response. If a controlled video bandwidth is available on the measurement receiver, it shall be set to its greatest value. Larger receiver bandwidths may be used; however, they may result in higher measured emission levels. NO BANDWIDTH CORRECTION FACTORS SHALL BE APPLIED TO TEST DATA DUE TO THE USE OF LARGER BANDWIDTHS.

TABLE II. Bandwidth and measurement time.

| Frequency Range | 6 dB Resolution Bandwidth | Dwell Time | | Minimum Measurement Time Analog-Tuned Measurement Receiver [1] |
		Stepped-Tuned Receiver [1] (Seconds)	FFT Receiver [2] (Seconds/ Measurement Bandwidth)	
30 Hz – 1 kHz	10 Hz	0.15	1	0.015 sec/Hz
1 kHz – 10 kHz	100 Hz	0.015	1	0.15 sec/kHz
10 kHz – 150 kHz	1 kHz	0.015	1	0.015 sec/kHz
150 kHz – 10 MHz	10 kHz	0.015	1	1.5 sec/MHz
10 MHz - 30 MHz	10 kHz	0.015	0.15	1.5 sec/MHz
30 MHz – 1 GHz	100 kHz	0.015	0.15	0.15 sec/MHz
Above 1 GHz	1 MHz	0.015	0.015	15 sec/GHz

[1] **Alternative scanning technique.** Multiple faster sweeps with the use of a maximum hold function may be used if the total scanning time is equal to or greater than the Minimum Measurement Time defined above.

[2] **FFT receivers.** FFT measurement techniques may be used provided that FFT operation is in accordance with ANSI C63.2. The user interface of the measurement receiver must allow for the direct input of the parameters in Table II for both FFT Time Domain and Frequency Stepped modes of measurement in the same manner, without the necessity or opportunity to control FFT functions directly.

Discussion: The bandwidths specified in Table II are consistent with the recommended available bandwidths and the bandwidth specification technique for receivers contained in ANSI C63.2. Existing receivers have bandwidths specified in a number of different ways. Some are given in terms of 3 dB down points. The 6 dB bandwidths are usually about 40% greater than the 3 dB values. Impulse bandwidths are usually very similar to the 6 dB bandwidths. For Gaussian shaped bandpasses, the actual value is 6.8 dB.

The frequency break point between using a 1 kHz and 10 kHz bandwidth was modified from 250 kHz to 150 kHz in this version of the standard to harmonize with commercial EMI standards.

In order not to restrict the use of presently available receivers that do not have the specified bandwidths, larger bandwidths are permitted. The use of larger bandwidths can produce higher detected levels for wide bandwidth signals. The prohibition against the use of correction factors is included to avoid any attempts to classify signals. A previous version of this standard eliminated the concept of classification of emissions as broadband or narrowband in favor of fixed bandwidths and single limits. Emission classification was a controversial area often poorly understood and handled inconsistently among different facilities.

The sensitivity of a particular receiver is an important factor in its suitability for use in making measurements for a particular requirement. RE102 is usually the most demanding requirement. The sensitivity of a receiver at room temperature can be calculated as follows:

Sensitivity in dBm = -114 dBm/MHz + bandwidth (dBMHz) + noise figure (dB)

As noted in the equation, reducing the noise figure is the only way (cryogenic cooling is not practical) to improve sensitivity for a specified bandwidth. The noise figure of receivers can vary substantially depending on the front end design. System noise figure can be improved through the use of low noise preamplifiers. The resulting noise figure of a preamplifier/receiver combination can be calculated from the following. All numbers are real numbers. Conversion to decibels (10 log) is necessary to determine the resulting sensitivity in the above formula:

System noise figure = preamp noise figure + (receiver noise figure)/(preamp gain)

Since preamplifiers are broadband devices, issues of potential overload need to be addressed. Separate preselectors, which are available for some spectrum analyzers, usually combine a tracking filter with a low noise preamplifier to eliminate overload. Preselection is an integral part of many receivers.

Example of multiple scan times derived from Table II are shown below. The frequency bands listed do not imply that those entire bands should be scanned at one time. The requirements for frequency resolution defined in 4.3.10.3.4 "Emission data presentation" must be met.

C1	C2	C3	C4	C5	C6	C7	C8	C9
Start Freq (Hz)	Stop Freq (Hz)	Span (Hz)	Resolution Bandwidth (Hz)	# of steps	Dwell time per step (sec)	Table II single sweep time (sec)	Single fast sweep time (sec)	# of fast sweeps to equal one Table II sweep
From Table II	From Table II	C2 – C1	From Table II	2*(C3/C4)	From Table II	C5 * C6	C5/C4	C7/C8
30	1000	970	10	194	0.15	29.1	19.4	1.5
1 k	10 k	9 k	100	180	0.015	2.7	1.8	1.5
10 k	150 k	140 k	1 k	280	0.015	4.2	0.28	15
0.15 M	30 M	29.85 M	10 k	5970	0.015	89.55	0.597	150
30 M	1000 M	970 M	100 k	19400	0.015	291	0.194	1500
1 G	18 G	17 G	1 M	34000	0.015	510	0.034	15000

The multiple scan option can be an effective method for capturing signals that are intermittent with a low duty cycle rate "On" time and significant "Off" time. Scan times and number of scans should be controlled for known signal characteristics to enhance the probability of capturing these signals. Scan times and sweep speeds are subject to limitations per column 8 of the above table which provides for enough dwell time for the IF filter to respond. Modern spectrum analyzers/ receivers have inhibits to prevent an uncalibrated sweep resulting from sweep speeds that are too fast for the final IF filter to respond. These types of signals form a Binomial type probability distribution for chance of capturing. Given the signal characteristics and the scanning parameters, the probability of capturing a signal can be reasonably estimated.

Measurement receivers need to operate in a maximum hold mode such that the highest levels across the frequency band are recorded over the sequence of scans. The signal characteristics (cycle times) should be included in the EMITR, if available.

The 0.015 second dwell time specified in Table II for step-tuned and analog-tuned receivers was selected to capture signals that had a minimum repetition rate of ~ 60 Hz. For lower frequency signals with lower repetition rates, traditional receivers will typically display individual pulses (in contrast to spectral lines) depending on the scan rate of the receiver (see 4.3.10.3 discussion). The 1 second dwell time for FFT receivers below 10 MHz is intended to capture baseband (no carrier frequency) emission profiles that have repetition rates as low as 1 Hz. The 10 MHz upper frequency was selected to correspond with the upper frequency of CE102 where power supplies may produce conducted noise with lower repetition rate profiles.

A.4.3.10.3.2 (4.3.10.3.2) Emission identification.
All emissions regardless of characteristics shall be measured with the measurement receiver bandwidths specified in Table II and compared against the applicable limits. Identification of emissions with regard to narrowband or broadband categorization is not applicable.

Discussion: Requirements for specific bandwidths and the use of single limits are intended to resolve a number of problems. Versions of MIL-STD-461 and MIL-STD-462 prior to the "D" revision had no controls on required bandwidths and provided both narrowband and broadband limits over much of the frequency range for most emission requirements. The significance of the particular bandwidths chosen for use by a test facility was addressed by classification of the appearance of the emissions with respect to the chosen bandwidths. Emissions considered to be broadband had to be normalized to equivalent levels in a 1 MHz bandwidth. The bandwidths and classification techniques used by various facilities were very inconsistent and resulted in a lack of standardization. The basic issue of emission classification was often poorly understood and implemented. Requiring specific bandwidths with a single limit eliminates any need to classify emissions.

An additional problem is that emission profiles from modern electronics are often quite complex. Some emission signatures have frequency ranges where the emissions exhibit white noise characteristics. Normalization to a 1 MHz bandwidth using spectral amplitude assumptions based on impulse noise characteristics is not technically correct. Requiring specific bandwidths eliminates normalization and this discrepancy.

A.4.3.10.3.3 (4.3.10.3.3) Frequency scanning.
For emission measurements, the entire frequency range for each applicable test shall be scanned. Minimum measurement time for analog measurement receivers during emission testing shall be as specified in Table II. Synthesized measurement receivers shall step in one-half bandwidth increments or less, and the measurement dwell time shall be as specified in Table II. For equipment that operates such that potential emissions are produced at only infrequent intervals, times for frequency scanning shall be increased as necessary to capture any emissions.

Discussion: For each emission test, the entire frequency range as specified for the applicable requirement must be scanned to ensure that all emissions are measured.

Continuous frequency coverage is required for emission testing. Testing at discrete frequencies is not acceptable unless otherwise stated in a particular test procedure. The minimum scan times listed in *Table II* are based on two considerations. The first consideration is the response time of a particular bandwidth to an applied signal. This time is 1/(filter bandwidth). The second consideration is the potential rates (that is modulation, cycling, and processing) at which electronics operate and the need to detect the worst case emission amplitude. Emission profiles usually vary with time. Some signals are present only at certain intervals and others vary in amplitude. For example, signals commonly present in emission profiles are harmonics of microprocessor clocks. These harmonics are very stable in frequency; however, their amplitude tends to change as various circuitry is exercised and current distribution changes.

The first entry in the table for analog measurement receivers of 0.015 sec/Hz for a bandwidth of 10 Hz is the only one limited by the response time of the measurement receiver bandpass. The response time is 1/bandwidth = 1/10 Hz = 0.1 seconds. Therefore, as the receiver tunes, the receiver bandpass must include any particular frequency for 0.1 seconds implying that the minimum scan time = 0.1 seconds/10 Hz = 0.01 seconds/Hz. The value in the table has been increased to 0.015 seconds/Hz to ensure adequate time. This increase by a multiplication factor of 1.5 results in the analog receiver having a frequency in its bandpass for 0.15 seconds as it scans. This value is the dwell time specified in the table for synthesized receivers for 10 Hz bandwidths. Since synthesized receivers are required to step in one-half bandwidth increments or less and dwell for 0.15 seconds, test time for synthesized receivers will be greater than analog receivers.

The measurement times for other table entries are controlled by the requirement that the receiver bandpass include any specific frequency for a minimum of 15 milliseconds (dwell time in table), which is associated with a potential rate of variation of approximately 60 Hz. As the receiver tunes, the receiver bandpass is required to include any particular frequency for the 15 milliseconds. For the fourth entry in the table of 1.5 seconds/MHz for a 10 kHz bandwidth, the minimum measurement time is 0.015 seconds/0.01 MHz = 1.5 seconds/MHz. A calculation based on the response time of the receiver would yield a response time of 1/bandwidth = 1/10 kHz = 0.0001 seconds and a minimum measurement time of 0.0001 seconds/0.01 MHz = 0.01 seconds/MHz. The longer measurement time of 1.5 seconds/MHz is specified in the table. If the specified measurement times are not adequate to capture the maximum amplitude of the EUT emissions, longer measurement times should be implemented.

Caution must be observed in applying the measurement times. The specified parameters are not directly available on measurement receiver controls and must be interpreted for each particular receiver. Also, the specified measurement times may be too fast for some data gathering devices such as real-time X-Y recording. Measurement receiver peak hold times must be sufficiently long for the mechanical pen drive on X-Y recorders to reach the detected peak value. In addition, the scan speed must be sufficiently slow to allow the detector to discharge after the signal is detuned so that the frequency resolution requirements of 4.3.10.3.4 are satisfied.

For measurement receivers with a "maximum hold" feature that retains maximum detected levels after multiple scans over a particular frequency range, multiple faster sweeps that produce the same minimum test times as implied by Table II are acceptable. For the situation noted in the requirement concerning equipment that produces emissions at only infrequent intervals, using the multiple scan technique will usually provide a higher probability of capturing intermittent data than using one slower scan.

FFT based measurement receivers perform time samples of signals in a relatively large bandwidth (typically in the MHz range) and mathematically convert the results to the frequency domain representation of the emission profile using the bandwidths specified by the standard. Two primary advantages of the FFT technique are reduced measurement time and the ability to capture frequency agile signals that jump around in a designated frequency band.

Disadvantages are that the receiver can saturate at lower signal levels and that low repetition rate signals can be totally missed if the dwell time is shorter than the pulse repetition interval of the emission. For example, an emission signature that occurs at one pulse/second rate with a short duration (~ 10 microseconds) will typically be captured at a number of measurement points with a traditional measurement receiver but would have only about a 1.5 % probability of being captured by the FFT receiver (0.015 second measurement time for 1 second period). A one pulse/second repetitive signal produces spectral lines that are 1 Hz apart extending well up in frequency based on the pulse width of the signal. If a traditional measurement receiver had a 1 Hz bandwidth, the individual spectral lines would be detected and would be continuously present. Larger receiver bandwidths start to reform the pulse and the detected pulse continues to get closer to its true shape with increasing bandwidth. The effect is that a traditional measurement receiver with bandwidths that are significantly larger than 1 Hz will detect a version of the pulse when it is on. If a particular frequency scan is required to last 10 seconds based on Table II in the standard, the above signal would produce 10 events (pulse responses rather than spectral lines) during the scan. The solution for the FFT receiver would be to increase the dwell time to at least 1 second to detect the pulse. If the FFT receiver does detect the pulse, a continuous spectral profile will be presented. The figures below illustrate the results for the postulated situation (1 pulse/second, 10 microsecond duration, 0.1 volt amplitude).

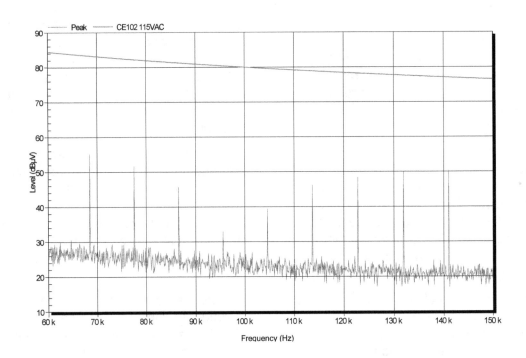

FIGURE A-5. Traditional Measurement Receiver with 10 Second Scan Time (Minimum Required by Table II)

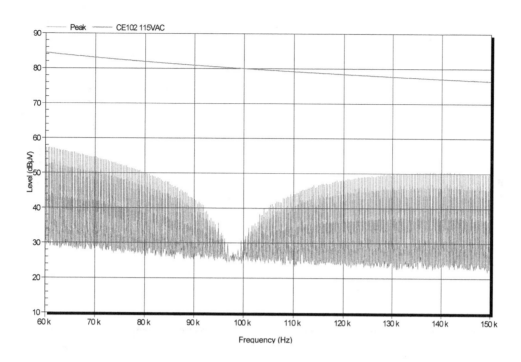

FIGURE A-6. Traditional Measurement Receiver with 300 Second Scan Time

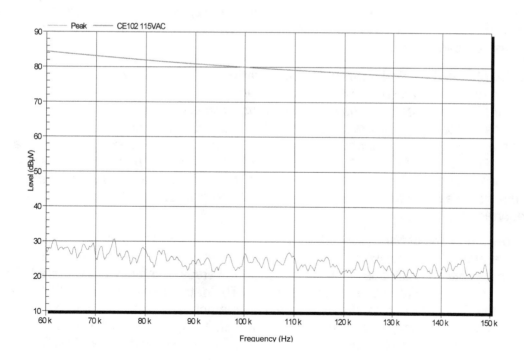

FIGURE A-7. FFT Measurement Receiver with 15 Millisecond Dwell Time

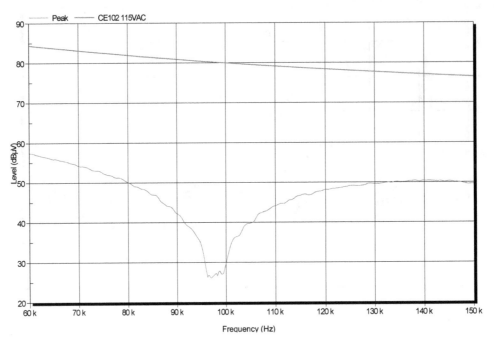

FIGURE A-8. FFT Measurement Receiver with 1 Second Dwell Time

Due to the larger measurement bandwidths associated with FFT receivers, there is an increased chance of saturation of the receiver for detected signals with a spectral density content that is broad with respect to the receiver bandpass. The detected signal level which is the bandpass times the spectral density (x MHz * y µV/MHz) will be larger for wider bandwidths. Depending on the architecture of the receiver, this may result in saturation sooner for FFT receivers as compared to traditional receivers.

A.4.3.10.3.4 (4.3.10.3.4) Emission data presentation.

Amplitude versus frequency profiles of emission data shall be automatically generated and displayed at the time of test and shall be continuous. The displayed information shall account for all applicable correction factors (transducers, attenuators, cable loss, and the like) and shall include the applicable limit. Manually gathered data is not acceptable except for verification of the validity of the output. Plots of the displayed data shall provide a minimum frequency resolution of 1% or twice the measurement receiver bandwidth, whichever is less stringent, and minimum amplitude resolution of 1 dB. The above resolution requirements shall be maintained in the reported results of the EMITR.

Discussion: Versions of MIL-STD-462 prior to the "D" revision permitted data to be taken at the three frequencies per octave for the highest amplitude emissions. **This approach is no longer acceptable**. Continuous displays of amplitude versus frequency are required. This information can be generated in a number of ways. The data can be plotted real-time as the receiver scans. The data can be stored in computer memory and later dumped to a plotter. Photographs of video displays are acceptable; however, it is generally more difficult to meet resolution requirements and to reproduce data in this form for submittal in an EMITR.

Placement of limits can be done in several ways. Data may be displayed with respect to actual limit dimensions (such as dBµV/m) with transducer, attenuation, and cable loss corrections made to the data. An alternative is to plot the raw data in dBμv (or dBm) and convert the limit to equivalent dBμv (or dBm) dimensions using the correction factors. This second technique has the advantage of displaying the proper use of the correction factors. Since both the emission level and the required limit are known, a second party can verify proper placement. Since the actual level of the raw data is not available for the first case, this verification is not possible.

An example of adequate frequency and amplitude resolution is shown on Figure A-9. 1% frequency resolution means that two sinusoidal signals of the same amplitude separated by 1% of the tuned frequency are resolved in the output display so that they both can be seen. As shown in the figure, 1% of the measurement frequency of 5.1 MHz is 0.051 MHz and a second signal at 5.151 MHz (1 dB different in amplitude on the graph) is easily resolved in the display. The "2 times the measurement receiver bandwidth" criteria means that two sinusoidal signals of the same amplitude separated by twice the measurement receiver bandwidth are resolved. For the example shown on Figure A-9, the bandwidth is 0.01 MHz and 2 times this value is 0.02 MHz. Therefore, the 1% criterion is less stringent and is applicable. 1 dB amplitude resolution means that the amplitude of the displayed signal can be read within 1 dB. As shown in the figure, the reviewer can determine whether the signal amplitude is 60 dBμV or 61 dBμV.

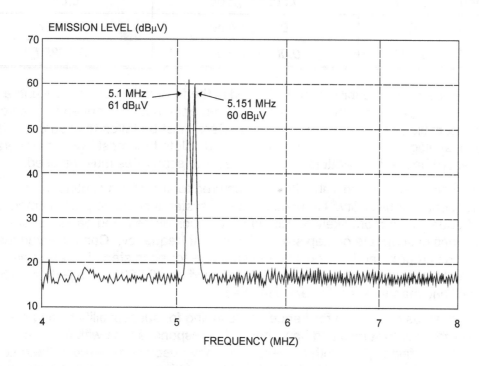

FIGURE A-9. Example of data presentation resolution.

The difference between resolution and accuracy is sometimes confusing. Paragraph 4.3.1 of the standard requires 3 dB measurement system accuracy for amplitude while 4.3.10.3.4 of the standard requires 1 dB amplitude resolution. Accuracy is an indication how precisely a value needs to be known while resolution is an indication of the ability to discriminate between two values. A useful analogy is reading time from a watch. A watch typically indicates the time within one second (resolution) but may be 30 seconds different than the absolute correct time (accuracy).

A.4.3.10.4 (4.3.10.4) Susceptibility testing.

A.4.3.10.4.1 (4.3.10.4.1) Frequency scanning.

For susceptibility measurements, the entire frequency range for each applicable test shall be scanned. For swept frequency susceptibility testing, frequency scan rates and frequency step sizes of signal sources shall not exceed the values listed in Table III. The rates and step sizes are specified in terms of a multiplier of the tuned frequency (f_o) of the signal source. Analog scans refer to signal sources which are continuously tuned. Stepped scans refer to signal sources which are sequentially tuned to discrete frequencies. Stepped scans shall dwell at each tuned frequency for the greater of 3 seconds or EUT response time. Scan rates and step sizes shall be decreased when necessary to permit observation of a response.

TABLE III. Susceptibility scanning.

Frequency Range	Analog Scans Maximum Scan Rates	Stepped Scans Maximum Step Size
30 Hz - 1 MHz	$0.0333 f_o$/sec	$0.05 f_o$
1 MHz – 30 MHz	$0.00667 f_o$/sec	$0.01 f_o$
30 MHz - 1 GHz	$0.00333 f_o$/sec	$0.005 f_o$
1 GHz - 18 GHz	$0.00167 f_o$/sec	$0.0025 f_o$

Discussion: For any susceptibility test performed in the frequency domain, the entire frequency range as specified in the applicable requirement must be scanned to ensure that all potentially susceptible frequencies are evaluated. Care must be taken to ensure that the scanning type, analog or stepped, is correctly selected. Note that most 'Sweep Generators' are actually digital synthesized generators and the "Stepped" scan rates must be used.

The scan rates and step sizes in Table III are structured to allow for a continuous change in value with frequency for flexibility. Computerized test systems could be programmed to change values very frequently. A more likely application is to block off selected bands for scanning and to base selections of scan rate or step size on the lowest frequency. Computerized test systems could be programmed to calculate the step size for each step. For example, if 1 - 2 GHz were selected, the maximum step at 1.5 GHz would be: 0.0025 x 1.5 GHz = 3.75 MHz. Both automatic and manual scanning are permitted.

The two primary areas of concern for frequency scanning for susceptibility testing are response times for EUTs to react to stimuli and how sharply the responses tune with frequency, normally expressed as quality factor (Q). Both of these items have been considered in the determination of the scan rates and step sizes in Table III. The table entries are generally based on the assumption of a maximum EUT response time of three seconds and Q values of 10, 50, 100, 500, and 1000 (increasing values as frequency increases in Table III). Since EUT responses are more likely to occur in approximately the 1 to 200 MHz range due to efficient cable coupling based on wavelength considerations, Q values have been increased somewhat to slow the scan and allow additional time for observation of EUT responses. More detailed discussions on these items follow.

The assumption of a maximum response time of three seconds is considered to be appropriate for a large percentage of possible cases. There are several considerations. While the electronics processing the interfering signal may respond quickly, the output display may take some time to react. Outputs that require mechanical motion such as meter movements or servo driven devices will generally take longer to show degradation effects than electronic displays such as video screens. Another concern is that some EUTs will only be in particularly susceptible states periodically. For example, sensors feeding information to a microprocessor are typically sampled at specific time intervals. It is important that the susceptibility stimuli be located at any critical frequencies when the sensor is sampled. The time intervals between steps and sweep rates in Table III may need to be modified for EUTs with unusually long response times.

Some concern has been expressed on the susceptibility scan rates and the impact that they would have on the length of time required to conduct a susceptibility test. The criteria of Table III allow the susceptibility scan rate to be adjusted continually as the frequency is increased; however, as a practical matter, the rate would most likely only be changed once every octave or decade. As an example, Table A-I splits the frequency spectrum up into ranges corresponding to Table III and frequency ranges of some of the requirements. Actual test times were measured in a laboratory allowing for settling time and leveling. The total test time to run RS103 from 2 MHz to 18 GHz for a stepped scan is 168 minutes for one polarization. Similarly, an analog scan would result in a total test time of approximately 100 minutes. These times are based on continuously calculating the next frequency using the present tuned frequency and the allowed step size. It must be emphasized that the scan speeds should be slowed down if the EUT response time or Q are more critical than those used to establish the values in Table III. Note that the sweep times in the table should be used as programmed times for a scan. Maximum allowable step sizes must be used. If scanning techniques employing alternative calculations, such as using the step size at the beginning frequency of an octave for the entire octave, larger test times will result.

Q is expressed as f_o/BW where f_o is the tuned frequency and BW is the width in frequency of the response at the 3 dB down points. For example, if a response occurred at 1 MHz at a susceptibility level of 1 V and the same response required 1.414 V (3 dB higher in required drive) at 0.95 and 1.05 MHz, the Q would be 1 MHz/(1.05 - 0.95 MHz) or 10. Q is primarily influenced by resonances in filters, interconnecting cabling, physical structure, and cavities. The assumed Q values are based on observations from various types of testing. The step sizes in Table III are one half of the 3 dB bandwidths of the assumed value of Q ensuring that test frequencies will lie within the resonant responses.

TABLE A-I. Susceptibility testing times.

Frequency Range	Maximum Step Size	Actual Scan Time (minutes)
30 Hz - 150 kHz	$0.05\ f_o$	16
150 kHz – 1 MHz	$0.05\ f_o$	4
1 MHz – 2 MHz	$0.01\ f_o$	5
2 MHz – 30 MHz	$0.01\ f_o$	20
30 MHz – 1 GHz	$0.005\ f_o$	54
1 GHz – 18 GHz	$0.0025\ f_o$	94
18 GHz – 40 GHz	$0.0025\ f_o$	28

Below approximately 200 MHz, the predominant contributors are cable and interface filter resonances. There is loading associated with these resonances which dampens the responses and limits most values of Q to less than 50. Above 200 MHz, structural resonances of enclosures and housings start playing a role and have higher values of Q due to less dampening. Above approximately 1 GHz, aperture coupling with excitation of cavities will be become dominant. Values of Q are dependent on frequency and on the amount of material contained in the cavity. Larger values of Q result when there is less material in the volume. A densely packaged electronics enclosure will exhibit significantly lower values of Q than an enclosure with a higher percentage of empty volume. Q is proportional to Volume/(Surface Area X Skin Depth). The value of Q also tends to increase with frequency as the associated wavelength becomes smaller. EUT designs with unusual configurations that result in high Q characteristics may require that the scan rates and step sizes in Table III be decreased for valid testing.

RF processing equipment presents a special case requiring unique treatment. Intentionally tuned circuits for processing RF can have very high values of Q. For example, a circuit operating at 1 GHz with a bandwidth of 100 kHz has a Q of 1 GHz/100 kHz or 10,000. Automatic leveling used to stabilize the amplitude of a test signal for stepped scans may require longer dwell times than one second at discrete frequencies. The signal will take time to settle and any EUT responses during the leveling process should be ignored.

A.4.3.10.4.2 (4.3.10.4.2) Modulation of susceptibility signals.
Susceptibility test signals for CS114 and RS103 shall be pulse modulated (on/off ratio of 40 dB minimum) at a 1 kHz rate with a 50% duty cycle.

Discussion: Modulation is usually the effect that degrades EUT performance. The wavelengths of the RF signal cause efficient coupling to electrical cables and through apertures (at higher frequencies). Non-linearities in the circuit elements detect the modulation on the carrier. The circuits may then respond to the modulation depending upon detected levels, circuit bandpass characteristics, and processing features.

Pulse modulation at a 1 kHz rate, 50% duty cycle, (alternately termed 1 kHz square wave modulation) is specified for several reasons. One kHz is within the bandpass of most analog circuits such as audio or video. The fast rise and fall times of the pulse causes the signal to have significant harmonic content high in frequency and can be detrimental to digital circuits. Response of electronics has been associated with energy present and a square wave results in high average power. The modulation encompasses many signal modulations encountered in actual use. The square wave is a severe form of amplitude modulation used in communications and broadcasting. It also is a high duty cycle form of pulse modulation representative of radars.

Care needs to be taken in implementing 1 kHz, 50% duty cycle, pulse modulation (on/off ratio of 40 dB) using some signal sources. Most higher frequency signal sources have either internal pulse modulation or an external port for pulse modulation. This function switches the output on and off without affecting the amplitude of the unmodulated signal, provided that the strength of the modulation signal is adequate. For other signal sources, particularly at lower frequencies, the external amplitude modulation (AM) port needs to be driven to a minimum of 99 % depth of modulation (equivalent to 40 dB on/off ratio) to simulate pulse modulation. The output signal will essentially double in amplitude compared to an unmodulated signal for this type of input. Depending on the type of testing being performed and the technique of monitoring applied signals, this effect may or may not influence the results. Use of an AM port can be substantially more involved than using a pulse modulation port. The amplitude of the input signal directly influences the depth of modulation. There is a potential of exceeding 100% depth of modulation, which will result in signal distortion. Since the on/off ratio requirement is stringent, it is necessary to view the output signal on an oscilloscope to set the appropriate depth of modulation. Another complication is that the bandwidth of AM ports is usually less than pulse ports. Driving the port with a pulse shape may result in difficulty in setting the source for a minimum of 99%.

MIL-STD-461A required that the worst case modulation for the EUT be used. Worst case modulation usually was not known or determined. Also, worst case modulation may not be related to modulations seen in actual use or may be very specialized. The most typical modulations used below approximately 400 MHz have been amplitude modulation at either 400 or 1000 Hz (30 to 80%) or pulse modulation, 50% duty cycle, at 400 or 1000 Hz. These same modulations have been used above 400 MHz together with pulse modulation at various pulse widths and pulse repetition frequencies. Continuous wave (CW - no modulation) has also occasionally been used. CW typically produces a detected DC level in the circuitry and affects certain types of circuits. In general, experience has shown that modulation is more likely to cause degradation. CW should be included as an additional requirement when assessing circuits that respond only to heat such as electroexplosive devices. CW should not normally be used as the only condition.

Consideration should be given to applying a secondary 1 Hz modulation (where the normal 1 kHz square wave modulated waveform is completely turned on and off every 500 milliseconds) for certain subsystems with low frequency response characteristics, such as aircraft flight control subsystems. This modulation simulates characteristics of some transmitters such as high frequency (HF) radios in single sideband operation (no carrier), where a transmitted voice signal will cause the RF to be present only when a word is spoken. The dilemma with using this modulation is that the potential response of some subsystems may be enhanced, while others may be less responsive. In the latter case, the 500 millisecond off period allows the subsystem to recover from effects introduced during the "on" period.

Starting in MIL-STD-461G, verification of the presence of correct modulation by monitoring output signals is specified in the CS114 and RS103 sections. Correct modulation is essential for evaluating EUT performance. Many items will respond readily to a modulated signal and not to a continuous wave source. Modulation sources are internal to some signal generators. Other signal generators require an external source. Simple forgetfulness to apply modulation, improper settings, or lack of visible indications of modulation on instrumentation displays can all result in deficient testing.

A.4.3.10.4.3 (4.3.10.4.3) Thresholds of susceptibility.
Susceptibilities and anomalies that are not in conformance with contractual requirements are not acceptable. However, all susceptibilities and anomalies observed during conduct of the test need to be documented. When susceptibility indications are noted in EUT operation, a threshold level shall be determined where the susceptible condition is no longer present. Thresholds of susceptibility shall be determined as follows and described in the EMITR:

a. *When a susceptibility condition is detected, reduce the interference signal until the EUT recovers.*

b. *Reduce the interference signal by an additional 6 dB.*

c. *Gradually increase the interference signal until the susceptibility condition reoccurs. The resulting level is the threshold of susceptibility.*

    d. Record this level, frequency range of occurrence, frequency and level of greatest susceptibility, and other test parameters, as applicable.

Discussion: It is usually necessary to test at levels above the limits to ensure that the test signal is at least at the required level. Determination of a threshold of susceptibility is necessary when degradations or anomalies are present to assess whether requirements are met. This information should be included in the EMITR. Threshold levels below limits are unacceptable.

The specified steps to determine thresholds of susceptibility standardize a particular technique. An alternative procedure sometimes utilized in the past was to use the value of the applied signal where the EUT recovers (step a above) as the threshold. Hysteresis type effects are often present where different values are obtained for the two procedures.

Distortion of sinusoidal susceptibility signals caused by non-linear effects in power amplifiers can lead to erroneous interpretation of results. When distortion is present, the EUT may actually respond to a harmonic of the intended susceptibility frequency, where the required limit may be lower. When frequency selective receivers are used to monitor the injected level, distortion itself does not prevent a valid susceptibility signal level from being verified at the intended frequency. However, harmonic levels should be checked when susceptibility is present to determine if they are influencing the results. When broadband sensors are being used such as in portions of RS103, distortion can result in the sensor incorrectly displaying the required signal level at the intended frequency. In this case, distortion needs to be controlled such that correct levels are measured.

A.4.3.11 (4.3.11) Calibration of measuring equipment.
Test equipment and accessories required for measurement in accordance with this standard shall be calibrated in accordance with ANSI/ISO/IEC 17025 or ISO 10012 or under an approved calibration program traceable to the National Institute for Standards and Technology. In particular, measurement antennas, current probes, field sensors, and other devices used in the measurement loop shall be calibrated at least every 2 years unless otherwise specified by the procuring activity, or when damage is apparent.

Discussion: Calibration is typically required for any measurement device whose characteristics are not verified through use of another calibrated item during testing. For example, it is not possible during testing to determine whether an antenna used to measure radiated emissions is exhibiting correct gain characteristics. Therefore, these antennas require periodic calibration. Conversely, a power amplifier used during radiated susceptibility testing often will not require calibration since application of the proper signal level is verified through the use of a separate calibrated field sensing device. Other amplifier applications such as the use of a signal pre-amplifier in front of a measurement receiver would require calibration of the amplifier characteristics since the specific gain versus frequency response is critical and is not separately verified.

A.4.3.11.1 (4.3.11.1) Measurement system test.
At the start of each emission test, the complete test system (including measurement receivers, cables, attenuators, couplers, and so forth) shall be verified by injecting a known signal, as stated in the individual test procedure, while monitoring system output for the proper indication. When the emission test involves an uninterrupted set of repeated measurements (such as evaluating different operating modes of the EUT) using the same measurement equipment, the measurement system test needs to be accomplished only one time.

Discussion: The end-to-end system check prior to emission testing is valuable in demonstrating that the overall measurement system is working properly. It evaluates many factors including proper implementation of transducer factors and cable attenuation, general condition and setting of the measurement receiver, damaged RF cables or attenuators, and proper operation of software. Details on implementation are included in the individual test procedures.

A.4.3.11.2 (4.3.11.2) Antenna factors.

Factors for test antennas shall be determined in accordance with SAE ARP958.

Discussion: SAE ARP958 provides a standard basis for determining antenna factors emission testing. A caution needs to be observed in trying to apply these factors in applications other than EMI testing. The two antenna technique for antennas such as the biconical and double ridge horns is based on far field assumptions which are not met over much of the frequency range. Although the factors produce standardized results, the true value of the electric field is not necessarily being provided through the use of the factor. Different measuring sensors need to be used when the true electric field must be known.

A.5. DETAILED REQUIREMENTS

A.5.1 (5.1) General.

This section specifies detailed emissions and susceptibility requirements and the associated test procedures. Table IV is a list of the specific requirements established by this standard identified by requirement number and title. General test procedures are included in this section. Specific test procedures are implemented by the Government approved EMITP. All results of tests performed to demonstrate compliance with the requirements are to be documented in the EMITR and forwarded to the Command or agency concerned for evaluation prior to acceptance of the equipment or subsystem. Design procedures and techniques for the control of EMI shall be described in the EMICP. Approval of design procedures and techniques described in the EMICP does not relieve the supplier of the responsibility of meeting the contractual emission, susceptibility, and design requirements.

TABLE IV. Emission and susceptibility requirements.

Requirement	Description
CE101	Conducted Emissions, Power Leads, 30 Hz to 10 kHz
CE102	Conducted Emissions, Power Leads, 10 kHz to 10 MHz
CE106	Conducted Emissions, Antenna Terminal, 10 kHz to 40 GHz
CS101	Conducted Susceptibility, Power Leads, 30 Hz to 150 kHz
CS103	Conducted Susceptibility, Antenna Port, Intermodulation, 15 kHz to 10 GHz
CS104	Conducted Susceptibility, Antenna Port, Rejection of Undesired Signals, 30 Hz to 20 GHz
CS105	Conducted Susceptibility, Antenna Port, Cross-Modulation, 30 Hz to 20 GHz
CS109	Conducted Susceptibility, Structure Current, 60 Hz to 100 kHz
CS114	Conducted Susceptibility, Bulk Cable Injection, 10 kHz to 200 MHz
CS115	Conducted Susceptibility, Bulk Cable Injection, Impulse Excitation
CS116	Conducted Susceptibility, Damped Sinusoidal Transients, Cables and Power Leads, 10 kHz to 100 MHz
CS117	Conducted Susceptibility, Lightning Induced Transients, Cables and Power Leads
CS118	Conducted Susceptibility, Electrostatic Discharge
RE101	Radiated Emissions, Magnetic Field, 30 Hz to 100 kHz
RE102	Radiated Emissions, Electric Field, 10 kHz to 18 GHz
RE103	Radiated Emissions, Antenna Spurious and Harmonic Outputs, 10 kHz to 40 GHz
RS101	Radiated Susceptibility, Magnetic Field, 30 Hz to 100 kHz
RS103	Radiated Susceptibility, Electric Field, 2 MHz to 40 GHz
RS105	Radiated Susceptibility, Transient Electromagnetic Field

Discussion: The applicability of individual requirements in Table IV for a particular equipment or subsystem is dependent upon the platforms where the item will be used. The electromagnetic environments present on a platform together with potential degradation modes of electronic equipment items play a major role regarding which requirements are critical to an application. For example, emissions requirements are tied to protecting antenna-connected receivers on platforms. The operating frequency ranges and sensitivies of the particular receivers on-board a platform, therefore, influence the need for certain requirements.

The EMICP, EMITP, and EMITR are important elements in documenting design efforts for meeting the requirements of this standard, testing approaches which interpret the generalized test procedures in this standard, and reporting of the results of testing. The EMICP is a mechanism instituted to help ensure that contractors analyze equipment design for EMI implications and include necessary measures in the design for compliance with requirements. Approval of the document does not indicate that the procuring activity agrees that all the necessary effort is stated in the document. It is simply a recognition that the design effort is addressing the correct issues.

The susceptibility limits are the upper bound on the range of values for which compliance is required. The EUT must also provide required performance at any stress level below the limit. For example, if the limit for radiated susceptibility to electric fields is 10 V/m, the EUT must also meet its performance requirements at 5 V/m or any other field less than or equal to 10 V/m. There have been cases documented where equipment (such as equipment with automatic gain control circuitry) was not susceptible to radiated electric fields at given frequencies at the limit level but was susceptible to the environment at the same frequencies when exposed to fields below the limit level.

In the "B" and "C' versions of MIL-STD-461, separate requirements were included to deal specifically with mobile electric power units as UM04 equipment. The intent of the present version of MIL-STD-461 is that the requirements for this type of equipment are platform dependent and should simply be the same as any other equipment associated with that platform as listed in Table IV.

A.5.1.1 (5.1.1) Units of frequency domain measurements.
All frequency domain limits are expressed in terms of equivalent Root Mean Square (RMS) value of a sine wave as would be indicated by the output of a measurement receiver using peak envelope detection (see 4.3.10.1).

Discussion: A detailed discussion is provided on peak envelope detection in 4.3.10.1. A summary of output of the detector for several input waveforms is as follows. For an unmodulated sine wave, the output simply corresponds to the RMS value of the sine wave. For a modulated sine wave, the output is the RMS value of an unmodulated sine wave with the same absolute peak value. For a signal with a bandwidth greater than the bandwidth of the measurement receiver, the output is the RMS value of an unmodulated sine wave with the same absolute peak value as the waveform developed in the receiver bandpass.

A.5.2 (5.2) EMI control requirements versus intended installations.
Table V summarizes the requirements for equipment and subsystems intended to be installed in, on, or launched from various military platforms or installations. When an equipment or subsystem is to be installed in more than one type of platform or installation, it shall comply with the most stringent of the applicable requirements and limits. An "A" entry in the table means the requirement is applicable. An "L" entry means the applicability of the requirement is limited as specified in the appropriate requirement paragraphs of this standard; the limits are contained herein. An "S" entry means the procuring activity must specify the applicability and limit requirements in the procurement specification. Absence of an entry means the requirement is not applicable.

TABLE V. Requirement matrix.

Equipment and Subsystems Installed In, On, or Launched From the Following Platforms or Installations	CE101	CE102	CE106	CS101	CS103	CS104	CS105	CS109	CS114	CS115	CS116	CS117	CS118	RE101	RE102	RE103	RS101	RS103	RS105
	Requirement Applicability																		
Surface Ships	A	A	L	A	S	S	S	L	A	S	A	L		A	A	L	L	A	L
Submarines	A	A	L	A	S	S	S	L	A	S	L			A	A	L	L	A	L
Aircraft, Army, Including Flight Line	A	A	L	A	S	S	S		A	A	A	L		A	A	L	A	A	L
Aircraft, Navy	L	A	L	A	S	S	S		A	A	A	L		L	A	L	L	A	L
Aircraft, Air Force		A	L	A	S	S	S		A	A	A	L		A	L		A		
Space Systems, Including Launch Vehicles		A	L	A	S	S	S		A	A	A	L		A	L		A		
Ground, Army		A	L	A	S	S	S		A	A	A	S		A	L	L	A		
Ground, Navy		A	L	A	S	S	S		A	A	A			A	L	L	A		L
Ground, Air Force		A	L	A	S	S	S		A	A	A			A	L		A		

Equipment and Subsystems Installed In, On, or Launched From the Following Platforms or Installations	CE101	CE102	CE106	CS101	CS103	CS104	CS105	CS109	CS114	CS115	CS116	CS117	CS118	RE101	RE102	RE103	RS101	RS103	RS105
	Requirement Applicability																		
Surface Ships	A	A	L	A	S	S	S	L	A	S	A	L	A	A	A	L	L	A	L
Submarines	A	A	L	A	S	S	S	L	A	S	L			A	A	A	L	L	A
Aircraft, Army, Including Flight Line	A	A	L	A	S	S	S		A	A	A	L	A	A	A	L	A	A	L
Aircraft, Navy	L	A	L	A	S	S	S		A	A	A	L	A	L	A	L	L	A	L
Aircraft, Air Force		A	L	A	S	S	S		A	A	A	L	A		A	L		A	
Space Systems, Including Launch Vehicles		A	L	A	S	S	S		A	A	A	L			A	L		A	
Ground, Army		A	L	A	S	S	S		A	A	A	S	A		A	L	L	A	
Ground, Navy		A	L	A	S	S	S		A	A	A		A		A	L	L	A	L
Ground, Air Force		A	L	A	S	S	S		A	A	A		A		A	L		A	

Discussion: Discussion on each requirement as it relates to different platforms is contained in the sections on the individual requirements.

A.5.3 (5.3) Emission and susceptibility requirements, limits, and test procedures.
Individual emission or susceptibility requirements and their associated limits and test procedures are grouped together in the following sections. The applicable frequency range and limit of many emission and susceptibility requirements varies depending on the particular platform or installation. The test procedures included in this section are valid for the entire frequency range specified in the procedure; however, testing only needs to be performed over the frequency range specified for the particular platform or installation.

Discussion: In this version of MIL-STD-461, the test procedures for individual requirements follow directly after the applicability and limit statements. The discussion for the individual requirements is separated into these two areas.

A.5.4 (5.4) CE101, conducted emissions, power leads.
Applicability and limits: The requirements are applicable from 30 Hz to 10 kHz for leads that obtain power from sources that are not part of the EUT. There is no requirement on output leads from power sources. Since power quality standards are normally used to govern the characteristics of output power, there is no need for separate EMI requirements on output leads.

The limits are in terms of current because of the difficulty in controlling the power source impedance in test facilities at lower frequencies. This type of control would be necessary to specify the limits in terms of voltage. Emission current levels will be somewhat independent of power source impedance variations as long as the impedance of the emission source is large relative to the power source impedance.

For surface ships and submarines, the intent of this requirement is to control the effects of conducted emissions peculiar to the shipboard power distribution system. Harmonic line currents are limited for each electrical load connected to the power distribution system. Power quality for surface ships and submarines is controlled by MIL-STD-1399-300.

The surface ships and submarine power distribution systems (ship's primary power) supplied by the ship's alternators is 440 V, 60 Hz, 3-phase, 3-wire, ungrounded. Although ship's primary power is ungrounded, there exists a virtual alternating current (AC) ground at each electrical load due to capacitance to chassis. The unbalance between the virtual grounds at each electrical load causes AC currents to flow in the hull of the submarine. These hull currents can degrade the performance of electronic equipment, upset ground detectors, and counteract degaussing.

Hull currents are controlled by limiting the amplitude of harmonic currents conducted on the power distribution system wiring for each electrical load. The limit is based on maintaining total harmonic voltage distortion of the ship power distribution system within 5% of the supply voltage with the contribution from any single harmonic being less than 3%. In addition to the hull current concern, total harmonic distortion of the supply voltage waveform greater than 5% is above the tolerance of most electronic equipment, induction motors, magnetic devices, and measuring devices.

For Army aircraft, the primary concern is to ensure that the EUT does not corrupt the power quality (allowable voltage distortion) on the power buses present on the platform. The Army aircraft limits are based on relating the allowable current into a 1.0 ohm impedance to MIL-STD-704 requirements on voltage distortion. The Army limit includes approximately a 20 dB margin with respect to MIL-STD-704 to allow for contributions from multiple emission sources.

For Navy aircraft, the requirement is applicable for installations using anti-submarine warfare (ASW) equipment, specifically equipment in the same cabinet or avionics bay, or that share the same power bus or same cable bundles, as the ASW equipment. In addition, the requirement should apply to any equipment that uses more than 6 amps of current on-board an ASW aircraft. The primary mission of ASW aircraft is to detect and locate submarines. Unacceptable levels of emission currents in the frequency range of this test would limit the detection and processing capabilities of the Magnetic Anomaly Detection (MAD) and Acoustic Sensor systems. The MAD systems must be able to isolate a magnetic disturbance in the earth's magnetic field of less than one part in 50,000. In present aircraft, the full sensitivity of the MAD systems is not available due to interference produced by onboard equipment. Low frequency interference effects in the 30 Hz to 10 kHz can be a problem for Acoustic Sensor systems.

Possible tailoring of the requirements by the procuring activity is to impose the requirement if sensitive receivers operating in the frequency range of the requirement are to be installed on a platform or to modify the limit based on the particular characteristics of the power system onboard the platform.

Another possible tailoring of the requirement by the procuring activity is for cases where high current loads exist (filter size may be massive to meet limit), where power distribution wiring has short lengths, or where dedicated returns run with the high sides (versus structure return). For these cases, the use of a 5 µH LISN may be appropriate, but it must be approved by the procuring activity. If a 5 µH LISN is used, the following modifications to the CE101 requirement could be applicable. Figure A-10 shows limits that will preserve MIL-STD-704 power quality and minimize filter size, regardless of EUT current load. The low frequency plateau of each curve is shown for a 1 Amp load at the power frequency. The low frequency plateau shifts upward for higher currents by adding a factor of 20*log (load current in Amperes). The limit extends to 150 kHz instead of 10 kHz. The limit at 150 kHz is fixed and calculated to coincide with the CE102 limit at 150 kHz, based on the impedance of a 5 µH LISN. Thus the slope of the limit curve between the scaled 2 kHz point and the fixed 150 kHz is a function of load current. For an AC load, the scan should start just below 400 cycles so that the 400 cycle load current can be used to properly scale the limit, even though the AC limit does not begin until the second harmonic.

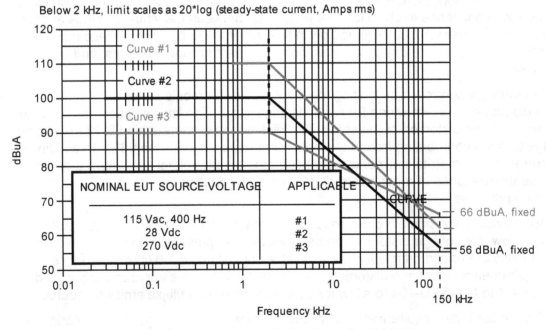

FIGURE A-10. CE101 limits for a 5 µH LISN.

Test procedures: Emission levels are determined by measuring the current present on each power lead. The LISNs will have little influence on the results of this testing. The circuit characteristics of the LISN will help stabilize measurements near 10 kHz; however, the LISN parameters will not be significant over most of the frequency range of the test.

Current is measured because of the low impedances present over most of the frequency range of the test. Current levels will be somewhat independent of power source impedance variations as long as the impedance of the emission source is significant in relation to the power source impedance. However, at frequencies where the shielded room filters in the test facility resonate (generally between 1 and 10 kHz), influences on measured currents can be expected.

During the measurement system check, the signal generator may need to be supplemented with a power amplifier to obtain the necessary current 6 dB below the applicable limit.

The value of the resistor "R" on Figure CE101-5 is not specified because a particular value is not critical. Whatever value is convenient for measurement and possible matching of the signal generator can be used.

A possible alternative measurement tool in this frequency range is a wave analyzer using a Fast Fourier Transform algorithm. Use of this type of instrumentation requires specific approval by the procuring activity.

An alternative test procedure for high current loads from 30 Hz – 150 kHz may be desirable. While the CE101 test method can be used without modification with these load current-dependent limits, it is desirable, especially for 400 Hz loads, to eliminate the LISN altogether, since it is not relevant to the measurement. A 5 µH LISN as described in the DISCUSSION of 4.3.6 may be used; however, it will influence the measurement somewhat. Another contributor to high power source impedance is the EMI test facility electrical filters, which typically resonate below 10 kHz and can have impedance as high as 50 ohms at a resonance. For AC loads, which are drawing harmonic currents below 10 kHz, it may be desirable to short out the EMI filters. For DC power, this effect is easily accomplished by placing a large capacitor across the power source. For AC power this approach is not practical. For AC power, the input and output ends of the facility filter would have to be shorted together to bypass the series inductance. If the line-to-ground capacitance of the filter then causes power factor problems, it may be necessary to bypass the filters altogether and bring power into the test chamber from an unfiltered source. The technical criterion for low source impedance is that the power waveform as loaded by the EUT has suitably low distortion. The distortion as measured when the EUT is energized is:

Allowable distortion (%) = (MIL-STD-704 total distortion (%)) x (EUT load current/power source rated load current)

For an AC bus, use of a distortion meter is desirable rather than a measurement receiver. If a distortion meter is not available, then the peak AC voltage should be measured open circuit and as loaded by the EUT, the difference between these divided by the open-circuit peak potential is subject to the limit above.

A.5.5 (5.5) CE102, conducted emissions, power leads.

Applicability and limits: The requirements are applicable from 10 kHz to 10 MHz for leads that obtain power from sources that are not part of the EUT. There is no requirement on output leads from power sources.

The basic concept in the lower frequency portion of the requirement is to ensure that the EUT does not corrupt the power quality (allowable voltage distortion) on the power buses present on the platform. Examples of power quality documents are MIL-STD-704 for aircraft, MIL-STD-1399 for ships, MIL-STD-1539 for space systems, and MIL-STD-1275 for military vehicles.

Since power quality standards govern allowable distortion on output power, there is no need for separate EMI requirements on output leads. The output power leads are treated no differently than any other electrical interface. This standard does not directly control the spectral content of signals present on electrical interfaces. Waveform definitions and distortion limits are specified in documents such as interface control documents. In the case of output power, the quality of the power must be specified over an appropriate frequency range so that the user of the power can properly design for its characteristics. This situation is true whether the power source is a primary source such as 115 V, 400 Hz, or a ±15 VDC low current supply. A significant indirect control on spectral content exists in the RE102 limits which essentially require that appropriate waveform control and signal transmission techniques be used to prevent unacceptable radiation (see discussion on CE102 limit placement and RE102 relationship below).

Since voltage distortion is the basis for establishing power quality requirements, the CE102 limit is in terms of voltage. The use of standardized line impedance over the frequency range of this test provides for the convenient measurement of the voltage as developed across this impedance. In previous versions of MIL-STD-461, a current measurement into a 10 µF feedthrough capacitor was specified. The intent of the capacitor was to provide an RF short of the power lead to the ground plane. It was difficult to interpret the significance of the current limit with respect to platform applications. The presence of standardized impedance is considered to reflect more closely the electrical characteristics of the power buses in platforms.

Of the power quality documents reviewed, MIL-STD-704 is the only one with a curve specifying an amplitude versus frequency relationship for the allowable distortion. The CE102 limits require that amplitude decays with increasing frequency similar to the requirements of MIL-STD-704. Common requirements are specified for all applications since the concerns are the same for all platforms.

The basic limit curve for 28 V is placed approximately 20 dB below the power quality curve in MIL-STD-704. There are several reasons for the placement. One reason is that a number of interference sources present in different subsystems and equipment on a platform may be contributing to the net interference voltage present at a given location on the power bus. Assuming that the interference sources are not phase coherent, the net voltage will be the square root of the sum of the squares of the voltages from the individual sources. A second reason is that the actual impedance in an installation will vary from the control impedance with actual voltages being somewhat higher or lower than that measured during the test. Therefore, some conservatism needs to be included in the limit.

The relaxation for other higher voltage power sources is based on the relative levels of the power quality curves on ripple for different operating voltages.

At higher frequencies, the CE102 limit serves as a separate control from RE102 on potential radiation from power leads that may couple into sensitive antenna-connected receivers. The CE102 limits have been placed to ensure that there is no conflict with the RE102 limit. Emissions at the CE102 limit should not radiate above the RE102 limit. Laboratory experiments on coupling from a 2.5 meter power lead connected to a line impedance stabilization network have shown that the electric field detected by the RE102 rod antenna is flat with frequency up to approximately 10 MHz and is approximately equal to (x-40) dBµV/m, where "x" is the voltage expressed in dBµV. For example, if there is a signal level of 60 dBµV on the lead, the detected electric field level is approximately 20 dBµV/m.

Tailoring of the requirements in contractual documents may be desirable by the procuring activity. Adjusting the limit line to more closely emulate a spectral curve for a particular power quality standard is one possibility. Contributions from multiple interference sources need to be considered as noted above. If antenna-connected receivers are not present on the platform at the higher frequencies, tailoring of the upper frequency of the requirement is another possibility. The requirement is limited to an upper frequency of 10 MHz due to the allowable 2.5 meter length of power lead in the test setup approaching resonance. Any conducted measurements become less meaningful above this frequency. If tailoring is done to impose the requirement at higher frequencies, the test setup should be modified for CE102 to shorten the allowable length of the power leads.

If the alternate CE101 limit and procedure for high current loads has been used below 150 kHz, then CE102 may start at 150 kHz instead of 10 kHz. In this case, a 5 μH LISN (such as the one described in the DISCUSSION under 4.3.6) should be used. While the CE102 limit does not change, the use of the 5 μH LISN provides relief in EMI filter design for both differential and common mode noise. Differential mode noise is a voltage source which will establish the same voltage in a 5 or 50 μH LISN, but the 5 μH LISN allows more current to flow for the same potential, so the filter attenuation requirements are lower. Common mode noise is a current source, and the lower impedance of the 5 μH LISN means that for a given current less measured voltage results below about 3 MHz. At 3 MHz and above the 5 and 50 μH LISNs have the same impedance, but it is much easier to filter in this high frequency 50 ohm region than between 10 kHz and 3 MHz.

Test procedures: Emission levels are determined by measuring the voltage present at the output port on the LISN.

The power source impedance control provided by the LISN is a critical element of this test. This control is imposed due to wide variances in characteristics of shielded room filters and power line impedances among various test agencies and to provide repeatability through standardization. The LISN standardizes this impedance. The impedance present at the EUT electrical interface is influenced by the circuit characteristics of the power lead wires to the LISNs. The predominant characteristic is inductance. The impedance starts to deviate noticeably at approximately 1 MHz where the lead inductance is about 13 ohms.

A correction factor must be included in the data reduction to account for the 20 dB attenuator and for voltage drops across the coupling capacitor. This capacitor is in series with a parallel combination of the 50 ohm measurement receiver and the 1 kilohm LISN resistor. The two parallel resistances are equivalent to 47.6 ohms. The correction factor equals:

$$20 \log_{10}(1 + 5.60 \times 10^{-9}f^2)^{1/2}/(7.48 \times 10^{-5}f)$$

where f is the frequency of interest expressed in Hz. This equation is plotted on Figure A-11. The correction factor is 4.45 dB at 10 kHz and drops rapidly with frequency.

The upper measurement frequency is limited to 10 MHz because of resonance conditions with respect to the length of the power leads between the EUT and LISN. As noted in 4.3.8.6.2 of the main body of the standard, these leads are between 2.0 and 2.5 meters long. Laboratory experimentation and theory show a quarter-wave resonance close to 25 MHz for a 2.5 meter lead. In the laboratory experiment, the impedance of the power lead starts to rise significantly at 10 MHz and peaks at several thousand ohms at approximately 25 MHz. Voltage measurements at the LISN become largely irrelevant above 10 MHz.

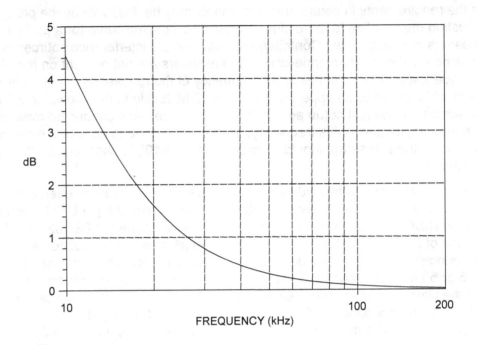

FIGURE A-11. Correction factor for 50 µH LISN coupling capacitor.

The 0.25 µF coupling capacitor in the LISN allows approximately 3.6 V to be developed across the 50 ohm termination on the signal port for 115 V, 400 Hz, power sources. The 20 dB attenuator is specified in the test procedure to protect the measurement receiver and to prevent overload. Sources of 60 Hz pose less of a concern.

An oscilloscope is necessary for the measurement system check on Figure CE102-1 to ensure that the actual applied voltage is measured accurately at 10 kHz and 100 kHz and maintains a sinusoidal shape. The LISN presents a 50 ohm load impedance to a 50 ohm signal generator only for frequencies of approximately 300 kHz or higher (see Figure 11). Since a 50 ohm signal generator is essentially an ideal voltage source in series with 50 ohms, the amplitude display setting of the generator is correct only when it is terminated in a matched impedance of 50 ohms. Under this condition the voltage splits between the two 50 ohm resistances. If the output is measured directly with a high impedance instrument, such as an oscilloscope, the indicated voltage is twice the amplitude setting. The load seen by the signal generator varies with frequency and the voltage at the LISN will also vary.

An area of concern for this test procedure is the potential to overload the measurement receiver due to the line voltage at the power frequency. Overload precautions are discussed in paragraph 4.3.7.3 of this standard. When an overload condition is predicted or encountered, a rejection filter can be used to attenuate the power frequency. A correction factor must be then included in the emission data to account for the filter loss with respect to frequency.

The CE102 test procedure for a 5 µH LISN is identical to that using a 50 µH LISN. The only difference is starting the test at 150 kHz. No correction factor is necessary for the coupling capacitor in the 5 µH LISN above 150 kHz.

As part of the measurement system integrity check, LISN impedance is spot-checked at the same frequencies as the traditional MSI check that verifies the test set-up and measurement procedures are correct. At 2 and 10 MHz, the 50 uH LISN impedance is automatically verified

208

by the traditional method, because at these frequencies the LISN impedance is 50 Ohms, so the signal generator level is what appears across the LISN, and if the LISN impedance is off, that will show up in the traditional check.

At 10 and 100 kHz, the 50 uH LISN impedance is lower than 50 Ohms and it loads a 50 Ohm signal source more than would a 50 Ohm load. The ratio of the rf potential across the LISN relative to that delivered into a 50 Ohm load is termed the insertion loss. Insertion loss is easily measured as an adjunct to the traditional MSI check.

Insertion loss is given by:

$$IL \ (dB) = 20 \log [2 * Z_{LISN} / (Z_{LISN} + 50)]$$

At 10 kHz, the 50 uH LISN impedance is 5 Ohms, so the insertion loss is -14.8 dB.
At 100 kHz, the 50 uH LISN impedance is 27 Ohms, so the insertion loss is -3.2 dB.
The tolerance on LISN impedance is +/- 20%, and that translates into +1.6 dB, -2 dB.

When using a 5 uH LISN, the impedance is 50 Ohms at and above 5 MHz, so the 50 Ohm portion of the LISN can be checked at 5 and 10 MHz in the traditional manner.

At 200 kHz, the 5 uH LISN impedance is 5.6 Ohms, so the insertion loss is 14 dB.
At 1 MHz, the 5 uH LISN impedance is 27 Ohms, so the insertion loss is -3.2 dB.

A.5.6 (5.6) CE106, conducted emissions, antenna terminal.

Applicability and limits: The requirement is applicable from 10 kHz to 40 GHz for transmitters, receivers and amplifiers. The basic concern is to protect antenna-connected receivers both on and off the platform from being degraded due to radiated interference from the antenna associated with the EUT. The limit for transmitters in the transmit mode is placed primarily at levels which are considered to be reasonably obtainable for most types of equipment. Suppression levels that are required to eliminate all potential electromagnetic compatibility situations are often much more severe and could result in significant design penalties. The limit for receivers and transmitters in standby is placed at a level that provides reasonable assurance of compatibility with other equipment. Common requirements are specified for all applications since the concerns are the same for all platforms.

As an example of an antenna coupling situation, consider a 10 watt VHF-AM transmitter operating at 150 MHz and a UHF-AM receiver with a sensitivity of -100 dBm tuned to 300 MHz with isotropic antennas located 10 meters apart. The requirement is that the transmitter second harmonic at 300 MHz must be down 50 + 10 log 10 = 60 dB. The free space loss equation. $P_R/P_T = (\lambda^2 G_T G_R)/(4\pi R)^2$ indicates an isolation of 42 dB between the two antennas.

P_R	= Received Power	G_R	= Receive Antenna Gain = 1
P_T	= Transmitted Power	G_T	= Transmitter Antenna Gain = 1
λ	= Wavelength = 1 meter	R	= Distance between Antennas = 10 meters

A second harmonic at the limit would be 60 + 42 = 102 dB down at the receiver. 102 dB below 10 Watts (40 dBm) is -62 dBm which is still 38 dB above the receiver sensitivity. The level that is actually required not to cause any degradation in the receiver is -123 dBm. This value results because the worst-case situation occurs when the interfering signal is competing with the sidebands of the intentional signal with a signal amplitude at the receiver sensitivity. For a standard tone of 30% AM used to verify sensitivity, the sidebands are 13 dB down from the carrier and a 10 dB signal-to-noise ratio is normally specified. To avoid problems, the interfering signal must, therefore, be 13 + 10 = 23 dB below -100 dBm or -123 dBm. This criterion would require the second harmonic to be 121 dB down from the transmitter carrier that could be a difficult task. Harmonic relationships can sometimes be addressed through frequency management actions to avoid problems.

Assessing the 34 dBμV (-73 dBm) requirement for standby, the level at the receiver would be -115 dBm which could cause some minimal degradation in the presence of a marginal intentional signal.

Greater antenna separation or antenna placement not involving direct line of sight would improve the situation. Also, the VHF antenna may be poorer than isotropic in the UHF band. CE106 does not take into account any suppression associated with frequency response characteristics of antennas; however, the results of the case cited are not unusual. RE103, which is a radiated emission control on spurious and harmonic outputs, includes assessment of antenna characteristics.

Since the free space loss equation indicates that isolation is proportional to the wavelength squared, isolation values improve rapidly as frequency increases. Also, antennas are generally more directional in the GHz region and receivers tend to be less sensitive due to larger bandwidths.

The procuring activity may consider tailoring contractual documents by establishing suppression levels based on antenna-to-antenna coupling studies on the particular platform where the equipment will be used. Another area could be relaxation of requirements for high power transmitters. The standard suppression levels may result in significant design penalties. For example, filtering for a 10,000 watt HF transmitter may be excessively heavy and substantially attenuate the fundamental frequency. Engineering trade-offs may be necessary.

For Navy surface ships, there are many instances of sensitive receivers operating within 10 m of high and medium power transmitters. These sensitive receivers are also installed on nearby surface and air platforms which operate within a few nautical miles of the transmitters. The frequency separation between these transmitters and receivers is often only a few percent of the fundamental, and sometimes their frequency ranges even overlap. To maximize the Navy's ability to use these systems simultaneously, the emissions of all of these transmitters must be kept as low as possible across a broad frequency range. For transmitters with peak transmit power less than 1 kW, the existing 5% frequency exclusion is considered appropriate. For transmitters with higher peak power additional relaxation is required and a range of 5 - 9% is considered achievable for the updated Navy limits. Many sensitive receivers have noise figures between 1 - 5 dB which results in a system noise floor between -113 to -109 dBm/MHz. To eliminate the risk of EMI, all spurious emissions would have to be greater than 10 dB below those levels in all configurations and operational scenarios. In many shipboard topside configurations, the isolation between systems can be as low as 60 dB. Taking this isolation into account results in an ideal limit of -63 dBm/MHz. Realizing that this ideal limit is very challenging, a level of -40 dBm/MHz has been selected. Compliance with this limit line is feasible and it will reduce the risk for EMI for typical installation geometries and scenarios. Compliance with this new limit will not always be enough to ensure that out of band emissions do not cause EMI for all geometries and as such tailoring is encouraged where warranted.

It should be noted that for simplification the absolute measurement limits are given in terms of power and not power spectral density. To be accurate the measured power should be given in terms of power per receiver bandwidth e.g. above 1 GHz the limit is more correctly stated in units of dBm/MHz since in that frequency range the receiver bandwidth is 1 MHz per Table II.

Test procedures: Since the test procedures measure emissions present on a controlled impedance, shielded, transmission line, the measurement results should be largely independent of the test setup configuration. Therefore, it is not necessary to maintain the basic test setup described in the main body of this standard.

The CE106 procedure uses a direct coupled technique and does not consider the effect that the antenna system characteristics will have on actual radiated levels.

The selection of modulation for transmitters and frequency, input power levels, and modulation for amplifiers can influence the results. The procedure requires that parameters that produce the worst case emission spectrum be used. The most complicated modulation will typically produce the worst case spectrum. The highest allowable drive level for amplifiers usually produces the worst harmonics and spurious outputs. However, some amplifiers with automatic gain controls may produce higher distortion with drive signals set to the lowest allowable input due to the amplifier producing the highest gain levels. The details of the analysis on the selection of test parameters should be included in the EMITP.

Figure CE106-3 is used for receivers and transmitters in the stand-by mode. The purpose of the attenuator pad on Figure CE106-3 is to establish a low voltage standing wave ratio (VSWR) for more accurate measurements. Its nominal value is 10 dB, but it can be smaller, if necessary, to maintain measurement sensitivity.

The setup on Figure CE106-1 is used for low power transmitters in which the highest intentionally generated frequency does not exceed 40 GHz. The attenuator pad should be approximately 20 dB or large enough to reduce the output level of the transmitter sufficiently so that it does not damage or overload the measurement receiver. The rejection network in the figure is tuned to the fundamental frequency of the EUT and is intended to reduce the transmitter power to a level that will not desensitize or induce spurious responses in the measurement receiver. Both the rejection network and RF pad losses must be adjusted to maintain adequate measurement system sensitivity. The total power reaching the measurement receiver input should not exceed the maximum allowable level specified by the manufacturer. All rejection and filter networks must be calibrated over the frequency range of measurement.

The setup of Figure CE106-2 is for transmitters with high average power. For transmitters with an integral antenna, it is usually necessary to measure the spurious emissions by the radiated procedures of RE103.

Some caution needs to be exercised in applying Table II. For spurious and harmonic emissions of equipment in the transmit mode, it is generally desirable for the measurement receiver bandwidth to be sufficiently large to include at least 90% of the power of the signal present at a tuned frequency. This condition is required if a comparison is being made to a power requirement in a specification. Spurious and harmonic outputs generally have the same modulation characteristics as the fundamental. Since this procedure measures relative levels of spurious and harmonic signal with respect to the fundamental, it is not necessary for the measurement receiver to meet the above receiver bandwidth to signal bandwidth criterion. However, if the measurement receiver bandwidth does not meet the criterion and spurious and harmonic outputs are located in frequency ranges where this standard specifies a bandwidth different than that used for the fundamental, the measurement receiver bandwidth should be changed to that used at the fundamental to obtain a proper measurement.

For EUTs having waveguide transmission lines, the measurement receiver needs to be coupled to the waveguide by a waveguide to coaxial transition. Since the waveguide acts as a high-pass filter, measurements are not necessary at frequencies less than 0.8 f_{co}, where f_{co} is the waveguide cut-off frequency.

A.5.7 (5.7) CS101, conducted susceptibility, power leads.

Applicability and limits: The requirement is applicable from 30 Hz to 150 kHz for power input leads that obtain power from other sources that are not part of the EUT. There is no requirement on power output leads. The basic concern is to ensure that equipment performance is not degraded from ripple voltages associated with allowable distortion of power source voltage waveforms.

The required signal is applicable only to the high sides on the basis that the concern is developing a differential voltage across the power input leads to the EUT. The series injection technique in the test procedure results in the voltage dropping across the impedance of the EUT power input circuitry. The impedance of the power return wiring is normally insignificant with respect to the power input over most of the required frequency range. Common mode voltages evaluations are addressed by other susceptibility tests such as CS114 and RS103. Injection on a power return will result in the same differential voltage across the power input; however, the unrealistic condition will result in a large voltage at the return connection to the EUT with respect to the ground plane.

Similar to CE102, the limits are based on a review of the power quality standards with emphasis toward the spectral content curves present in MIL-STD-704. Rather than having a separate curve for each possible power source voltage, only two curves are specified. The voltage amplitude specified is approximately 6 dB above typical power quality limits, although the limit has been somewhat generalized to avoid complex curves. The margin between the limit and the power quality standard is necessary to allow for variations in performance between manufactured items.

The difference between the limits for CE102 and CS101 of approximately 26 dB should not be viewed as a margin. The CE102 limit is placed so that ripple voltages do not exceed that allowed by the power quality standards due to interference contributions from multiple EUTs. Therefore, the power quality standard is the only valid basis of comparison.

The primary tailoring consideration for the procuring activity for contractual documents is adjustment of the limit to follow more closely a particular power quality standard.

Test procedures: Since the applied voltage is coupled in series using a transformer, Kirchhoff's voltage law requires that the voltage appearing across the transformer output terminals must drop around the circuit loop formed by the EUT input and the power source impedance. The voltage level specified in the limit is measured across the EUT input because part of the transformer induced voltage can be expected to drop across the source impedance.

The procedure allows the use of either an oscilloscope to make a time domain measurement or a measurement receiver with a transducer to make a frequency domain measurement. The transducer is used to isolate the 50 ohm measurement receiver from the power source voltage and to lower the signal amplitudes to safe levels. The transfer characteristics of the transducer with respect to the amplitude versus frequency need to be characterized across the frequency range of the test and applied to determine the actual signal level.

Earlier EMI standards introduced a circuit for a phase shift network which was intended to cancel out AC power waveforms and allow direct measurement of the ripple present across the EUT. While these devices very effectively cancel the power waveform, they return the incorrect value of the ripple and are not acceptable for use. The networks use the principle of inverting the phase of the input power waveform, adding it to the waveform (input power plus ripple) across the EUT, and presumably producing only the ripple as an output. For a clean power waveform, the network would perform properly. However, the portion of the ripple that drops across the power source impedance contaminates the waveform and gets recombined with the ripple across the EUT resulting in an incorrect value.

Below 10 kHz there is a possibility that a portion of the injected signal will drop across the power source rather than the test sample power input. Therefore, below 10 kHz when the specification limit potential cannot be developed across the test sample power input and the precalibrated power limit has been reached, it is incumbent on the tester to check that the missing signal level is not being dropped across the power source. If the missing potential is there (usually due to high impedance test facility EMI filters), then steps should be taken to lower the source impedance. This can be done on DC power by using a larger capacitor (~10,000 uF) in parallel with the 10 uF capacitor. With AC power that isn't possible and the best approach is to bypass facility EMI filters entirely, bringing unfiltered power into the room.

Voltages will appear across the primary side of the injection transformer due to the EUT current load at the power frequency. Larger current loads will result in larger voltages and are the predominant concern. These voltages can cause potential problems with the power amplifier. The circuit arrangement on Figure A-12 will substantially reduce this voltage and provide protection for the amplifier. This effect is accomplished by using a dummy load equal to the EUT and wiring the additional transformer so that its induced voltage is equal to and 180 degrees out of phase with the induced voltage in the injection transformer. If possible, the dummy load should have the same power factor as the EUT.

On initial turn on, DC to DC power switching converters can create large voltages on the primary side of the injection transformer that can damage the power amplifier. A precaution is to place a 5 ohm resistor across the primary and to disconnect the transformer during initial turn on.

The injected signal should be maintained as a sinusoid. Saturation of the power amplifier or coupling transformer may result in a distorted waveform.

If the return side of power is not connected to the shielded room ground, the oscilloscope may need to be electrically "floated" using an isolation transformer to correctly measure the injected voltage resulting in a potential shock hazard. Differential probe amplifiers are available which will convert a differential measurement between the high side and an isolated ground to a single-ended measurement where the measurement device can be grounded. These probes have an output that is suitable for measurement with either an oscilloscope or a high impedance, frequency selective, receiver (provided the receiver can tolerate the high input voltage).

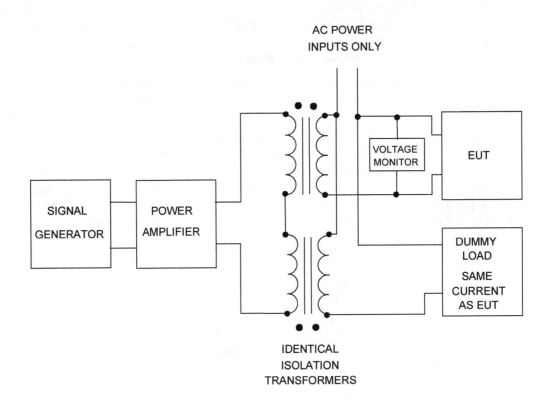

FIGURE A-12. CS101 power amplifier protection.

A.5.8 (5.8) CS103, conducted susceptibility, antenna port, intermodulation.

Applicability and limits: This receiver front-end susceptibility requirement is applicable from 15 kHz to 10 GHz for equipment and subsystems, such as communications receivers, RF amplifiers, transceivers, radar receivers, acoustic receivers, and electronic warfare receivers as specified in the individual procurement specification. The intent of this requirement is to control the response of antenna-connected receiving subsystems to in-band signals resulting from potential intermodulation products of two signals outside of the intentional passband of the subsystem produced by non-linearities in the subsystem. The requirement can be applied to receivers, transceivers, amplifiers, and the like. Due to the wide diversity of subsystem designs being developed, the applicability of this type of requirement and appropriate limits need to be determined for each procurement. Also, requirements need to be specified that are consistent with the signal processing characteristics of the subsystem and the particular test procedures to be used to verify the requirement.

One approach for determining levels required for the out-of-band signals is from an analysis of the electromagnetic environments present and characteristics of receiving antennas. However, levels calculated by this means will often place unreasonable design penalties on the receiver. For example, if an external environment of 200 V/m is imposed on a system, an isotropic antenna at 300 MHz will deliver 39 dBm to the receiver. This level represents a severe design requirement to many receivers. An alternative approach is to simply specify levels that are within the state-of-the-art for the particular receiver design.

This requirement is most applicable to fixed frequency, tunable, superheterodyne receivers. Previous versions of this standard required normal system performance with the two out-of-band signals to be 66 dB above the level required to obtain the standard reference output for the receiver. One signal was raised to 80 dB above the reference in the 2 to 25 MHz and 200 to 400 MHz bands to account for transmissions from HF and UHF communication equipment. Maximum levels for both signals were limited to 10 dBm. As an example, conventional communication receivers commonly have sensitivities on the order of -100 dBm. For this case, the 66 dB above reference signal is at -34 dBm and the 80 dB above reference signal is at -20 dBm. Both are substantially below the 10 dBm maximum used in the past.

For other types of receivers, application of this requirement is often less straightforward and care must be taken to ensure that any applied requirements are properly specified. Many receivers are designed to be interference or jam resistant and this feature may make application of this requirement difficult or inappropriate.

One complicating factor is that one of the out-of-band signals typically is modulated with a waveform normally used by the receiver. For receivers that process a very specific modulation, the issue exists whether an out-of-band signal can reasonably be expected to contain that modulation. Another complicating factor is related to the potential intermodulation products resulting from two signals. Responses from intermodulation products can be predicted to occur when $f_o = mf_1 \pm nf_2$ where f_o is the operating frequency of the receiver, m and n are integers, and f_1 and f_2 are the out-of-band signals. For receivers which continuously change frequency (such as frequency agile or frequency hopping), the relationship will be true only for a portion of the operating time of the receiver, unless the out-band-signals are also continuously tuned or the receiver operating characteristics are modified for the purpose of evaluation.

Test procedures: No test procedures are provided in the main body of this standard for this requirement. Because of the large variety of receiver designs being developed, the requirements for the specific operational characteristics of a receiver must be established before meaningful test procedures can be developed. Only general testing techniques are discussed in this appendix.

Intermodulation testing can be applied to a variety of receiving subsystems such as receivers, RF amplifiers, transceivers and transponders.

Several receiver front-end characteristics must be known for proper testing for intermodulation responses. These characteristics generally should be determined by test. The maximum signal input that the receiver can tolerate without overload needs to be known to ensure that the test levels are reasonable and that the test truly is evaluating intermodulation effects. The bandpass characteristics of the receiver are important for determining frequencies near the receiver fundamental f_o that will be excluded from test. Requirements for this test are generally expressed in terms of a relative degree of rejection by specifying the difference in level between potentially interfering signals and the established sensitivity of the receiver under test. Therefore, determination of the sensitivity of the receiver is a key portion of the test.

The basic concept with this test is to combine two out-of-band signals and apply them to the antenna port of the receiver while monitoring the receiver for an undesired response. One of the out-of-band signals is normally modulated with the modulation expected by the receiver. The second signal is normally continuous wave (CW). Figure A-13 shows a general setup for this test.

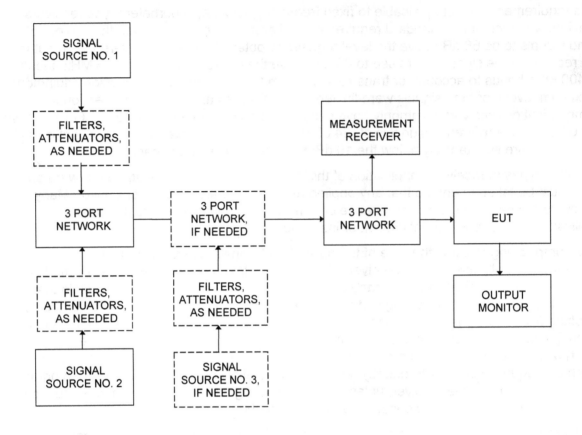

FIGURE A-13. CS103 General test setup.

For applications where the receiver would not provide an indication of interference without a receive signal being present, a third signal can be used at the fundamental. This arrangement may also be suitable for some receivers that process a very specialized type of modulation which would never be expected on an out-of-band signal. An option is for the two out-of-band signals to be CW for this application.

The frequency of the two out-of-band signals should be set such that $f_o = 2f_1 - f_2$ where f_o is the tuned frequency of the receiver and f_1 and f_2 are the frequencies of the signal sources. This equation represents a third order intermodulation product, which is the most common response observed in receivers. f_1 and f_2 should be swept or stepped over the desired frequency range while maintaining the relationship in the equation. It is important to verify that any responses noted during this test are due to intermodulation responses. Responses can result from simply lack of rejection to one of the applied signals or from harmonics of one of the signal sources. Turning off each signal source in turn and noting whether the response remains can demonstrate the source of the response.

For receivers with front-end mixing and filtering in an antenna module, the test may need to be designed to be performed on a radiated basis. All signals would need to be radiated and assurances provided that any observed intermodulation products are due to the receiver and not caused by items in the test area. The EMITP would need to address antenna types, antenna locations, antenna polarizations and field measurement techniques. This test would probably need to be performed in an anechoic chamber.

For frequency hopping receivers, one possible approach is choose an f_o within the hop set and set up the signals sources as described above. The performance of the receiver could then be evaluated as the receiver hops. If the frequency hopping receiver has a mode of operation using just one fixed frequency, this mode should also be tested.

A common error made in performing this test procedure is attributing failures to the EUT which are actually harmonics of the signal source or intermodulation products generated in the test setup. Therefore, it is important to verify that the signals appearing at the EUT antenna port are only the intended signals through the use of a measurement receiver as shown on Figure A-13. Damaged, corroded, and faulty components can cause signal distortion resulting in misleading results. Monitoring will also identify path losses caused by filters, attenuators, couplers, and cables.

Typical data for this test procedure for the EMITR are the sensitivity of the receiver, the levels of the signal sources, frequency ranges swept, operating frequencies of the receivers, and frequencies and threshold levels associated with any responses.

A.5.9 (5.9) CS104, conducted susceptibility, antenna port, rejection of undesired signals.

Applicability and limits: This receiver front-end susceptibility requirement is applicable from 30 Hz to 20 GHz for equipment and subsystems, such as communications receivers, RF amplifiers, transceivers, radar receivers, acoustic receivers, and electronic warfare receivers as specified in the individual procurement specification. The intent of this requirement is to control the response of antenna-connected receiving subsystems to signals outside of the intentional passband of the subsystem. The requirement can be applied to receivers, transceivers, amplifiers, and the like. Due to the wide diversity of subsystem designs being developed, the applicability of this type of requirement and appropriate limits need to be determined for each procurement. Also, requirements need to be specified that are consistent with the signal processing characteristics of the subsystem and the particular test procedures to be used to verify the requirement.

One approach for determining levels required for the out-of-band signal can be determined from an analysis of the electromagnetic environments present and characteristics of receiving antennas. However, levels calculated by this means will often place unreasonable design penalties on the receiver. For example, if an external environment of 200 V/m is imposed on a system, an isotropic antenna at 300 MHz will deliver 39 dBm to the receiver. This level represents a severe design requirement to many receivers. An alternative approach is to simply specify levels that are within the state-of-the-art for the particular receiver design.

This requirement is most applicable to fixed frequency, tunable, superheterodyne receivers. Previous versions of this standard required normal system performance for a 0 dBm signal outside of the tuning range of the receiver and a signal 80 dB above the level producing the standard reference output within the tuning range (excluding the receiver passband within the 80 dB points on the selectivity curve). As an example, a conventional UHF communication receiver operating from 225 MHz to 400 MHz commonly has a sensitivity on the order of -100 dBm. For this case, the 0 dBm level applies below 225 MHz and above 400 MHz. Between 225 MHz and 400 MHz (excluding the passband), the required level is -20 dBm.

For other types of receivers, application of this requirement is often less straightforward and care must be taken to ensure that any applied requirements are properly specified. Many receivers are designed to be interference or jam resistant and this feature may make application of this requirement difficult or inappropriate.

This requirement is usually specified using either one or two signals. With the one signal requirement, the signal is out-of-band to the receiver and is modulated with a waveform normally used by the receiver. No in-band signal is used. For receivers that process a very specific modulation, the issue exists whether an out-of-band signal can reasonably be expected to contain that modulation. An alternative is to specify the requirement for two signals. An in-band signal can be specified which contains the normal receiver modulation. The out-of-band signal can be modulated or unmodulated with the criterion being that no degradation in reception of the intentional signal is allowed.

Test procedures: No test procedures are provided in the main body of this standard for this requirement. Because of the large variety of receiver designs being developed, the requirements for the specific operational characteristics of a receiver must be established before meaningful test procedures can be developed. Only general testing techniques are discussed in this appendix.

Front-end rejection testing can be applied to a variety of receiving subsystems such as receivers, RF amplifiers, transceivers, and transponders.

Several receiver front-end characteristics must be known for proper testing. These characteristics generally should be determined by test. The maximum signal input that the receiver can tolerate without overload needs to be known to ensure that the test levels are reasonable. The bandpass characteristics of the receiver are important for determining frequencies near the receiver fundamental that will be excluded from testing. Requirements for this test are often expressed in terms of a relative degree of rejection by specifying the difference in level between a potentially interfering signal and the established sensitivity of the receiver under test. Therefore, determination of the sensitivity of the receiver is a key portion of the test.

The basic concept with this test procedure is to apply out-of-band signals to the antenna port of the receiver while monitoring the receiver for degradation. Figure A-14 shows a general test setup for this test. There are two common techniques used for performing this test using either one or two signal sources. For the one signal source procedure, the signal source is modulated with the modulation expected by the receiver. It is then swept over the appropriate frequency ranges while the receiver is monitored for unintended responses. With the two signal source procedure, a signal appropriately modulated for the receiver is applied at the tuned frequency of the receiver. The level of this signal is normally specified to be close to the sensitivity of the receiver. The second signal is unmodulated and is swept over the appropriate frequency ranges while the receiver is monitored for any change in its response to the intentional signal.

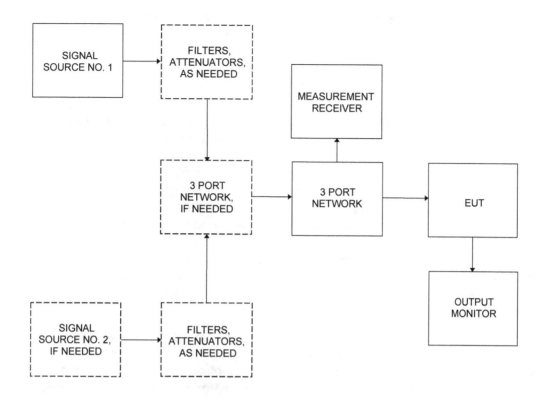

FIGURE A-14. CS104 General test setup.

The two signal source procedure is more appropriate for most receivers. The one signal source procedure may be more appropriate for receivers that search for a signal to capture since they may respond differently once a signal has been captured. Some receivers may need to be evaluated using both procedures to be completely characterized.

For frequency hopping receivers, one possible approach is to use a one signal procedure as if the EUT did not have a tuned frequency (include frequency scanning across the hop set) to evaluate the jamming/interference resistance of the receiver. If a frequency hopping receiver has a mode of operation using just one fixed frequency, this mode should also be tested.

For receivers with front-end mixing and filtering in an antenna module, the test may need to be designed to be performed on a radiated basis. All signals would need to be radiated and assurances provided that any observed responses are due to the receiver and not caused by items in the test area. The EMITP would need to address antenna types, antenna locations, antenna polarizations, and field measurement techniques. This test would probably need to be performed in an anechoic chamber.

A common error made in performing this test procedure is attributing failures to the EUT which are actually harmonics or spurious outputs of the signal source. Therefore, it is important to verify that the signals appearing at the EUT antenna port are only the intended signals through the use of a measurement receiver as shown on Figure A-14. Damaged, corroded, and faulty components can cause signal distortion resulting in misleading results. Monitoring will also identify path losses caused by filters, attenuators, couplers, and cables.

Typical data for this test procedure for the EMITR are the sensitivity of the receiver, the levels of the signal sources, frequency ranges swept, operating frequencies of the receivers, degree of rejection (dB), and frequencies and threshold levels associated with any responses.

A.5.10 (5.10) CS105, conducted susceptibility, antenna port, cross modulation.

Applicability and limits: This receiver front-end susceptibility requirement is applicable from 30 Hz to 20 GHz only for receivers that normally process amplitude-modulated RF signals, as specified in the individual procurement specification. The intent of this requirement is to control the response of antenna-connected receiving subsystems to modulation being transferred from an out-of-band signal to an in-band signal. This effect results from a strong, out-of-band signal near the operating frequency of the receiver that modulates the gain in the front-end of the receiver and adds amplitude varying information to the desired signal. The requirement should be considered only for receivers, transceivers, amplifiers, and the like, which extract information from the amplitude modulation of a carrier. Due to the wide diversity of subsystem designs being developed, the applicability of this type of requirement and appropriate limits need to be determined for each procurement. Also, requirements need to be specified that are consistent with the signal processing characteristics of the subsystem and the particular test procedure to be used to verify the requirement.

One approach for determining levels required for the out-of-band signal can be determined from an analysis of the electromagnetic environments present and characteristics of receiving antennas. However, levels calculated by this means will often place unreasonable design penalties on the receiver. For example, if an external environment of 200 V/m is imposed on a system, an isotropic antenna at 300 MHz will deliver 39 dBm to the receiver. This level represents a severe design requirement to many receivers. An alternative approach is to simply specify levels that are within the state-of-the-art for the particular receiver design.

This requirement is most applicable to fixed frequency, tunable, superheterodyne receivers. Previous versions of this standard required normal system performance with an out-of-band signal to be 66 dB above the level required to obtain the standard reference output for the receiver. The maximum level for the signal was limited to 10 dBm. As an example, conventional communication receivers commonly have sensitivities on the order of -100 dBm. For this example, the 66 dB above reference signal is at -34 dBm that is substantially below the 10 dBm maximum used in the past.

For other types of receivers, application of this requirement is often less straightforward and care must be taken to ensure that any applied requirements are properly specified. Many receivers are designed to be interference or jam resistant and this feature may make application of this requirement difficult or inappropriate.

One complicating factor is that one of the out-of-band signals typically is modulated with a waveform normally used by the receiver. For receivers that process a very specific modulation, the issue exists whether an out-of-band signal can reasonably be expected to contain that modulation. Another factor is that the out-of-band signal is normally specified to be close to the receiver operating frequency. For receivers that continuously change frequency (such as frequency agile or frequency hopping), an appropriate relationship may exist for only short periods for a fixed frequency out-of-band signal.

Test procedures: No test procedures are provided in the main body of this standard for this requirement. Because of the large variety of receiver designs being developed, the requirements for the specific operational characteristics of a receiver must be established before meaningful test procedures can be developed. Only general testing techniques are discussed in this appendix.

Cross modulation testing should be applied only to receiving subsystems such as receivers, RF amplifiers, transceivers and transponders which extract information from the amplitude modulation of a carrier.

Several receiver front-end characteristics must be known for proper testing for cross modulation responses. These characteristics generally should be determined by test. The maximum signal input that the receiver can tolerate without overload needs to be known to ensure that the test levels are reasonable. The bandpass characteristics of the receiver are important for determining frequencies near the receiver fundamental that will be excluded from test. Requirements for this test are generally expressed in terms of a relative degree of rejection by specifying the difference in level between potentially interfering signals and the established sensitivity of the receiver under test. Therefore, determination of the sensitivity of the receiver is a key portion of the test.

The basic concept with this test is to apply a modulated signal out-of-band to the receiver and to determine whether the modulation is transferred to an unmodulated signal at the receiver's tuned frequency resulting in an undesired response. There may be cases where the in-band signal needs to be modulated if the receiver characteristics so dictate. The level of the in-band signal is normally adjusted to be close to the receiver's sensitivity. The out-of-band signal is modulated with the modulation expected by the receiver. It is then swept over the appropriate frequency ranges while the receiver is monitored for unintended responses. Testing has typically been performed over a frequency range ± the receiver intermediate frequency (IF) centered on the receiver's tuned frequency. Figure A-12 shows a general setup for this test.

For receivers with front-end mixing and filtering in an antenna module, the test may need to be designed to be performed on a radiated basis. All signals would need to be radiated and assurances provided that any responses are due to the receiver and not caused by items in the test area. The EMITP would need to address antenna types, antenna locations, antenna polarizations and field measurement techniques. This test would probably need to be performed in an anechoic chamber.

For frequency hopping receivers, one possible approach is choose an f_o within the hop set and set up the signals sources as described above. The performance of the receiver could then be evaluated as the receiver hops. If the frequency hopping receiver has a mode of operation using just one fixed frequency, this mode should also be tested.

It is important to verify that the signals appearing at the EUT antenna port are only the intended signals through the use of a measurement receiver as shown on Figure A-15. Damaged, corroded, and faulty components can cause signal distortion resulting in misleading results. Monitoring will also identify path losses caused by filters, attenuators, couplers, and cables.

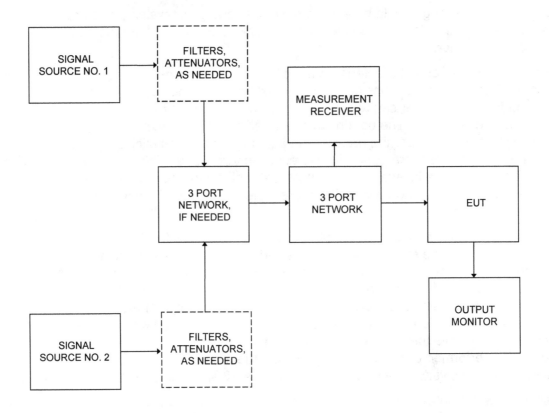

FIGURE A-15. CS105 General test setup.

Typical data for this test procedure for the EMITR are the sensitivity of the receiver, the levels of the signal sources, frequency ranges swept, operating frequencies of the receivers, and frequencies and threshold levels associated with any responses.

A.5.11 (5.11) CS109, conducted susceptibility, structure current.

Applicability and limits: This requirement is specialized and is intended to be applied from 60 Hz to 100 kHz only for very sensitive equipment (1 µV or better), such as tuned receivers operating over the frequency range of the test. The basic concern of the requirement is to ensure that equipment does not respond to magnetic fields caused by currents flowing in platform structure and through EUT housing materials. The magnetic fields are sufficiently low that there is no concern with most circuitry.

An estimate can be made of induced voltages that may result from the required CS109 currents. Magnetic fields act by inducing voltages into loop areas in accordance with Faraday's law ($V = -d\phi/dt$). For a constant magnetic field perpendicular to a given loop area, Faraday's law reduces to $V = -2\pi f B A$ where:

f = Frequency of Interest

B = Magnetic Flux Density

A = Loop Area

Since Faraday's law indicates that these voltages are proportional to frequency, the maximum voltage from the CS109 currents will result at the 20 kHz knee of the curve for a given loop area. A drop of 20 dB/decade would result in a constant voltage. Since the curve is dropping at only 10 dB/decade below 20 kHz, the induced voltage will rise as frequency increases. The sharp drop off above 20 kHz results in decreasing voltages with increasing frequency.

If the 103 dBμA current at 20 kHz specified in the requirement is assumed to spread uniformly over a cross-sectional dimension of 10 cm, the surface current density and the resulting magnetic field intensity at the surface would be 1.41 amperes/meter. In air, this value corresponds to magnetic flux density of 1.77×10^{-6} Tesla. If it is further assumed that this magnetic field is uniform over a circuit loop area of 0.001 m^2 (such as 20 cm by 0.5 cm) within the enclosure, Faraday's Law predicts an induced voltage of 222 μV.

Similar calculations at 400 Hz and 100 kHz yield values of 31 μV and 8 μV, respectively.

It is apparent that design considerations such as proper grounding techniques, minimizing of loop areas, and common mode rejection concepts need to be implemented to prevent potential problems with very sensitive circuits used in submarines such as low frequency tuned receivers. However, these levels are well below the sensitivity of typical circuits used in other equipment.

The limit is derived from operational problems due to current conducted on equipment cabinets and laboratory measurements of response characteristics of selected receivers.

No tailoring is recommended.

Test procedures: Electrical connection needs to be made to the external structure of the EUT and damage to the external finish should be minimized. Screws or protuberances at ground potential near the diagonal corners of the EUT should normally be used as test points. Connections should be made with clip or clamp type leads. If convenient test points are not available at the diagonal corners, a sharply pointed test probe should be used to penetrate the finish in place of the clip or clamp type lead.

The requirement to maintain the leads perpendicular to the surface for at least 50 cm is to minimize effects on the path of current along the surface from the magnetic fields caused by the current in the leads.

Coupling transformers used to perform CS101 testing are normally suitable for this test. The electrical isolation provided by the coupling transformer eliminates the need to electrically "float" the amplifier and signal source that could result in a potential shock hazard.

A.5.12 (5.12) CS114, conducted susceptibility, bulk cable injection.

Applicability and limits: The requirements are applicable from 10 kHz to 200 MHz for all electrical cables interfacing with the EUT enclosures. The basic concept is to simulate currents that will be developed on platform cabling from electromagnetic fields generated by antenna transmissions both on and off the platform. Investigation into aircraft carrier hangar deck electromagnetic environment test data from nine aircraft carriers showed that significant HF electric field levels are present. Measurements from on-board HF transmitters showed field levels in the 2 to 30 MHz band up to 42 V/m in the hanger deck. Therefore, for equipment located in the aircraft hangar deck, the same limit that is used for non-metallic ships (below decks), is being used in the 2 to 30 MHz frequency range. In addition, a low frequency limit (77 dBμA) has been added from 4 kHz to 1 MHz for EUTs on surface ships and submarines with solid state power generation (in contrast to electromechanical generation equipment) to simulate common mode currents that have been found to be present on AC power cables. The measured common mode currents have exceeded the previous CS114 Ships (metallic, below decks) and submarines (internal) limits by up to 50 dB.

An advantage of this type of requirement is that it provides data that can be directly related to induced current levels measured during platform-level evaluations. An increasingly popular technique is to illuminate the platform with a low level, relatively uniform field while monitoring induced levels on cables. Then, either laboratory data can be reviewed or current injection done at the platform with the measured currents scaled to the full threat level. This same philosophy has been applied to lightning and electromagnetic pulse testing.

Due to size constraints and available field patterns during radiated susceptibility testing (such as RS103), it has long been recognized that cabling cannot be properly excited to simulate platform effects at lower frequencies. The most notable example of this situation is experience with HF (2 - 30 MHz) radio transmissions. HF fields have caused numerous problems in platforms through cable coupling. However, equipment items rarely exhibit problems in this frequency range during laboratory testing.

The limits are primarily derived from testing on aircraft that were not designed to have intentionally shielded volumes. The basic structure is electrically conductive; however, there was no attempt to ensure continuous electrical bonding between structure members or to close all apertures. The shape of the limit reflects the physics of the coupling with regard to resonant conditions and the cable length with respect to the interfering frequency wavelength. At frequencies below resonance, coupling is proportional to frequency (20 dB/decade slope). Above resonance, coupled levels are cyclic with frequency with a flat maximum value. The 10 dB/decade decrease in the limit level at the upper frequency portion is based on actual induced levels in the aircraft testing data base when worst-case measurements for the various aircraft are plotted together. From coupling theory for a specific cable, the decrease would be expected to be cyclic with frequency with an envelope slope of 40 dB/decade.

The basic relationship for the limit level in the resonance (flat) portion of the curve is 1.5 mA per V/m that is derived from worst-case measurements on aircraft. For example, 110 dBμA corresponds to 200 V/m. At resonance, the effective shielding effectiveness of the aircraft can be zero. Application of these results to other platforms is reasonable.

The frequency range of 10 kHz to 200 MHz is now standardized for all applications. The optional frequency range of 200 MHz to 400 MHz is deleted because of the questionable validity of performing bulk cable measurements at higher frequencies.

For submarines, the CS114 limit now distinguishes between equipment located internal versus external to the pressure hull. For equipment installed internal to the pressure hull, the curve 2 limit is now specified above 30 MHz to account for portable transmitters used within the submarine. For equipment located external to the pressure hull, stricter limits are imposed to more closely reflect the electromagnetic environment. The external CS114 limits should be applied only to equipment that is required to be fully operational when located above the waterline. Separate limits are specified, which are less severe, for equipment that is "external" to the pressure hull but located within the submarine superstructure (metallic boundary).

The limit may be tailored by the procuring activity in contractual documents with a curve whose amplitude is based on the expected field intensity for the installation and with a breakpoint for the curve based on the lowest resonance associated with the platform. Tailoring of the frequency of application can be done based on the operating frequencies of antenna-radiating equipment. Tailoring should also include transmitters that are not part of the platform. For equipment used in benign environments, the requirement may not be necessary.

Test procedures: This type of test is often considered as a bulk current test since current is the parameter measured. However, it is important to note that the test signal is inductively coupled and that Faraday's law predicts an induced voltage in a circuit loop with the resultant current and voltage distribution dependent on the various impedances present. For this reason, the test method under MIL-STD-461G reverts to an older method than was used in MIL-STD-461D and MIL-STD-462D. Instead of leveling primarily on the cable-induced current, the pre-calibrated forward power is the primary target, with only a frequency-independent induced cable current limit equal to 6 dB above the flat (maximum) portion of the applicable limit. With this older method, which is found in SAE ARP1972, and RTCA DO-160C/D, the relationship between the Bulk Cable Injection (BCI) cable currents and those induced by radiated fields will agree more closely for shielded cables, while being no different for unshielded cables.

It should be noted that the method used for MIL-STD-461E and MIL-STD-461F works well with heuristically determined cable currents such as in DEF STAN 59-411, because there the previously measured cable current is in fact the target, not the precalibrated forward power. With limits based on the physics of field-to-wire coupling as described in previous paragraphs, controlling the induced potential and allowing the current to be determined by the cable impedance is the proper technique.

The calibration fixture with terminations is a 50 ohm transmission line. Since the injection probe is around the center conductor within the fixture, a signal is being induced in the loop formed by the center conductor, the two 50 ohm loads, and the structure of the fixture to which the 50 ohm loads are terminated. From a loop circuit standpoint, the two 50 ohm loads are in series, providing a total loop impedance of 100 ohms. Because of the transmission line configuration, inductance effects are minimized. Measurement of induced current levels is performed by measuring a corresponding voltage across one of the 50 ohm loads. Since the 50 ohm loads are in series for the induced signal, the total drive voltage is actually two times that being measured.

The actual current that appears on a tested cable from the pre-calibrated drive signal depends on the loop impedance associated with the cable and the source impedance characteristics of the drive probe and amplifier. If the loop impedance is low, such as would often result with an overall shielded cable, currents greater than those in the calibration fixture will result. The maximum required current is limited to 6 dB above the flat plateau portion of the pre-calibration current limit.

In the past, MIL-STD-462 included a test procedure, CS02, which specified capacitive coupling of a voltage onto individual power leads. As is the case for this test procedure, CS02 assessed the effect of voltages induced from electromagnetic fields. CS114 improves on CS02 by inducing levels on all wires at a connector interface simultaneously (common mode) which better simulates actual platform use. Also, a deficiency existed with CS02 since the RF signals were induced only on power leads. This test procedure is applicable to all EUT cabling.

The requirement to generate loop circuit characterization data has been removed from this version of the standard. The information was not being used as it was originally envisioned.

A commonly used calibration fixture is shown on Figure A-16. Other designs are available. The top is removable to permit the lower frequency probes to physically fit. The calibration fixture can be scaled to accommodate larger injection probes. Figure A-17 displays the maximum VSWR that this calibration fixture should exhibit when measured without a current probe installed in the fixture. The presence of a probe will usually improve the VSWR of the fixture.

NOTE: VERTICAL CROSS-SECTION AT CENTER OF FIXTURE SHOWN

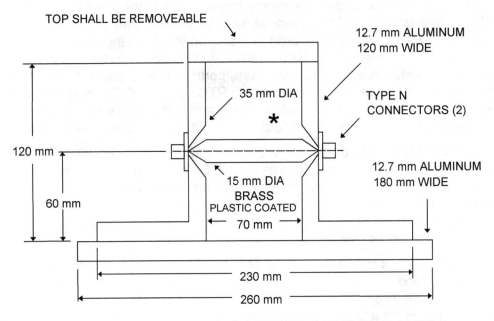

FIGURE A-16. Typical CS114 calibration fixture.

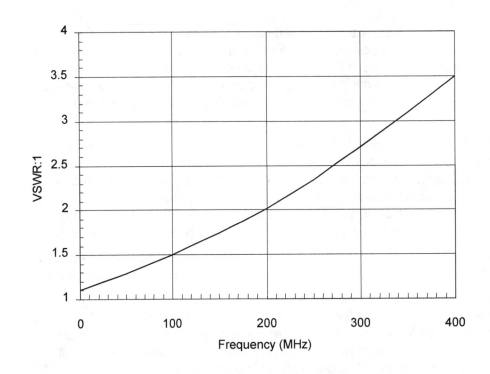

FIGURE A-17. Maximum VSWR of calibration fixture.

An advantage of this type of conducted testing as compared to radiated susceptibility testing is that voltage and current levels can be more easily induced on the interfaces that are comparable to those present in installations. The physical dimensions of the EUT cabling in a test setup are often not large enough compared to the installation for efficient coupling at lower frequencies.

In the past, some platform-level problems on Navy aircraft could not be duplicated in the laboratory using the standard test procedures in earlier versions of this standard. It was determined that differences between the aircraft installation and laboratory setups regarding the laboratory ground plane and avionics (aircraft electronics) mounting and electrical bonding practices were responsible. Most avionics are mounted in racks and on mounting brackets. At RF, the impedances to general aircraft structure for the various mounting schemes can be significantly different than they are with the avionics mounted on a laboratory ground plane. In the laboratory, it is not always possible to produce a reasonable simulation of the installation. A ground plane interference (GPI) test was developed to detect potential failures due to the higher impedance. In the GPI test, each enclosure of the EUT, in turn, is electrically isolated above the ground plane and a voltage is applied between the enclosure and the ground plane to simulate potential differences that may exist in the installation. Since CS114 provides similar common mode stresses at electrical interfaces as the GPI, the GPI is not included in this standard. However, the Navy may prefer to perform an additional susceptibility scan for aircraft applications with an inductor placed between the EUT enclosure and ground plane to more closely emulate the results of a GPI setup. The primary side of a typical CS101 injection transformer is considered to be an appropriate inductor.

CS114 has several advantages over the GPI as a general evaluation procedure. The GPI often results in significant current with little voltage developed at lower frequencies. CS114 is a controlled current test. A concern with the GPI test, which is not associated with CS114, is that the performance of interface filtering can be altered due to isolation of the enclosure from the ground plane. The results of CS114 are more useful since the controlled current can be compared with current levels present in the actual installation induced from fields. This technique has commonly been used in the past for certification of aircraft as safe to fly.

Testing is required on both entire power cables and power cables with the returns removed to evaluate common mode coupling to configurations that may be present in different installations. In some installations, the power returns are routed with the high side wiring. In other installations, power returns are tied to system structure near the utilization equipment with system structure being used as the power return path.

Insertion loss characteristics of injection probes are specified on Figure CS114-2 of the test procedure. A control on insertion loss has been found to be necessary to obtain consistency in test results. Insertion loss is measured as shown on Figure A-18. It is the difference in dB of the power applied to the probe installed in the calibration fixture and the power level detected by the measurement receiver. Lower insertion loss indicates more efficient coupling. Since the signal level that is induced in the calibration fixture is equally divided between the 50 ohm coaxial load and the measurement receiver, the lowest possible loss is 3 dB. The use of a network analyzer or measurement receiver that includes a tracking generator can simplify the measurement.

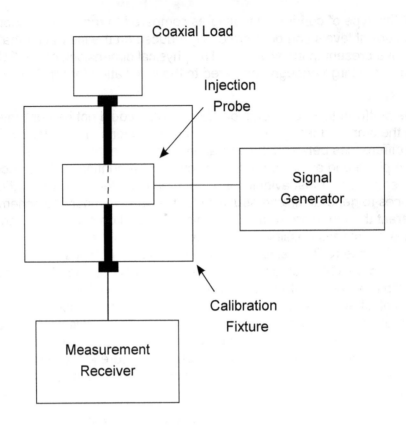

FIGURE A-18. Insertion loss measurement.

Techniques using network analyzers or spectrum analyzers with tracking generators can simplify the measurements for both 5.13.3.4b calibration and 5.13.3.4c EUT testing portions of the procedure. For example, the output signal can first be set to a predetermined value such as one mW and the flatness of the signal with frequency can be separately verified through a direct connection to the receiver. With this same signal then applied to the directional coupler, the induced level in the calibration fixture can be directly plotted.

Ideal bulk cable monitor probes would have no effect on the circuit under test. In reality, there is a transfer function associated with insertion into the calibration or test circuit (not to be confused with insertion loss). However, a well-engineered probe might introduce only a 1 dB response change after introduction into the 100 Ω calibration circuit. There are other problems that might be encountered when conducting a bulk cable test; loose or damaged connections and center pins, damaged cables, bad attenuators and terminations; overheated injection or monitor probe, and incorrect monitor probe factors. In computer controlled systems, it is possible to cross the two spectrum analyzers or use of the probe outside of an appropriate band without realizing it. These will never be discovered while conducting the test.

The lower frequency limit for ships and submarines has been extended to 4 kHz to simulate common mode currents that have been found to be present on AC power cables for EUTs installed on platforms with solid state power generation (ships and submarines). The calibration limit from 4 kHz to 10 kHz is 77 dBμA. This limit is achievable with 100 watt power amplifier and an injection probe which complies with the insertion loss requirement of Figure CS114-2b. A possible alternative to the injection probe method below 10 kHz is to utilize a CS101 injection transformer in each power lead and to drive all in parallel. The common mode current is measured between the injection transformers and the EUT power input. The alternative method for a three-phase ungrounded power system is shown schematically on Figure A-19.

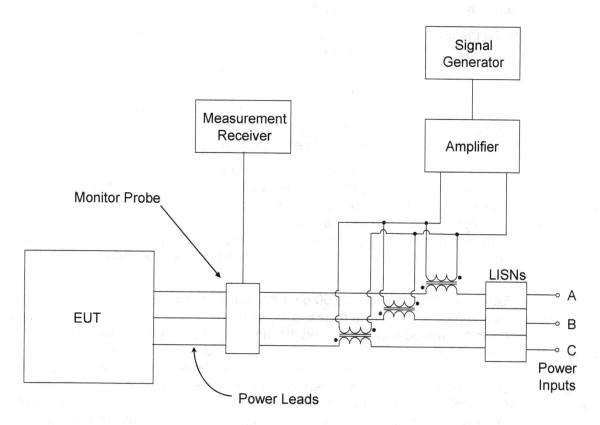

FIGURE A-19. CS114 alternate test setup, three phase ungrounded power system.

A.5.13 (5.13) CS115, conducted susceptibility, bulk cable injection, impulse excitation.

Applicability and limits: The requirements are applicable to all electrical cables interfacing with EUT enclosures. The basic concern is to protect equipment from fast rise and fall time transients that may be present due to platform switching operations and external transient environments such as lightning and electromagnetic pulse. The requirement is intended to replace "chattering relay" type requirements (RS06 in MIL-STD-461C) commonly used in procurements of equipment for aircraft applications in the past. The chattering relay has been criticized as unscientific and non-repeatable. The CS115 requirement has a defined waveform and a repeatable coupling mechanism.

The 2 nanosecond rise time is consistent with rise times possible for the waveforms created by inductive devices interrupted by switching actions. The 30 nanosecond pulse width standardizes the energy in individual pulses. In addition, it separates the rising and falling portions of the pulse so that each may act independently. Also, each portion may affect different circuits. The 5 ampere amplitude (500 V across 100 ohm loop impedance calibration fixture) covers most induced levels that have been observed during system-level testing of aircraft to transient environments. The 30 Hz pulse rate is specified to ensure that a sufficient number of pulses are applied to provide confidence that the equipment will not be upset.

Many circuit interfaces are configured such that potential upset is possible for only a small percentage of the total equipment operating time. For example, a microprocessor may sequentially poll various ports for input information. A particular port may continuously update information between polling intervals. If the transient occurs at the time the port is accessed, an upset condition may result. At other times, no effect may occur.

Possible tailoring by the procuring activity for contractual documents is lowering or raising the required amplitude based on the expected transient environments in the platform. Another option is to adjust the pulse width based on a particular environment onboard a platform or for control of the energy content of the pulse.

Test procedures: The excitation waveform from the generator is a trapezoidal pulse. The actual waveform on the interconnecting cable will be dependent on natural resonance conditions associated with the cable and EUT interface circuit parameters.

A circuit diagram of the 50 ohm, charged line, pulse generator required by CS115 is shown on Figure A-20. Its operation is essentially the same as impulse generators used to calibrate measurement receivers except that the pulse width is much longer. A direct current power supply is used to charge the capacitance of an open-circuited 50 ohm coaxial line. The high voltage relay is then switched to the output coaxial line to produce the pulse. The pulse width is dependent upon the length of the charge line. The relay needs to have bounce-free contact operation.

The calibration fixture with terminations is a 50 ohm transmission line. Since the injection probe is around the center conductor within the fixture, a signal is being induced in the loop formed by the center conductor, the two 50 ohm loads, and the structure of the fixture to which the 50 ohm loads are terminated. From a loop circuit standpoint, the two 50 ohm loads are in series, providing a total loop impedance of 100 ohms. Because of the transmission line configuration, inductance effects are minimized. Measurement of induced current levels is performed by measuring a corresponding voltage across one of the 50 ohm loads. Since the 50 ohm loads are in series for the induced signal, the total drive voltage is actually two times that being measured.

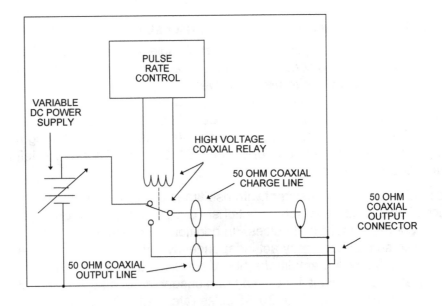

FIGURE A-20. Circuit diagram of CS115 pulse generator.

Paragraph 5.14.3.4b(3) of CS115 requires verification that the rise time, fall time, and pulse width portions of the applied waveform are present in the observed waveform induced in the calibration fixture. Figure A-21 shows a typical waveform that will be present. Since the frequency response of injection probes falls off at lower frequencies, the trapezoidal pulse supplied to the probe sags in the middle portion of the pulse that is associated with the lower frequency content of the applied signal. The relevant parameters of the waveform are noted. It is critical that an injection probe be used with adequate response at higher frequencies to produce the required rise time and fall time characteristics.

As also specified in CS114, testing is required on both entire power cables and power cables with the returns removed to evaluate common mode coupling to configurations which may be present in different installations. In some installations, the power returns are routed with the high side wiring. In other installations, power returns are tied to system structure near the utilization equipment with system structure being used as the power return path.

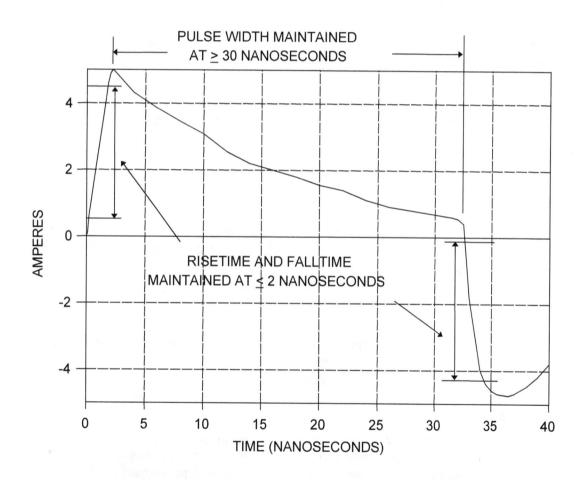

FIGURE A-21. Typical CS115 calibration fixture waveform.

RS06 was previously included in MIL-STD-462. RS06 was a formalization of the "chattering relay" test used widely throughout the military aircraft industry. This test procedure improves on RS06. The chattering relay has been found to be effective for determining upset conditions of equipment. The basic concept was to electrically connect the relay coil in series with a normally closed contact and allow the relay to continuously interrupt itself. The wire between the coil and contact was used to couple the transient onto EUT cables. The greatest concern with the chattering relay is that it does not produce a repeatable waveform since an arcing process is involved. The particular relay being used and the condition of its contact and coil mechanics play a large role. CS115 retains the most important characteristic of the chattering relay which is the fast rise time waveform and also has the important advantage of a consistent excitation waveform.

The same calibration fixture used for CS114 can be used for this test procedure. An available design is shown on Figure A-16.

A.5.14 (5.14) CS116, conducted susceptibility, damped sinusoid transients, cables and power leads.

Applicability and limits: The requirements are applicable from 10 kHz to 100 MHz for all electrical cables interfacing with each EUT enclosure and also individually on each power lead. The basic concept is to simulate electrical current and voltage waveforms occurring in platforms from excitation of natural resonances.

In contrast to CS115 that excites natural resonances, the intent of this requirement is to control the waveform as a damped sine. Damped sine waveforms (sometimes complex combinations) are a common occurrence on platforms from both external stimuli such as lightning and electromagnetic pulse and from platform electrical switching phenomena. Waveforms appearing on cables can be due to the cable itself resonating or to voltage and current drives resulting from other resonances on the platform. Wide frequency coverage is included to account for a wide range of conditions. Transients caused from switching actions within the platform can also result in similar waveforms.

A consideration for the requirement is whether momentary upsets are allowable if the EUT is capable of self-recovery to normal operation. Some upsets may occur that are not even noticed by an operator due to self-correcting mechanisms in the equipment. There may be cases where longer term upset is acceptable which may possibly require action by an operator to reset the equipment. The EMITP should address any instances where the contractor proposes that observable upsets be accepted.

A limited set of damped sine waves is specified to address a sampling of the various ringing frequencies that may be present in the platform. An advantage of using a set of damped sine waves is that different circuit types are evaluated for various waveform attributes that may cause worst-case effects. Some circuits may respond to peak amplitude while others may respond to total energy or rate of rise.

The requirement to test at resonant frequencies determined through loop circuit characterization evaluation has been removed from this version of the standard. Test experience had shown that equipment was no more susceptible at these frequencies than the standard frequencies.

The current limits are set at levels that cover most induced levels found in platforms during system-level testing to external transient environments. The lower frequency breakpoints are at worst-case platform resonant frequencies below which the response will fall off at 20 dB/decade. The upper frequency breakpoint is located where the spectral content of the transient environments falls off.

Possible tailoring of the requirements by the procuring activity in contractual documents is to adjust the curve amplitude either higher or lower based on the degree of protection provided in the area of the platform where the equipment and interconnecting cabling will be located. A caution with this particular requirement based on past experiences is that the platform designer should be required to share in the burden of the hardening process by providing stress reduction measures in the platform. The equipment should not be expected to provide the total protection. Protection against transients generated internal to the platform needs to remain a consideration. Another potential tailoring area is adjusting the lower frequency breakpoint to be more consistent with the lowest resonance of a particular platform.

Test procedures: The calibration fixture with terminations is a 50 ohm transmission line. Since the injection probe is around the center conductor within the fixture, a signal is being induced in the loop formed by the center conductor, the two 50 ohm loads, and the structure of the fixture to which the 50 ohm loads are terminated. From a loop circuit standpoint, the two 50 ohm loads are in series, providing a total loop impedance of 100 ohms. Because of the transmission line configuration, inductance effects are minimized. Measurement of induced current levels is performed by measuring a corresponding voltage across one of the 50 ohm loads. Since the 50 ohm loads are in series for the induced signal, the total drive voltage is actually two times that being measured.

In the past, MIL-STD-462 included test procedures CS10, CS11, CS12, and CS13, which addressed various types of damped sine testing on both cables and individual circuits or connector pins. This test procedure is a single replacement for all those procedures. CS116 addresses testing of cables (interconnecting, including power) and individual power leads. The common mode cable portion of the test is the best simulation of the type of condition present on platforms from electromagnetic field excitation. The individual power lead test addresses differential type signals present on platforms from switching functions occurring in the power system.

As necessary, the test can be applied in a straightforward manner to wires on individual pins on an EUT connector or to individual circuits (twisted pairs, coaxial cables, and so forth).

Since the quality factor (Q) of the damped sine signal results in both positive and negative peaks of significant value regardless of the polarity of the first peak, there is no requirement to switch the polarity of the injected signal.

The common mode injection technique used in this procedure and other procedures such as CS114 is a partial simulation of the actual coupling mechanism on platforms. The magnetic field in the injection device is present at the physical location of the core of the injection device. In the platform, the electromagnetic field will be distributed in space. The injection probe induces a voltage in the circuit loops present with the voltage dropping and current flowing based on impedances present in the loop. There is a complex coupling relationship among the various individual circuits within the cable bundle. The injection probe is required to be close to the EUT connector for standardization reasons to minimize variations particularly for higher frequencies where the shorter wavelengths could affect current distribution.

Exercise caution to ensure that attenuators and current injection probes are rated such that they will not be damaged nor have their characteristics altered by the injected signals. Attenuators are generally rated in terms of their ability to handle average power. The peak power and voltages associated with the injected susceptibility signal can damage attenuators.

For example, the 10 A current limit for CS116, exposes the attenuator to 500 V (10 A x 50 ohms) levels, which corresponds to a peak power of 5 kW ((500 V)^2/50 ohms). Similarly, current injection probes can have their magnetic properties altered by the pulsed signals.

For measurement of Q of the injected waveform, Figure CS116-1 specifies the use of the peak of the first half-sine wave and the associated peak closest to being 50% down in amplitude. Some facilities use a damped cosine waveform rather than a damped sine. Since this waveform is more severe than the damped sine because of the fast rise time on the leading edge, there is no prohibition from using it. Because of potential distortion caused by leading edge effects, the first peak should not be used to determine Q for damped cosine waveforms. The next half peak (negative going) should be used together with the associated negative peak closest to 50% down. Equipment may exhibit failures with this waveform that would not be present with the damped sine.

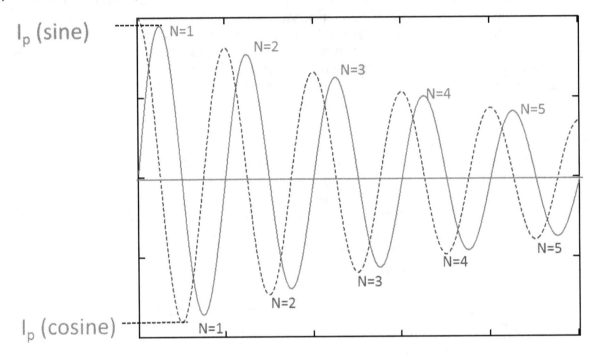

FIGURE A-22. Typical CS116 calibration fixture sine and cosine waveforms.

A5.15 (5.15) CS117, conducted susceptibility, lightning transients, cables and power leads.

Applicability and limits: These levels and waveforms were derived from general and civil aviation experience and are considered applicable to military aircraft equipment and subsystems. This requirement is intended to address the equipment-level indirect effects of lightning as outlined in the platform electromagnetic environments defined within MIL-STD-464, specifically Figure 2 and Table 7.

Test method CS117 does not provide test coverage for either the Direct Effects or Nearby Lightning requirement from MIL-STD-464. However, for most equipment, testing with some combination of CS116 and CS115 may provide sufficient coverage to address the environment for nearby lightning called out in MIL-STD-464. This is because the changing electromagnetic fields primarily result in currents being induced on equipment cables. Equipment with antennas and receivers that respond to low frequency fields (for example AM radio band or ADF sensors) may require additional testing to satisfy MIL-STD-464, Nearby Lightning requirements.

The requirements are defined as default values for the identified equipment classifications. The intent was to give high confidence test levels for design assurance and equipment qualification that is primarily targeted for aircraft flight/safety critical equipment within various installation locations and types of aircraft construction/shielding. In the event that actual lightning threat levels from the host aircraft are available, tailoring of the equipment test levels to match the host threat levels (with appropriate margins) is encouraged and must be approved by the procuring agency. More detailed discussion on this approach can be found in SAE ARPs 5412, 5414, 5415 and 5416.

The EUT will be specified as either internal or external by the procuring authority. Table CS117-1 defines external located equipment as being located on a platform where it is exposed to the external electromagnetic environment. The lightning induced coupling to wiring that is external to the aircraft is expected to be significantly higher than coupling to wiring fully contained inside the protection of the aircraft main fuselage/shielded interior. Often there are line–replaceable units (LRUs) that are installed within the aircraft fuselage, but have wire bundles routed through exterior portions of the aircraft. This situation would require the LRU to be tested to external levels even though the LRU itself was inside the fuselage. In addition, aircraft with portions of structure that are constructed of non-conductive materials would be considered external and any LRUs or wiring installed inside such structures would therefore need to meet the external lightning threat. Examples of such could be an empennage or fairing made of non-conductive composite materials. Aircraft often have wiring routed in wheel wells, bomb bays and leading edge areas of the wings that are exposed to external threats during certain flight phases, therefore wiring or LRUs in these areas would need to meet the external threat levels.

The waveform sets and levels of Table CS117-1 were chosen based on information gathered from SAE ARP5412 and RTCA DO-160. The applicability of each waveform set is highly dependent on the location, routing and design of the EUT cable harness. For the purposes of this procedure it is assumed that the majority of cable bundles under test are shielded. In this case, it is expected that current will be driven down the low impedance bundles and that the required current test levels of waveform set 2/1 and 4/5A will be achieved. Waveform set 3/3 is always defined as a voltage test level due to the higher frequency content of the transient compared to its double exponential counterparts and the typical interaction in cable harnesses in actual aircraft environments. The other factor to take into account when selecting waveform sets is the cable bundle routing on an aircraft and the type of coupling that may occur during a lightning event. In most cases the lightning transients will predominantly be coupled through aperture coupling in which case waveform set 2/1 is applicable. This type of coupling is dominant in metallic type aircraft. However, in situations where a cable harness is routed through an area of the aircraft that is made of composite material, the coupling may also consist of resistive coupling in addition to the aperture coupling. This resistive coupling from the lightning transient passing through the composite material stretches the double exponential waveforms typically seen in aperture coupling environments. In these cases, the longer duration waveform set 4/5A is applicable in addition to waveform set 2/1 to cover the additional resistive coupling from the composite material. Waveform 6 will typically only be present on very well shielded cable bundles, with the shielding terminated with a 360-degree shield to connector terminations at the connectors on both ends of the bundle. These types of very low impedance cables are typically found in areas of the aircraft that are electromagnetically exposed outside the fuselage, such as landing gear regions, engines, flight control surfaces, wingtips, or empennage regions. Cable bundles that are both not heavily shielded and not routed outside the fuselage or wing structures will typically not to be tested for Waveform 6.

The current test/limit level specified for individual power lines (identified in parenthesis in Table CS117-1) is the expected worst-case current for an individual core wire in an actual aircraft installation. These worst-case current levels are based on information gathered from SAE ARP5412 and RTCA DO-160. In a typical cable bundle made up of multiple leads, the total bundle current is distributed in each lead and the larger current level is applicable. However, since power lines are required to be tested separate from the bundle and the high sided tested individually, it is necessary to define a worst-case current limit for these individual leads (the value in parenthesis in Table CS117-1) so as not to force an extreme over-test condition.

There may also be similar situations where there are signal bundles to be tested with a relatively low wire count. Bundles with only a few wires shall utilize a current limit that is based upon the individual wire limit (stated current limits in parenthesis of Table CS117-1). The test shall be performed and the injection currents controlled so as not to exceed these individual wire limits for each individual wire. This may require an initial survey by testing the bundle to lower levels and see how the currents are distributing amongst the wires within the bundle. Once this distribution is known, then judiciously applying the transients so that the individual wire currents are well controlled and do not exceed the individual wire limits. This control may drive a need to break the test point into individual leads and test them separately, using the individual wire limits.

The requirement definition includes the timing effects associated with a Multiple Stroke and Multiple Burst lightning event. RTCA DO-160 allows the Single Stroke and Multiple Stroke tests to be performed separately. CS117 applies the Single Stroke and Multiple Stroke waveforms as a combined test. For this reason the first stroke of the Multiple Stroke application has been adjusted to the applicable Single Stroke test level from RTCA DO-160. The Multiple Stroke and Multiple Burst tests are not synchronized to any particular EUT critical frequency so an irregular pattern is applied and is not intended to be synchronized with the EUT timing processes. This excites the system so that the probability of upsetting periodic signals in the EUT is increased. The timing for the waveforms is defined in 5.15.3.4b(3). This irregular timing approach results in excitation of the cable resonance points.

Test Procedures: It is desired to initially test to the current test levels I_T for Waveform 1 and 5A. For low impedance bundles, this is generally not an issue. However, for unshielded and hybrid (mix of shielded and unshielded wiring) bundles, the higher impedance may result in the voltage test limit (V_L) being achieved before I_T which will then require a Waveform 2 and 4 test to be completed. In the case that V_L is achieved during a Waveform 1 or 5A test, it can be acceptable to go over V_L to meet the I_T requirements. Caution is urged during this test condition as it may induce core voltages in excess of hardware design limits. Consultation with engineering design is recommended.

Transient amplitude determination can be a significant source of test variability and error. The techniques used not only determine the susceptibility threat level applied to the EUT, but they are also the basis of timing measurements that determine whether the wave-shape is compliant during generator calibration/verification. Variability and error can be minimized by using consistent oscilloscope measurement techniques when making transient measurements. The proper time scale and the use/placement of cursors are critical to proper measurements.

Time Scale Selection: The second key to consistent transient amplitude measurements is to choose the proper time scale. This improves consistency in the identification of high frequency noise versus the transient being measured. During generator calibration/generator performance verification, the time scale should be set to the minimum time per division that displays all of the waveform parameters necessary to show compliance. For example, for most oscilloscopes, 1 µs per division is the minimum time scale which displays the required waveform parameters for Waveform 3 at 1 MHz. Depending on transient generator design and waveform set, the open circuit voltage and short circuit current time scales may be different.

Cursor Placement: Whenever a voltage or current transient amplitude measurement determines the level applied to the EUT, including cable bundle test's generator performance verification, and cable bundle test's test sequences, peak amplitude should be determined by manually placing the oscilloscope's horizontal cursors rather than by using automatic measurement functions which just report the absolute peaks. The possibility of under-testing is the reason the use of cursors is advisable when the measurement determines the level applied to the EUT. Transient characteristics described in this section such as high frequency noise and the inductive kick effect, which are not uncommon, cause the absolute peak of the transient to be higher than the actual transient amplitude. If a transient is free of these characteristics, both measurement techniques will yield the same amplitude. One transient characteristic that may appear during both generator calibration/generator performance verification and the EUT test sequence is high frequency (high with respect to the intended transient's frequency components) noise. High frequency noise can appear on the leading edge and/or peak of both damped sine and double exponential waveforms and it should be ignored/not given credit.

Figure A-23 is an example of correct amplitude determination of a Waveform 3 damped sine transient with high frequency noise. The narrow spike on the peak of this transient's first cycle is the high frequency noise that should be ignored during amplitude determination. The narrow spike gradually opens as amplitude decreases, requiring a subjective judgment of where to place the cursor. The narrow spike should be minimized or not exist during the generator calibration/generator performance verification, but may be unavoidable as a loading effect during the EUT test sequence. As shown in this example, place the cursor at the peak where there is some discernable energy under the curve. This discernable energy under the curve amplitude determination criterion illustrates the importance of time scale choice.

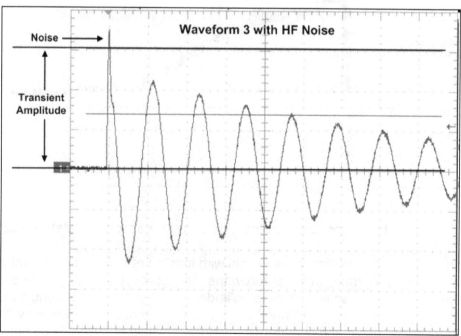

FIGURE A-23. High frequency noise - Waveform 3 amplitude determination.

Figure A-24 is an example of correct amplitude determination of a Waveform 4 double exponential transient with high frequency noise. Loading effect high frequency noise is present both as the narrow spikes on the leading edge and peak of the transient and as a hash around the decay of the transient. Since the double exponential test transient is masked by high frequency noise, a curve was drawn to represent the test transient based on the general underlying waveshape, which may differ from the generator calibration/generator performance verification waveshape. As shown in this example (and similar to Figure A-23), place the peak amplitude cursor at the peak of the curve representing the test transient. Understand that there is energy under the curve that is masked by the noise, in order to avoid overly conservative cursor placement at the base of the noise. The curve representing the test transient may be drawn on a printed waveform or may only be drawn mentally by an experienced operator. Ideally, transient generators do not produce even close to this amount of high frequency noise during generator calibration/generator performance verification, but some amount may be present. In this case, base the 50% amplitude point that determines T2 on the peak amplitude cursor. In both of these examples, the subjective judgment of the test operator is required, but that is unavoidable. The use of an automatic measurement function for either transient would result in amplitude over-reporting, an unacceptable under-test if the measurement determines the level applied to the EUT. Careless cursor placement can result in amplitude under-reporting, an unnecessary over-test.

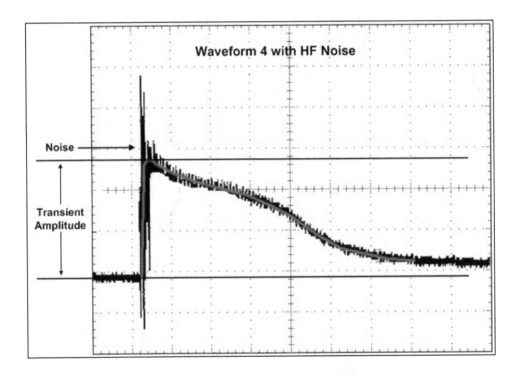

FIGURE A-24. High frequency noise - Waveform 4 amplitude determination.

In general, amplitude determination of transients with loading effects is no different than amplitude determination of transients that follow the ideal damped sine or double exponential waveforms: the peak of the transient is the amplitude if there is discernable energy under the peak. For example, Figure A-25 is a Waveform 5A double exponential transient with two notable loading effects- ripple and high frequency noise. Ripple should only be present as a loading effect, not during generator calibration/generator performance verification, if the generator is well designed. Ripple can appear on damped sine and double exponential waveforms, with or without higher frequency spikes included. Like most other loading effects, the peak of the test transient is the peak of the ripple, but high frequency noise should still be ignored. In this example, the upper cursor gives credit for the high frequency noise and is therefore incorrect amplitude determination that results in an under-test. The second cursor is correct amplitude determination because it ignores high frequency noise as described above, yet gives credit for the peak of the ripple. Like Figure A-24, a curve was drawn between the peaks of the ripple as another example of representing the test transient based on the general underlying waveshape, which may differ from the generator calibration/generator performance verification waveshape.

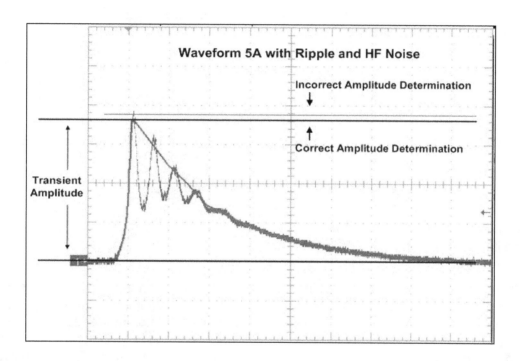

FIGURE A-25. Ripple with high frequency noise - Waveform 5A amplitude determination.

The most common damped sine loading effect is the inductive kick effect, which arises because of the ability of inductance in the load circuit (EUT) to store energy initially upon discharge of the transient generator. The stored energy is released later in the cycle, increasing the charge on the generator's tank capacitor above the open circuit level. The result is subsequent peak(s) of higher amplitude than the first peak and of higher amplitude than the generator was charged to, as shown on Figure A-26.

Figure A-26 is a Waveform 3 cable bundle test. Since the second positive peak is more than 20% higher than the first positive peak record the amplitude of the second positive peak, which is currently at the requirement level +20% (the maximum allowed amplitude tolerance). The goal is to reach the requirement level with the first peak, however to avoid overstressing the EUT, it is acceptable to stop leveling, if one of the subsequent peaks reaches the requirement level plus the maximum allowed amplitude tolerance (20%).

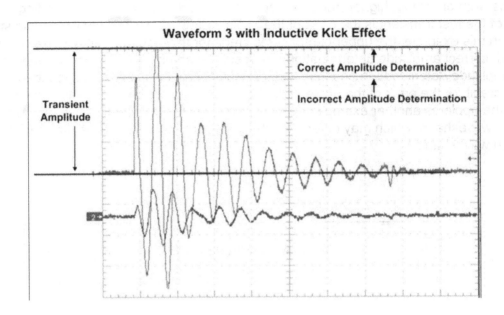

FIGURE A-26. Inductive kick effect - Waveform 3 amplitude determination.

A.5.16 (5.16) CS118, personnel borne electrostatic discharge.

Applicability and limits: The requirement is applicable to electrical, electronic, and electromechanical subsystems and equipment which does not interface with or control ordnance items. Implementation of this requirement at the subsystem level supports the requirements outlined in MIL-STD-464 for electrostatic charge control at the system level.

ESD will have its greatest effect on equipment with intentional seams and apertures, such as controls and displays: equipment designed to provide a man-machine interface. Equipment of the type labeled "black box," with six metal sides and only connector interfaces are much less likely to be susceptible to ESD, and less likely to be handled while operational. Therefore such "black box" type equipment are prime candidates for qualification by analysis. The analysis being that these "black boxes" are inherently hard, and inherently isolated from ESD events.

Failures caused by ESD are caused by the rapid transfer of charge (current) and the short duration, high-energy radiated electromagnetic fields generated during the ESD event. The effects of these failures may be immediate or latent (delayed), with the failure mode ranging from a temporary deviation in the subsystem's specified performance to damage requiring repair or replacement of the affected component(s) or subsystem. The failures may be subdivided into two categories: "soft" and "hard" ESD-induced failures.

Soft ESD-induced failures are typically characterized by the momentary disruption in operation of a subsystem's internal circuitry. The first source of this disruption is the short duration, high-energy radiated electromagnetic field generated by the ESD discharge. This field couples to traces on the circuit board. As the electromagnetic field decays, the circuit returns to normal operation without any lasting damage. The second source is the current associated with the rapid transfer of charge during the ESD event. This current may cause a momentary level shift such as a change in the voltage measured by an analog-to-digital converter, or momentary actuation of an active component (e.g.. Insulated Gate Bipolar Transistor or "H" bridge). The operation of the circuit returns to normal as this transient current approaches zero.

Hard ESD-induced failures typically involve physical damage to subsystem circuitry such as discrete and integrated bipolar and metal oxide semiconductor (MOS) components. Damage occurs through thermal and dielectric breakdown within the underlying semiconductor material, or metallization melt with damage to bond wires. Passive components such as filter capacitors may also be affected when repeated exposure to ESD causes a breakdown of the dielectric material. This results in the filter capacitor acting more like a resistor than a capacitor. Immunity to ESD is reduced, and the probability of subsystem susceptibility to the external electromagnetic environment (EME) and increased unintended emissions levels on conductors connected to the affected circuit increases.

Test procedures: The test procedure described in this section presents a controlled method to evaluate the susceptibility of electrical and electronic subsystems to ESD. The intent is to cover subsystem aspects accessible by personnel during EUT operations. The test equipment and procedures are based upon internationally recognized standards such as IEC 61000-4-2. The use of a single configuration with bonding as installed in actual usage is not a mistake. The insertion of an isolated handling test was considered, however the maximum charge transfer should occur when the system is bonded, which makes the installed configuration the worst case.

The verification of any ESD simulator prior to the start of testing is required to ensure the validity of the test results. An ESD simulator is subject to repeated physical handling by the test operator as hundreds, if not thousands of ESD events are applied to the EUT during a single test. Depending on the usage profile i.e., number of tests performed over a given period, an annual calibration interval is insufficient to detect and correct any ESD simulator-related issues. At a minimum, the tip voltage should be verified prior to the start of testing, preferably on a daily basis for a series of tests spanning several days. Verification of the peak discharge current and discharge network time constant should be done at the beginning of test. The ESD current target is available from several manufacturers of ESD test equipment.

Verification of the ESD simulator's performance using the contact discharge waveform is preferred over verification using the air discharge waveform. During application of an air discharge event to the ESD target, the approach speed and angle of approach to the target introduce variability into the waveform which is observable as a change in the rise time, peak current, and duration of the waveform. Repeatability of the air discharge waveform is highly dependent upon the skill of the operator. Annex E of ISO 10605:2008 provides further reading in regards to the use of air discharge to verify the ESD simulator's performance.

Exposure of the EUT to multiple discharges at different test points provides greater confidence that the EUT will operate as designed when fielded. Test points typically include apertures or seams in the case and connectors accessible to the user during operation. This also includes test points such as dials, indicators, lamp bezels, switches, etc. All of these points represent potential coupling paths, both direct and indirect, into the EUT. Exposure of these test points ensures the electrical and mechanical design of the EUT is robust to the effects of ESD. For example, the design of a commercially-available electronic module uses a printed circuit board, conformal coated and contained within a non-hermetically sealed, non-conductive plastic housing. The design of the housing has an integral one-way aperture which allows moisture to escape from within the housing and equalize pressure between inside the housing and the surrounding atmosphere. If this aperture is located near ESD-sensitive components, even if the size of the aperture is on the order of a pinhole, the aperture will allow ESD to couple into the components and disrupt its operation or damage the module beyond repair.

A.5.17 (5.17) RE101, radiated emissions, magnetic field.

Applicability and limits: This requirement is specialized and is intended primarily to control magnetic fields from 30 Hz to 100 kHz for applications where equipment is present in the installation which is potentially sensitive to magnetic induction at lower frequencies. The most common example is a tuned receiver that operates within the frequency range of the test.

RS101 is a complimentary requirement imposed on equipment to ensure compatibility with the anticipated magnetic fields. The RS101 limits are higher to allow for variations in performance between manufactured items and to account for the possibility that the emissions from the EUT may couple into a larger physical area than that evaluated under the RS101 test procedures.

For Navy aircraft, the requirement is applicable for installations using anti-submarine warfare (ASW) equipment, specifically equipment in the same cabinet or avionics bay, or that share the same power bus or same cable bundles, as the ASW equipment. In addition, the requirement should apply to any equipment that uses more than 6 amps of current on-board an ASW aircraft.

The Navy RE101 limit is based on preventing induction of more than 0.5 µV (nominal) in an RG-264A/U transmission line (loop area, A, of 0.65 square inches), with a maximum induced level of 4 µV at 60 Hz. The need to limit the low frequency magnetic field emissions from equipment is due to the close proximity of electronic and electrical systems and associated cables installed on the Navy platforms, and the essentiality of low frequency sensors and systems. The primary concerns are potential effects to low frequency acoustic systems and sensors, and ELF and VLF/LF communications systems and sensors that have sensitivities in the nV range.

Note that the limit does not take into account magnetic effects from equipment such as magnetic launchers, magnetic guns and the like.

An estimate can be made of the types of induced levels that will result in circuitry from the limits. Magnetic fields act by inducing voltages into loop areas in accordance with Faraday's law ($V = -d\phi/dt$). For a uniform magnetic field perpendicular to the loop area, the induced voltage from Faraday's law reduces to $V = -2\pi fBA$.

f = Frequency of Interest   B = Magnetic Flux Density   A = Loop Area

The Army RE101 limit is based on preventing induction of more than 2.5 mV (5 mV for RS101) in a 12.7 cm (5 inch) diameter loop. Since magnetic induction is proportional to frequency and the limit falls off at 20 dB/decade, the induced voltage in a given loop area is constant. Since the Army limit is greater than or equal to the Navy limit at all frequencies, this induced level represents the worst-case. The primary concerns are potential effects to engine, flight and weapon turret control systems and sensors that have sensitivities in the mV range.

There are certain limited applications in the Air Force where an RE101 requirement needs to be considered. These applications are primarily when a subsystem will be installed in an aircraft in close proximity to an antenna connected to a VLF/LF receiver. An appropriate limit needs to be chosen based upon distances between the equipment and the antenna.

For Army applications, possible tailoring is increasing the limit for single-use equipment that will be located a sufficient distance from any potentially susceptible systems or waiving of the requirement.

Test procedures: A 13.3 cm loop is specified for the test.
If the maximum level is always observed on one face or on one cable at all frequencies, then data only needs to be recorded for that face or cable.

Typical points of magnetic field emissions leakage from EUT enclosures are CRT yokes, transformers and switching power supplies.

MIL-STD-462D required measurement of emissions from electrical interface cables. This standard limits measurements to electrical interface connectors. This change recognizes that the connectors are the most likely place for emissions associated with electrical interfaces to occur due to a number of reasons. One is that signal paths transition from normal cable construction techniques (such as twisted pairs) to parallel routing through the connector pins. Also, there are potential contributions from shield termination techniques.

A possible alternative measurement tool in this frequency range is wave analyzer using a Fast Fourier Transform algorithm. Use of this type of instrumentation requires specific approval by the procuring activity.

A generic correction factor curve was included in MIL-STD-462D to convert from the voltage indicated by the measurement receiver to the magnetic field in dBpT. However, the various manufacturers use different construction techniques that cause the actual factor to vary somewhat. Therefore, it is necessary to use the manufacturers' supplied data.

Measurements are now required for each point of maximum radiation which exceeds the RE101 limit at 7 cm. These measurements are performed by increasing the measurement distance until the emission falls below the specified limit. The fall-off measurement data is intended to assist the equipment designer in determining the source of the magnetic field emissions and in the development of appropriate mitigation techniques. It should be noted the EUT is required to comply with the applicable RE101 limit at 7cm; this is not a change to the RE101 limit or measurement distance.

A.5.18 (5.18) RE102, radiated emissions, electric field.

Applicability and limits: The requirements are applicable from 10 kHz to 18 GHz for electric field emissions from the EUT and associated cables. The basic intent of the requirement is to protect sensitive receivers from interference coupled through the antennas associated with the receiver. Many tuned receivers have sensitivities on the order of 1 µV and are connected to intentional apertures (the antenna) that are constructed for efficient reception of energy in the operating range of the receiver. The potential for degradation requires relatively stringent requirements to prevent platform problems.

There is no implied relationship between this requirement and RS103 that addresses radiated susceptibility to electric fields. Attempts have been made quite frequently in the past to compare electric field radiated emission and susceptibility type requirements as a justification for deviations and waivers. While RE102 is concerned with potential effects with antenna-connected receivers, RS103 simulates fields resulting from antenna-connected transmitters.

Often, the same equipment item will be involved in influencing both requirements. A 30 watt VHF-AM radio with a typical blade antenna operating at 150 MHz can easily detect a 40 dBµV/m electric field (approximately -81 dBm developed at receiver input) while in the receive mode. When this same piece of equipment transmits at the same 150 MHz frequency, it will produce a field of approximately 150 dBµV/m (32 V/m) at a 1 meter distance. The two field levels are 110 dB apart.

The limit curves are based on experience with platform-level problems with antenna-connected receivers and the amount of shielding typically between antennas and equipment and associated wiring. The limits for surface ships, both topside and below decks, is based on numerous documented incidents of case and cable radiation coupling to receiver antennas and sensitive systems. The topside limit is more stringent than corresponding electric field radiation emissions requirements contained in military-related international agreements and standards such as those used by NATO. The below deck limit is comparable to many commercial/international standards.

For submarines, the RE102 limit distinguishes between equipment located internal versus external to the pressure hull. For equipment located external to the pressure hull, stricter limits are imposed. Possible tailoring is to apply the external RE102 requirement only to equipment that is located above the waterline.

The limit curves for equipment in internal installations on fixed wing aircraft are placed for air vehicles that are not designed to have intentionally shielded volumes that are effective across the frequency range of the test. Some minimal shielding is present. The curve for equipment in external installations and helicopters is 10 dB more stringent because even this minimal shielding is not available.

These limits for the 30 to 400 MHz band, in particular, have been validated as being properly placed. It has become standard practice on some aircraft programs to use spectral analysis equipment wired to aircraft antennas to assess degradation due to radiated emissions from onboard equipment. Many problems due to out-of-limit conditions in this band have been demonstrated. It has also been determined that equipment meeting the limit generally does not cause problems. Most of this experience is on fighter size aircraft. The 20 dB/decade increase in the limit above 100 MHz is due to the aperture size of a tuned antenna ($G\lambda^2/(4\pi)$) decreasing with frequency. The coupled power level from an isotropic tuned antenna will remain constant. The curve breaks at 100 MHz because of difficulty with maintaining a tuned antenna due to increasing physical size and the lower likelihood of coupling to the antenna with longer wavelengths.

For Air Force aircraft, there is no limit specified below 2 MHz for internal equipment. There are antennas on some aircraft that operate below 2 MHz; however, these antennas are usually magnetic loops that have an electrostatic shield. These antennas have very short electrical lengths with respect to the wavelength of frequencies below 2 MHz and any electric field coupling will be inefficient. The inefficient coupling to cabling at lower frequencies has been demonstrated innumerable times in EMI testing.

For Navy aircraft, the starting frequency was reduced to capture electrical switching noise sources to address their impact on sensitivities and range of specialized receivers. The increased use of switching power supplies can raise the noise floor of the ground plane the antennas are referencing and has been shown to affect the reception abilities of sensitive receivers.

The limits for Navy mobile and all Army ground equipment are the same. Also, the limits for Navy fixed and all Air Force ground equipment are identical. The 20 dB difference between the limits exists because of the general situations where the equipment is deployed. The Navy mobile is primarily oriented toward the Marines that operate in a fashion similar to the Army. Equipment is often very close to unprotected antennas such as installations in vehicles or tents or near physically small helicopter aircraft. The Navy fixed and most Air Force installations have less critical coupling situations with regard to antenna coupling.

The limit for surface ships is based on numerous documented incidents of case and cable radiation coupling to receiver antennas. The use of hand-held type transceivers below deck within a ship is increasing and can be plagued by excessive levels of interference below deck. The limit is more stringent than corresponding electric field radiation emissions requirements contained in military-related international agreements and standards such as those used by NATO.

Another issue is that there have been substantial conflicts between allowed radiated levels implied by the power quality limits of MIL-STD-704 and previous MIL-STD-461 requirements. For example, MIL-STD-704 allows approximately 0.63 V_{rms} on 115 V, 400 Hz, AC power buses at 15 kHz. Based on laboratory testing, this level will radiate at approximately 76 dBµV/m. This level is 31 dB above the previous MIL-STD-461 limit for aircraft equipment. It is interesting to note that if the rod antenna in the MIL-STD-462 setup were usable down to 400 Hz, an approximate 1 V/m level would be indicated because of the power source waveform.

Possible tailoring by the procuring activity for contractual documents is as follows. The limits could be adjusted based on the types of antenna-connected equipment on the platform and the degree of shielding present between the equipment, associated cabling, and the antennas. For example, substantial relaxations of the limit may be possible for equipment and associated cabling located totally within a shielded volume with known shielding characteristics. It may be desirable to tailor the frequency coverage of the limit to include only frequency bands where antenna-connected receivers are present. Some caution needs to be exercised in this regard since there is always the chance the equipment will be added in the future. For example, it is not uncommon to add communications equipment (such as HF radio) onboard an aircraft as different missions evolve.

Based on the above discussion concerning MIL-STD-704, relaxing of RE102 limits for aircraft should be considered at lower frequencies for power generation equipment to avoid conflicts between the two sets of requirements.

Test procedures: Specific antennas are required by this test procedure for standardization reasons. The intent is to obtain consistent results between different test facilities.

In order for adequate signal levels to be available to drive the measurement receivers, physically large antennas are necessary. Due to shielded room measurements, the antennas are required to be relatively close to the EUT, and the radiated field is not uniform across the antenna aperture. For electric field measurements below several hundred megahertz, the antennas do not measure the true electric field.

The 104 cm rod antenna has a theoretical electrical length of 0.5 meters and is considered to be a short monopole with an infinite ground plane. It would produce the true electric field if a sufficiently large counterpoise were used to form an image of the rod in the ground plane. However, there is not adequate room. The biconical and double ridged horn antennas are calibrated using far-field assumptions at a 1 meter distance. This technique produces standardized readings. However, the true electric field is obtained only above approximately 1 GHz where a far field condition exists for practical purposes.

The defined configuration for rod antennas measurements on Figure RE102-5 came from a study of various approaches to obtaining the most accurate results. A calibrated vertical field was first generated using a special structure and was measured with an electrically small broadband sensor (RS103) in an empty room, with the sensor located at the center position of the rod. The rod antenna was then placed at its normal location and a field level indicated by the rod antenna was measured (scaled to prevent saturation). Bonding the counterpoise to the bench ground plane or the floor with a wide strap was found to enhance readings at higher frequencies of the rod and depress readings at other frequencies. Floating the counterpoise with the coaxial cable electrically bonded at the floor with a weak ferrite sleeve (lossy with minimum inductance) on the cable produced the best overall results. Lowering the antenna such that the center point of the rod is 120 cm above the floor to be consistent with the other antennas improved the results further.

For shielded enclosures that do not have an available point for bonding the coaxial cable from the matching network to the floor directly beneath the counterpoise, a low inductance copper sheet should be installed from the nearest access point on the floor to the counterpoise location.

Another issue is that some rod antennas have output connectors that are not electrically bonded to the matching network enclosure. These antennas include a common choke that have the return side of the connector wired through the choke. It is required that these antennas be modified to bond the shell of the connector to the enclosure. This change does not affect the antenna factor but can have a large affect on the resulting measurements.

Antenna factors are determined using the procedures of SAE ARP958. They are used to convert the voltage at the measurement receiver to the field strength at the antenna. Any RF cable loss and attenuator values must be added to determine the total correction to be applied.

Previous versions of this standard specified conical log spiral antennas. These antennas were convenient since they did not need to be rotated to measure both polarizations of the radiated field. The double ridged horn is considered to be better for standardization for several reasons. At some frequencies, the antenna pattern of the conical log spiral is not centered on the antenna axis. The double ridged horn does not have this problem. The circular polarization of the conical log spiral creates confusion in its proper application. Electric fields from EUTs would rarely be circularly polarized. Therefore, questions are raised concerning the need for 3 dB correction factors to account for linearly polarized signals. The same issue is present when spiral conical antennas are used for radiated susceptibility testing. If a second spiral conical is used to calibrate the field correctly for a circularly polarized wave, the question arises whether a 3 dB higher field should be used since the EUT will respond more readily to linearly polarized fields of the same magnitude.

Other linearly polarized antennas such as log periodic antennas are not to be used. It is recognized that these types of antennas have sometimes been used in the past; however, they will not necessarily produce the same results as the double ridged horn because of field variations across the antenna apertures and far field/near field issues. Uniform use of the double ridge horn is required for standardization purposes to obtain consistent results among different test facilities.

The stub radiator required by the procedure is simply a short wire (approximately 10 cm) connected to the center conductor of a coaxial cable that protrudes from the end of the cable.

There are two different mounting schemes for baluns of available 104 cm rod antennas with respect to the counterpoise. Some are designed to be mounted underneath the counterpoise while others are designed for top mounting. Either technique is acceptable provided the desired 0.5 meter electrical length is achieved with the mounting scheme.

The nominal 10 pF capacitor used with the rod antenna in 5.17.3.4c(3) as part of the system check simulates the capacitance of the rod element to the outside world. The actual rod capacitance depends on its width, so the manufacturer's recommended value should be used if available. With the rod antenna, the electric field present induces a voltage in the rod that is applied to the matching network circuitry. One of the functions of the matching network is to convert the high impedance input of the antenna element to the 50 ohm impedance of the measurement receiver. The 10 pF capacitor ensures that the correct source impedance is present during the check. Some antennas have a nominal 10 pF capacitor built into the rod balun for calibration purposes and some require that an external capacitor be used.

For measurement system checks, establishing the correct voltage at the input to the 10 pF capacitor can be confusing dependent upon the design of the antenna and the associated accessories. Since, the electrical length of the 104 cm rod is 0.5 m, the conversion factor for the induced voltage at the input to the 10 pF capacitor is 6 dB/m. If the limit at the measurement system check frequency is 34 dBµV/m, the required field level to use for measurement system check is 6 dB less than this value or 28 dBµV/m. The voltage level that must be injected is:

28 dBµV/m – 6 dB/m = 22 dBµV

Since the input impedance at the 10 pF capacitor is very high, a signal source must be loaded with 50 ohms (termination load or measurement receiver) to ensure that the correct voltage is applied. A "tee" connection is used with the signal source connected to the first leg, the 50 ohm load connected to the second leg, and the center conductor of the third leg connected to the 10 pF capacitor.

Accessories provided for rod antennas, such as calibration networks or voltage dividers, to assist in signal injection and calibration have been found to have stray capacitance issues that produce incorrect readings. The technique shown on Figure RE102-7 must be used. This same technique should be used to determine calibration factors for the rod matching network. A network analyzer signal output can be used to drive the 10 pF capacitor with the 50 ohm termination connection routed to one of the analyzer receive ports (T) and the matching network routed to the second receive port (R). With the analyzer operating in the mode to produce T/R, the antenna factor is directly produced.

The stray capacitance issue mentioned above has also been found to result in incorrect factors being supplied by organizations that calibrate rod antennas due to the use of incorrectly designed calibration networks.

Some rod antennas include high pass filters that can be turned on and off by small switches internal to the matching network. Caution should be exercised to ensure that the antennas factors being used include the effect of any switches that are activated.

The antenna positioning requirements in this procedure are based on likely points of radiation and antenna patterns. At frequencies below several hundred MHz, radiation is most likely to originate from EUT cabling. The 104 cm rod and biconical antennas have wide pattern coverage. The equation on Figure RE102-7 is based on the rod and biconical being placed at least every 3 meters along the test setup boundary. The double ridge horns have narrower beamwidths. However, the shorter wavelengths above 200 MHz will result in radiation from EUT apertures and portions of cabling close to EUT interfaces. The requirements for antenna positioning above 200 MHz are based on including EUT apertures and lengths of cabling at least one quarter wavelength.

All the specified antennas are linearly polarized. Above 30 MHz, measurements must be performed to measure both horizontal and vertical components of the radiated field. Measurements with the 104 cm rod are performed only for vertical polarization. This antenna configuration is not readily adapted for horizontal measurements.

For equipment or subsystems that have enclosures or cabling in various parts of a platform, data may need to be taken for more than one configuration. For example, in an aircraft installation where a pod is located outside of aircraft structure and its associated cabling is internal to structure, two different limits may be applicable. Different sets of data may need to be generated to isolate different emissions from the pod housing and from cabling. The non-relevant portion of the equipment would need to be protected with appropriate shielding during each evaluation.

A.5.19 (5.19) RE103, radiated emissions, antenna spurious and harmonic outputs.

Applicability and limits: The requirements are essentially identical with CE106 for transmitters in the transmit mode from 10 kHz to 40 GHz. There are no requirements for receivers or transmitters in the standby mode. Most of the discussion under CE106 also applies to RE103. A distinction between the requirements is that RE103 testing includes effects due to antenna characteristics. The test itself is considerably more difficult.

It should be noted that for simplification the absolute measurement limits are given in terms of power and not power spectral density. To be accurate the measured power should be given in terms of power per receiver bandwidth e.g. above 1 GHz the limit is more correctly stated in units of dBm/MHz since in that frequency range the receiver bandwidth is 1 MHz per Table II.

Test procedures: Since the test procedure measures emissions radiating from an antenna connected to a controlled impedance, shielded, transmission line, the measurement results should be largely independent of the test setup configuration. Therefore, it is not necessary to maintain the basic test setup described in the main body of this standard.

The test procedure is laborious and will require a large open area to meet antenna separation distances. Equations in the test procedure specify minimum acceptable antenna separations based on antenna size and operating frequency of the EUT. Antenna pattern searches in both azimuth and elevation are required at the spurious and harmonic emissions to maximize the level of the detected signal and account for antenna characteristics.

Sensitivity of the measurement system may need enhancement by use of preamplifiers and the entire test needs to be coordinated with local frequency allocation authorities. All recorded data has to be corrected for space loss and antenna gain before comparisons to the limit.

As shown on Figures RE103-1 and RE103-2, shielding might be necessary around the measurement system and associated RF components to prevent the generation of spurious responses in the measurement receiver. The need for such shielding can be verified by comparing measurement runs with the input connector of the measurement receiver terminated in its characteristic impedance and with the EUT in both transmitting and stand-by modes or with the EUT turned off. Also, the receiving or transmit antenna may be replaced with a dummy load to determine if any significant effects are occurring through cable coupling.

The RF cable from the receive antenna to the measurement receiver should be kept as short as possible to minimize signal loss and signal pick-up.

The band-rejection filters and networks shown on Figures RE103-1 and RE103-2 are needed to block the transmitter fundamental and thus reduce the tendency of the measurement receiver to generate spurious responses or exhibit suppression effects because of the presence of strong out-of-band signals. These rejection networks and filters require calibration over the frequency range of test.

Some caution needs to be exercised in applying Table II of the main body of this standard. In 5.19.3.4d(4) of the test procedure, a power monitor is used to measure the output power of the EUT. In conjunction with the antenna gain, this value is used to calculate the effective radiated power (ERP) of the equipment. In 5.19.3.4d(5) of the test procedure, the measurement receiver is used to measure the power from a receiving antenna. This result is also used to calculate an ERP. For the two measurements to be comparable, the measurement receiver bandwidth needs to be sufficiently large to include at least 90% of the power of the signal present at the tuned frequency. If the bandwidth in Table II of the main body of the standard is not appropriate, a suitable measurement receiver bandwidth should be proposed in the EMITP.

For measurement of the magnitude of harmonic and spurious emissions with respect of the fundamental, the bandwidths of Table II will normally produce acceptable results, regardless of whether the bandwidth is large enough to process 90% of the power. Since the signal bandwidth of harmonic and spurious emissions is usually the same as the fundamental, use of a common bandwidth for measuring both the fundamental and the emissions will provide a correct relative reading of the amplitudes.

A.5.20 (5.20) RS101, radiated susceptibility, magnetic fields.

Applicability and limits: This requirement is specialized and intended primarily to ensure that performance of equipment potentially susceptible to low frequency magnetic fields from 30 Hz to 100 kHz is not degraded. RE101 is a complimentary requirement governing the radiated magnetic field emissions from equipment and subsystems. The RE101 discussion is also applicable to this requirement.

The Navy RS101 limit was established by measurement of magnetic field radiation from power distribution components (transformers and cables), and the magnetic field environment of Navy platforms. The Navy RS101 limit from 30 Hz to 2 kHz was derived from the worst case magnetic field radiation from a power transformer (~170 dBpT) and applicable cable types (DSGU-400), and takes into account the user equipment power line harmonic content and maximum anticipated power consumption. The Navy RS101 limit above 2 kHz is based on the measured magnetic field environment of Navy platforms.

The aircraft applicability is limited to equipment located next to or near high current devices such as generator equipment, de-icing equipment, or motor driven equipment like large cable reels. RS101 is not necessarily for ASW equipment, but rather systems exposed to ASW equipment, generators, cable reels, etc. It is also applicable to external systems exposed to magnetic fields from the Electromagnetic Aircraft Launch System (EMALS).

In past versions of this standard, the Navy RS101 and RE101 limits had the same general shape with the RS101 limit being higher than the RE101 limit. In this version, there is a deviation from this pattern where the difference between the two limits is greater in some regions than in the past. This change is due to a recognition that there are localized areas on the platforms where there are sources of higher level magnetic fields that must be tolerated. The acceptance of these higher levels within the platform is not justification for overall relaxation of the RE101 limit. Also, there is the possibility that the emissions from the EUT may couple into a larger physical area than that evaluated under the RS101 test procedure.

The Army has maintained the basic relationship of the RS101 and RE101 limits having the same shape. The RS101 limit is based on 5 mV (independent of frequency) being induced in a 12.7 cm (5 inch) diameter loop.

Test procedures: Laboratory tests have been performed to assess the possibility of using the 13.3 cm loop sensor specified in the RE101 test procedure instead of the 4 cm loop sensor used in this test procedure to verify the radiated field. The testing revealed that the 13.3 cm loop sensor did not provide the desired result due to variation of the radiated field over the area of the loop sensor. Due to its smaller size, the 4 cm loop sensor provides an accurate measure of the field near the axis of the radiating loop. A generic correction factor curve was included in MIL-STD-462D to convert from the voltage indicated by the measurement receiver to the magnetic field in dBpT. However, the various manufacturers use different construction techniques that cause the actual factor to vary somewhat. Therefore, it is necessary to use the manufacturers' supplied data.

The primary test procedure requires that testing be performed at each electrical interface connector. On some small size EUTs, connectors may be closely spaced such that more than one connector can be effectively illuminated for a particular loop position. The EMITP should address this circumstance.

Helmholtz coils generate a relatively uniform magnetic field that is more representative of the environment experienced on some platforms, particularly submarines. For this reason, the AC Helmholtz coil test option is preferred for submarine applications. In addition to providing a more realistic test bed, Helmholtz coils will, in general, reduce test time. Application of the guidelines and analytical expressions presented herein should enable users to design and construct Helmholtz coils for RS101 testing.

AC Helmholtz coils may be designed in accordance with the following guidance.

a. A closed form solution for the magnetic flux density produced along the axis of a series-driven system of two identical circular coils is:

$$B_z = \frac{\mu_o N I r^2}{2} \left(\frac{1}{\left(z^2 + r^2\right)^{3/2}} + \frac{1}{\left(\left(d - z\right)^2 + r^2\right)^{3/2}} \right)$$

where,

B_z = magnetic flux density, Teslas
μ_o = permeability of free space, Henrys/meter
N   = number of turns (same for each coil)
I   = current, Amperes
r   = coil radius, meters
d   = coil separation, meters
z   = distance along common axis, meters

For a standard Helmholtz coil configuration, d = r. At the center of the test volume (z = r/2), the above expression can be simplified:

$$B_z \approx \frac{\left(8.99 \times 10^{-7}\right) N I}{r}$$

b. The coil impedance can be estimated using general expressions for an *RL* series circuit. The dominant term for frequencies below 100 kHz is the coil inductance that is the sum of each coil's series inductance (L) and the mutual inductance (M) between the two coils:

L_{Total} = 2(L + M)

where:

M = $\mu r N$ Henrys/meter

The series inductance can be estimated using the following expression for the external inductance of a circular coil where the wire bundle cross section is circular in shape and small relative to the coil radius:

$$L = N^2 r \mu_0 \left[\ln\left(\frac{16r}{a}\right) - 2 \right]$$

where: a = diameter of wire bundle cross section, meters

There are several practical limitations that must be considered when designing AC Helmholtz coils.

a. The coil drive current is limited by coil impedance. The dominant term in the coil impedance is the coil inductive reactance. Because it is proportional to the square of the number of turns (N), the coils should be designed with a minimum number of turns needed to meet the low frequency test limit. Depending on coil size, it may be necessary to construct the coils with one or more taps so the number of turns can be reduced at higher frequencies.

b. The coil self-resonant frequency must be greater than 100 kHz. At self-resonance, it may not be practical to generate sufficient drive current to achieve the test limit.

c. A series voltage drop will exist across each coil that is proportional to the product of the coil impedance and coil drive current. Because the voltage drops are separated in space by the distance between the coils, a voltage gradient will exist (electric field in V/m). This field is maximum near the perimeter of circular coils. If the EUT is relatively small compared to the available test volume, this effect may not be a concern. However, if the EUT is near the coil perimeter, or if the electric field magnitude is significant relative to the RS103 electric field susceptibility requirement, then steps should be taken to minimize the electric field.

It may not be practical using commonly available laboratory power amplifiers to achieve the RS101 test limit for coils much larger than 4 feet in diameter. Consideration should be given to tailoring the test limit if a larger Helmholtz coil is used. For example, it may be proposed that the radiated test level exceed the limit by 3dB, rather than the 6 dB required for Helmholtz coils. Any tailoring requires approval from the procuring activity.

Prior to initial use, the coils must be tested to ensure they are capable of generating the required magnetic flux densities from 30 Hz to 100 kHz. Sufficient margin (2-3 dB) should be available to compensate for the potential loading effect of nearby metallic structures or magnetic material. It must be confirmed that the first indication of self-resonance appears above the RS101 upper frequency limit of 100 kHz. For frequencies above 10 kHz, the magnitude of the electric field component in the test volume should be determined either by direct measurement, or it should be approximated by measuring the voltage drop across the coils and dividing by coil separation distance. Unless the electric field component is much less than the RS103 electric field susceptibility limit, the coils should be enclosed in a non-continuous electrostatic shield to prevent ambiguity when interpreting susceptibility test results.

A.5.21 (5.21) RS103, radiated susceptibility, electric field.

Applicability and limits: The requirements are applicable from 10 kHz to 40 GHz for both the EUT enclosures and EUT associated cabling. The basic concern is to ensure that equipment will operate without degradation in the presence of electromagnetic fields generated by antenna transmissions both onboard and external to the platform.

There is no implied relationship between this requirement and RE102. The RE102 limit is placed primarily to protect antenna-connected receivers while RS103 simulates fields resulting from antenna transmissions.

The limits specified for different platforms are simply based on levels expected to be encountered during the service life of the equipment. They do not necessarily represent the worst-case environment to which the equipment may be exposed. RF environments can be highly variable, particularly for emitters not located on the platform. The limits are placed at levels that are considered to be adequate to cover most situations, including design levels for "back door" effects (excluding direct coupling to platform antennas or externally mounted devices) resulting from RF high power threat emitters. The aircraft carrier hanger deck is not a totally enclosed area. Investigation of the electromagnetic environment in the aircraft carrier hangar deck on 9 aircraft carriers showed levels in the HF band (2 to 30 MHz) up to 42 V/m. Therefore, equipment located in the hanger deck is required to meet the same 50 V/m level as equipment in non-metallic ships (below decks) from 2 to 30 MHz.

An example which demonstrates the variability of environments for ground installations and the need for effective tailoring of requirements is the installation of equipment in a large ground-based radar facility. Some of these facilities transmit power levels over one megawatt and the back lobes from the antennas can be substantial. Suitable design levels for equipment that will be used in the facility or nearby need to be imposed.

For aircraft and ships, different limits are specified depending on whether the equipment receives protection from platform structure. This distinction is not made for Army ground systems, such as tanks, because the same equipment used inside a structure is often used in other applications where protection is not available.

The 200 V/m requirement for Army aircraft regardless of the location or criticality of the equipment is based on the use of Army aircraft. Portions of the external environment accepted for most of the Army's aircraft is higher than 200 V/m. Army aircraft, especially rotary wing, have flight profiles that are almost exclusively nap-of-the-earth (NOE). The NOE profiles allow for much closer and longer duration encounters with high power emitters. This approach is similar to the FAA approach that recommends that Visual Flight Rules (VFR) helicopters be qualified to levels higher than fixed wing aircraft.

For submarines, the RS103 limit now distinguishes between equipment located internal versus external to the pressure hull. For equipment installed internal to the pressure hull, 10 V/m is now specified above 30 MHz to account for portable transmitters used within the submarine. For equipment located external to the pressure hull, stricter limits are imposed to more closely reflect the electromagnetic environment. The external RS103 limits should be applied only to equipment that is required to be fully operational when located above the waterline. Separate limits are specified, which are less severe, for equipment that is "external" to the pressure hull but located with the submarine superstructure (metallic boundary).

Using circularly polarized fields is not allowed due to problems with using the spiral conical antennas specified in versions of MIL-STD-462 in the past. Circularly polarized fields were convenient since they avoided the need to rotate a linearly polarized antenna to obtain both polarizations of the radiated field. However, problems existed with this antenna. At some frequencies, the antenna pattern of the conical log spiral is not centered on the antenna axis. Also, the circular polarization of the conical log spiral creates confusion in its proper application. The EUT and associated cabling can be expected to respond more readily to linearly polarized fields. If a second spiral conical were used to calibrate the field radiated from the first spiral conical antenna, it would indicate an electric field 3 dB higher than a linearly polarized antenna. The question arises whether a 3 dB higher field should be used for a spiral conical transmit antenna to obtain response characteristics similar to a linearly polarized field. Similarly, if a spiral conical antenna were used to calibrate a linearly polarized field, the indication would be 3 dB below the true electric field strength.

Possible tailoring by the procuring activity for contractual documents is to modify the required levels and required frequency ranges based on the emitters on and near a particular installation. Actual field levels can be calculated from characteristics of the emitters, distances between the emitters and the equipment, and intervening shielding. MIL-HDBK-235 provides information on land, air, and sea based RF emitters, both hostile and friendly, which contribute to the overall electromagnetic environment. The possible use of the equipment in other installations and the potential addition or relocation of RF emitters needs to be considered. Other possible tailoring is to change from the standard 1 kHz, square wave modulation or use additional modulations based on actual platform environments.

RS103 requirements for surface ships and submarines are included at the tuned frequency of antenna-connected receiver; there is no relaxation as for other platforms. The use of wireless devices such as radio frequency identification (RFID) tags, handheld transceivers, wireless local area network (WLAN), etc. is increasing rapidly for below decks applications. The requirement is to protect receivers at their tuned frequency, from the intentional emissions of wireless (RF generating) devices used in close proximity to the receiver when sufficient isolation is provided by the platform (for example, path loss from sea water between the emitter and receive antenna for submarines) such that the receiver's antenna does not detect significant levels from wireless devices. The requirement is intended to ensure the equipment (receiver) does not respond to the electric fields generated internal to the structure and is not to restrict signals received via the antenna. The electric field strength at a distance of 1.0 m from a typical wireless device with an effective isotropic radiated power (EIRP) of 100 mW (typical of 802.11 wireless LAN access points, RFID, and wireless communications) is 1.73 V/m. Federal Communications Commission (FCC) rules defines power limitations for WLANs in FCC Part 15.247 and requires effective isotropic radiated power (EIRP) to be 1 W or less; this equates to an electric field strength of 5.5 V/m at a distance of 1 m. It should be noted that for fixed, point-to-point systems that use higher gain directive antennas an EIRP of 4.0 W is permitted by the FCC.

For Navy aircraft, testing has shown susceptibilities below 100MHz that were not found with CS114, especially in EUTs with many connectors (think common vs. differential mode). In addition, use of HF has increased greatly in the Navy. The lower start frequency for Navy aircraft to 2MHz is due to increased HF exposure. Navy aircraft that are strictly land-based should start testing at 30 MHz.

Test procedures: Test facilities are permitted to select appropriate electric field generating apparatus. Any electric field generating device such as antenna, long wire, TEM cell, reverberating chamber (using mode tuned techniques) or parallel strip line capable of generating the required electric field may be used. Fields should be maintained as uniform as possible over the test setup boundary. Above 30 MHz, both horizontally and vertically polarized fields must be generated. This requirement may limit the use of certain types of apparatus. Only vertically polarized measurements are required below 30 MHz due to the difficulty of orienting available test equipment for horizontal measurements.

Electric field sensors are located at least 30 cm above the ground plane below 1 GHz to minimize electromagnetic boundary conditions of the ground plane affecting the field that is present at the longer wavelengths. At and above 1 GHz, these effects are less pronounced and the volumes being illuminated by antennas that typically have higher gain are smaller. Therefore, the sensors need to be positioned in the main antenna beam and located at a height where the EUT is being radiated.

The requirement to ensure that the E-field sensor is displaying the fundamental frequency is primarily concerned with the biconical antenna, which has poor characteristics at the lower frequencies. Harmonics, which are down from the fundamental in power, may radiate higher levels than the fundamental due to the antenna being more efficient at the harmonic frequencies. The primary way to avoid this effect is to use a transmission line radiator or a physically larger transmit antenna at the lower frequencies (approximately below 70 MHz).

This version of the MIL-STD-461 allows larger distances than 1 meter between the transmit antenna and the EUT boundary. This approach is actually preferable, where amplifier power is available to obtain the required field, since more of the EUT is illuminated at one antenna position.

When testing large equipment, there may be a need to use antennas with wider beamwidths so that the EUT and sensor are within the 3dB beamwidth. It may also be achieved by moving the antenna farther away to satisfy the requirement. This may require the use of more powerful amplifiers to achieve the required field strength.

Monitoring requirements emphasize measuring true electric field. While emission testing for radiated electric fields does not always measure true electric field, sensors with adequate sensitivity are available for field levels generated for susceptibility testing. Physically small and electrically short sensors are required so that the electric field does not vary substantially over the pickup element resulting in the measurement of a localized field. Broadband sensors not requiring tuning are available.

The use of more than one sensor is acceptable provided all sensors are within the beamwidth of the transmit antenna. The effective field is determined by taking the average of the readings. For example, if the readings of three sensors are 30, 22, and 35 V/m, the effective electric field level is (30 + 22 + 35)/3 = 29 V/m.

Different sensors may use various techniques to measure the field. At frequencies where far-field conditions do not exist, sensors must be selected which have electric field sensing elements. Sensors that detect magnetic field or power density and convert to electric field are not acceptable. Under far-field conditions, all sensors will produce the same result. Correction factors must be applied for modulated test signals for equivalent peak detection as discussed under 4.3.10.1. A typical procedure for determining the correction factor for these sensors is as follows:

    a.   Generate a field at a selected frequency using an unmodulated source.

    b.   Adjust the field to obtain a reading on the sensor display near full scale and note the value.

    c.   Modulate the field as required (normally 1 kHz pulse, 50% duty cycle) and ensure the field has the same peak value. A measurement receiver with the peak detector selected and receiving antenna can be used to make this determination.

    d.   Note the reading on the sensor display.

    e.   Divide the first reading by the second reading to determine the correction factor (Subtract the two readings if the field is displayed in terms of dB).

    f.   Repeat the procedure at several frequencies to verify the consistency of the technique.

Above 1 GHz, radiated fields usually exhibit far-field characteristics for test purposes due to the size of typical transmit antennas, antenna patterns, and distances to the EUT. Therefore, a double ridged horn together with a measurement receiver will provide true electric field.

Similarly, the particular sensing element in an isotropic sensor is not critical, and acceptable conversions to electric field can be made.

For equipment or subsystems that have enclosures or cabling in various parts of a platform, data may need to be taken for more than one configuration. For example, in an aircraft installation where a pod is located outside of aircraft structure and its associated cabling is internal to structure, two different limits may be applicable. Different sets of data may need to be generated to evaluate potential pod susceptibility due to coupling through the housing versus coupling from cabling. The non-relevant portion of the equipment would need to be protected with appropriate shielding.

Reverberating chambers, using mode tuned techniques, have been popular for performing shielded effectiveness evaluations and, in some cases, have been used for radiated susceptibility testing of equipment and subsystems. The concept used in reverberating chambers is to excite available electromagnetic wave propagation modes to set up variable standing wave patterns in the chamber. A transmit antenna is used to launch an electromagnetic wave. An irregular shaped tuner is rotated to excite the different modes and modify the standing wave pattern in the chamber. Any physical location in the chamber will achieve same peak field strength at some position of the paddle wheel.

Reverberation chambers have the advantage of producing relatively higher fields than other techniques for a particular power input. Also, the orientation of EUT enclosures is less critical since the all portions of the EUT will be exposed to the same peak field at some paddle wheel position. The performance of a particular reverberation chamber is dependent upon a number of factors including dimensions, Q of the chamber, number of available propagation modes, and frequency range of use.

Some issues with reverberation chambers are as follows. The field polarization and distribution with respect to the EUT layout are generally unknown at a point in time. If a problem is noted, the point of entry into the EUT may not be apparent.

Reverberation chambers are sometimes treated as a good tool to determine potential problem frequencies with conventional antenna procedures being used to evaluate areas of concern.

The performance of each chamber must be reviewed to determine the suitability of its use for reverberation testing over a particular frequency range.

Reverberation chambers should be constructed in accordance with the following guidance in order to function properly.

    a.   A tuner should be constructed of metal and installed with appropriate positioning equipment to allow the tuner to be rotated 360 degrees in at least 200 evenly spaced increments. The tuner should be constructed to be asymmetric with the smallest dimension of the tuner being at least $\lambda/3$ of lowest frequency to be tested and the longest dimension of the tuner being approximately 75% of the smallest chamber dimension.

    b.   The enclosure should be free of any materials that might exhibit absorptive properties such as tables, chairs, wood floors, sub-floors, shelves, and such. Support structures should be constructed from high density foam.

    c.   Transmit and receive antennas should be at least 1.0 meter ($\square/3$ is the actual limitation) from any wall or object and should be positioned to prevent direct alignment between the main lobes of the two antennas or between the EUT and the main lobe of either antenna.

d. The lower frequency limit is dependent on chamber size. To determine the lower frequency limit for a given chamber, use one of the following methods:

(1) Using the following formula, determine the number of possible modes (N) which can exist at a given frequency. If, for a given frequency, N is less than 100 then the chamber should not be used at or below that frequency.

$$N = \frac{8\pi}{3} abd \frac{f^3}{c^3}$$

where: a, b, and d are the chamber internal dimensions in meters

f is the operation frequency in Hz

c is the speed of propagation (3 x 10^8 m/s)

(2) Use the methods detailed in IEC 61000-4-21 for determining the lowest useable frequency based on field uniformity. NOTE: the MODE-TUNED calibration procedure outlined in IEC 6100-4-21 may be substituted for the procedure outlined in 5.21.4.4. Substitution of the data from the IEC procedure into the equations of 5.21.4.4 is not allowed.

e. In order to assure that the time response of the chamber is fast enough to accommodate pulsed waveform testing (other than the 1 kHz, 50% duty cycle, waveform specified), determination of the chamber time constant must be accomplished using the following procedure:

(1) Calculate the chamber Q using:

$$Q = \left(\frac{16\pi^2 V}{\eta_{Tx}\eta_{Rx}\lambda^3} \right) \left(\frac{P_{ave\ rec}}{P_{forward}} \right)$$

where η_{Tx} and η_{Rx} are the antenna efficiency factors for the Tx and Rx antennas respectively and can be assumed to be 0.75 for a log periodic antenna and 0.9 for a horn antenna, V is the chamber volume (m^3), λ is the free space wavelength (m) at the specific frequency, $P_{ave\ rec}$ is the average received power over one tuner rotation, and $P_{forward}$ is the forward power input to the chamber over the tuner rotation at which $P_{ave\ rec}$ was measured.

(2) Calculate the chamber time constant, τ, using:

$$\tau = \frac{Q}{2\pi f}$$

where Q is the value calculated above, and f is the frequency (Hz)

(3) If the chamber time constant is greater than 0.4 of the pulse width of the modulation waveform, absorber material must be added to the chamber or the pulse width must be increased. If absorber material is added, repeat the measurement and the Q calculation until the time constant requirement is satisfied with the least possible absorber material. A new $CLF(f)$ must be defined if absorber material is required.

f.   Prior to using the chamber, the effectiveness of the tuner should be evaluated at the upper and lower frequencies to be used and at points between the endpoints not to exceed 1 GHz spacing. To evaluate the stirring effectiveness, inject a CW signal into the chamber at the desired frequency and record the net received power at 200 positions of the tuner evenly spaced over a 360 degree rotation of the tuner. Determine the correlation coefficient between the original set of received power and subsequent sets obtained by rotating the last data point of the original set to the position of the first point and then shifting all the other points to the right as depicted below.

Original data	D1, D2, D3, D4, D5, . . . D200
Shifted data (1)	D200, D1, D2, D3, D4, . . . D199
Shifted data (2)	D199, D200, D1, D2, D3, . . . D198
Shifted data (3)	D198, D199, D200, D1, D2, . . . D197
Shifted data (4)	D197, D198, D199, D200, D1, . . . D196
Shifted data (5)	D196, D197, D198, D199, D200, D1, . . . D195

The correlation coefficient should drop to below 0.36 within five shifts of the data. This will ensure that the tuner is operating properly. If the tuner fails this test, then the tuner needs to be made either larger or more complex, or both.

g.   National Bureau of Standards Technical Note 1092 and National Institute of Standards and Technology Technical Note 1508 should be used as a guide in preparing a shielded room for reverberation measurements.

A.5.22 (5.22) RS105, radiated susceptibility, transient, electromagnetic field.

Applicability and limits: This requirement is primarily intended for EUTs to withstand the fast rise time, free-field transient environment of EMP. It applies for equipment enclosures which are directly exposed to the incident field outside of the platform structure or for equipment inside poorly shielded or unshielded platforms. This requirement may be tailored in adjustment of the curve amplitude either higher or lower based on degree of field enhancement or protection provided in the area of the platform where the equipment will be located. This requirement is applicable only for EUT enclosures. The electrical interface cabling should be protected in shielded conduit. Potential equipment responses due to cable coupling are controlled under CS116.

Test procedures: To protect the EUT and actual and simulated loads and signal equipment, all cabling should be treated with overall shielding; kept as short as possible within the test cell; and oriented to minimize coupling to the EMP fields.

The EMP field is simulated in the laboratory using bounded wave TEM radiators such as TEM cells and parallel plate transmission lines. To ensure the EUT does not significantly distort the field in the test volume, the largest EUT dimension should be no more than a third of the dimension between the radiating plates of the simulator. In these simulators the electric field is perpendicular to the surfaces of the radiator. Since the polarization of the incident EMP field in the installation is not known, the EUT must be tested in all orthogonal axes.

There is a requirement to first test at 10% of the specified limit and then increase the amplitude in steps of 2 or 3 until the specified limit is reached for several reasons. This test has the potential to burnout equipment and starting at lower levels provides a degree of protection.

Also, the equipment may exhibit susceptibility problems at lower test levels that do not occur at higher test levels due to the presence of terminal protection devices (TPDs). At lower test levels, the devices might not actuate resulting in higher stresses on circuits than for higher levels where they do actuate.

Common mode signals can result on cables with inadequate isolation or leaky connectors in the presence of radiated fields. A method of checking for potential problems is as follows:

    a.   Measure the E-field with the B-dot or D-dot probe.

    b.   Invert the probe by rotating it 180 degrees.

    c.   Measure the E-field again and invert the signal.

    d.   Overlay and subtract the two signals.

    e.   The result is the common mode signal.

If any significant level is present, corrections to the setup should be undertaken, such as tightening of connectors and introduction of additional isolation, such as better shielded cables, alternative routing, or shielding barriers.

CONCLUDING MATERIAL

Custodians:
    Army – AV
    Navy - AS
    Air Force - 11
    DISA/JSC – DC5

Preparing activity:
    Air Force - 11

(Project No. EMCS-2013-001)

Review activities:
    Army – AT, CR, MD, MI, MR, TE
    Navy – CG, EC, MC, OS, SH, TD
    Air Force – 13, 19, 84
    NSA – NS
    DTRA - DS

NOTE: The activities listed above were interested in this document as of the date of this document. Since organizations and responsibilities can change, you should verify the currency of the information above using the ASSIST Online database at https://assist.dla.mil.